CW01024148

Passionate politics

Manchester University Press

Passionate politics

Democracy, development and India's 2019 general election

edited by

Indrajit Roy

MANCHESTER UNIVERSITY PRESS

Published by Manchester University Press
Oxford Road, Manchester M13 9PL

www.manchesteruniversitypress.co.uk

British Library Cataloguing-in-Publication Data
A catalogue record for this book is available from the British Library

ISBN   978 1 5261 5772 0   hardback

First published 2023

Typeset by
New Best-set Typesetters Ltd

Contents

List of figures and tables

Figure

Tables

List of contributors

Sarah Ansari is a historian of South Asia, and places that are today part of Pakistan. Much of her recent research has focused on the largest population upheaval of the twentieth century, namely the 1947 Partition that took place alongside independence from British rule in South Asia, and particularly Partition's long-term impact on the lives of the millions of people displaced by it. Her latest publication (co-authored with William Gould) is *Boundaries of Belonging: Localities, Citizenship and Rights in India and Pakistan* (Cambridge University Press, 2019).

Shaswati Das is a PhD researcher at the University of York's Department of Politics. Her research examines jihadist violence and counterterrorism in Kashmir from the perspectives of Social Movement and Resource Mobilisation theories. Previously, Shaswati worked as a journalist in India for ten years, during which time she reported extensively on matters of internal security and jihadism in Kashmir, and Naxal violence in Bastar.

Mabel Denzin Gergan is Assistant Professor in the Asian Studies Department at Vanderbilt University. A geographer by training, her research focuses on postcolonial environmentalism, Tribal/Indigenous theorisation, anti-colonial politics and race and ethnicity in South Asia. So far, she has focused on the Indian Himalayan borderlands and the relationship between frontier territories and 'mainland' India, characterised on the one hand by state-led development interventions in the region, and on the other through the movement of racialised bodies from the borderland to India's urban heartland.

Ajay Gudavarthy is Associate Professor at the Centre for Political Studies, Jawaharlal Nehru University, New Delhi. His recent published work includes *India after Modi: Populism and the Right* (Bloomsbury, Delhi, 2018) and *Secular Sectarianism: Limits of Subaltern Politics* (edited, Sage, 2019). He was previously Visiting Professor, Centre for Modern Indian Studies at Gottingen University, Germany (2014); Visiting Fellow, Centre for Citizenship, Civil Society and Rule of Law at University of Aberdeen (2012); Visiting Fellow, Goldsmith College, University of London (2010); Charles Wallace Visiting Fellowship, SOAS, London (2008).

Charu Gupta is a Professor in the Department of History, University of Delhi. The focus of her work is gender, sexuality, masculinity, caste, religious identities and vernacular literatures in early twentieth-century north India. Her monographs include *Sexuality, Obscenity, Community: Women, Muslims and the Hindu Public in Colonial India* (Permanent Black, 2001), and *The Gender of Caste: Representing Dalits in Print* (University of Washington Press, 2016). She has been a Visiting Professor and ICCR Chair at the University of Vienna, and a Visiting Faculty at Yale University, the Washington University and the University of Hawaii. She has also been a Fellow at the Nehru Memorial Museum and Library, Delhi, the Social Science Research Council, New York, the Asian Scholarship Foundation, Thailand, the Wellcome Institute, London and the University of Oxford. She is presently working on social histories of particular genres and subjects through life narratives in Hindi.

Sneha Krishnan is an Associate Professor in Human Geography at the University of Oxford, and a Tutorial Fellow in Geography at Brasenose College, Oxford. As a feminist historical and cultural geographer, her work asks how childhood and youth are materialised in South Asia in entanglement with the endurance of imperialism. She is currently a British Academy-Wolfson Fellow and is writing her first book on hostels in South India. Her work has been published most recently in *Antipode* and *Gender, Place and Culture*.

Charisma K. Lepcha is an Assistant Professor in Anthropology at Sikkim University, India. Her research interests include religion, language, indigeneity, identity, material culture and visual anthropology in the eastern Himalayan borderlands. She was a Fellow at the Indian Institute of Advanced Study, Shimla (2018–19), and is currently Visiting Scholar at the Harvard-Yenching Institute, Cambridge, MA (2021–22).

Jens Lerche is Reader (Associate Professor) in Labour and Agrarian Studies in the Department of Development Studies at SOAS, University of London. His research interests include class, caste and race relations, and rural labour migration and social reproduction. Jens is an editor of the *Journal of Agrarian Change*. His publications include *Ground Down by Growth: Tribe, Caste, Class and Inequality in Twenty-First-Century India* (co-authored, Pluto Press, 2018, Hindi edition 2019) and 'The farm laws struggle 2020–2021: Class–caste alliances and bypassed agrarian transition in neoliberal India', *Journal of Peasant Studies* (2021).

Gurpreet Mahajan was Professor at the Centre for Political Studies, School of Social Sciences, Jawaharlal Nehru University. She has written extensively on issues of multiculturalism, minority rights, secularism and civil society. Her publications include *Explanation and Understanding in the Human Sciences* (Oxford University Press, 1992, 1997, 2011), *Identities and Rights: Aspects of Liberal Democracy in India* (Oxford University Press, 1998) and *India: Political Ideas and the Making of a Democratic Discourse* (Zed Books, 2013).

James Manor is the Emeka Anyaoku Professor Emeritus of Commonwealth Studies in the School of Advanced Study, University of London. He has previously taught at Yale, Harvard and Leicester universities, the Institute of Development Studies, University of Sussex, and the Institute for Social and Economic Change, Bengaluru, India. His most recent books include *Politics and State–Society Relations in India*; (with Rob Jenkins) *Politics and the Right to Work: India's National Rural Employment Guarantee Act*; and (with James Chiriyankandath, Diego Maiorano and Louise Tillin) *The Politics of Poverty Reduction in India: The UPA Government, 2004–14*.

Nitya Rao is Professor of Gender and Development at the University of East Anglia, Norwich. She has worked extensively as a researcher and advocate in the field of women's rights, employment and education for over three decades, with a particular focus on exploring the gendered changes in land and agrarian relations, migration and livelihoods, especially in contexts of climatic variability and economic precarity. She has published on these themes in international peer-reviewed journals and books, and has consistently engaged with policy and practice, at both the global and local levels. Nitya is currently a member of the Steering Group of the High-Level Panel of Experts to the Committee on World Food Security.

Mujibur Rehman teaches at Jamia Millia Central University, New Delhi. He is the author of the forthcoming book, *Shikwa-e-Hind: The Political Future of Indian Muslims* (Simon & Schuster). His other publications include *Communalism in Postcolonial India: Changing Contours*, whose second edition has a foreword by noted historian Romila Thapar; and *Rise of Saffron Power: Reflections on Indian Politics*. Both are published by Routledge. His latest publications include 'Subordinated citizenship: Muslims in Hindu Rashtra' in *P & S: Political Science & Politics*, 54(4), October 2021.

Indrajit Roy is Senior Lecturer in Global Development Politics at the University of York. He obtained his DPhil at the University of Oxford (2008–12) where he also held a Junior Research Fellowship (2012–14) and an ESRC Future Research Leader Fellowship (2014–17). Indrajit has publications in *World Development, Journal of Peasant Studies, Journal of Development Studies, Commonwealth and Comparative Politics* and *South Asia: Journal of South Asian Studies*. His first book, *Politics of the Poor: Negotiating Democracy in Contemporary India*, was published by Cambridge University Press in 2018. He is cowriting (with Samuel Hickey) a textbook on global development politics.

Kunal Sen is the Director of UNU-WIDER, and Professor of Development Economics at the Global Development Institute, University of Manchester. He is the author of eight books and the editor of five volumes on the economics and political economy of development. Kunal is a leading international expert on the political economy of growth and development. His research has focused primarily on India, but also East Asia and sub-Saharan Africa. His books include *The Political Economy of India's Growth Episodes* (2016), *The Process of Financial Liberalization in India* (1997), and *Economic Restructuring in East Asia and India: Perspectives on Policy Reform* (1995). He was awarded the Sanjaya Lall Prize in 2006 and the Dudley Seers Prize in 2003 for his publications.

Alpa Shah is Professor of Social Anthropology at the London School of Economics. She is the author of *Nightmarch: Among India's Revolutionary Guerrillas*, shortlisted for the 2019 Orwell Prize for Political Writing and the New India Foundation Prize, and winner of the 2020 Association for Political and Legal Anthropology book prize. She is also the author of *In the Shadows of the State: Indigenous Politics, Environment and Insurgency in Jharkhand, India* (2010) and co-author of *Ground Down by Growth: Tribe, Caste, Class and Inequality in Twenty-First-Century India* (2018).

Amogh Dhar Sharma (PhD, MPhil Oxon; BA Delhi) is currently an Economic and Social Research Council Postdoctoral Fellow at the University of Oxford. He has previously worked as a Departmental Lecturer in Modern South Asia Studies at the Oxford School of Global and Area Studies and as a Stipendiary Lecturer in Politics at The Queen's College, Oxford. His research interests include comparative politics, political communication and the political economy of development in South Asia. He is currently working on a book manuscript based on his doctoral dissertation where he explores the professionalisation of politics in India.

Suryakant Waghmore is Professor of Sociology at IIT (Indian Institute of Technology), Mumbai. He is the author of *Civility Against Caste* (Sage, 2013) and co-editor of *Civility in Crisis* (Routledge, 2020).

Ather Zia is a political anthropologist, poet, short fiction writer and columnist. She is an Associate Professor in the Department of Anthropology and Gender Studies programme at the University of Northern Colorado, Greeley. Ather is the author of the award-winning *Resisting Disappearances: Military Occupation and Women's Activism in Kashmir*. She is the founder-editor of Kashmir Lit and the cofounder of the Critical Kashmir Studies Collective.

Acknowledgements

This volume started life in early 2019 as *India Tomorrow*, a seven-part series by The Anthill, a podcast from The Conversation. I am grateful to Gemma Ware and Annabel Bligh for producing the series and for inviting me to co-host and curate it. Huge thanks to Uma Pradhan, who convinced me to consider turning the series into an edited volume. Tia patiently kept me company throughout the recordings, for which I am very thankful. Most of the contributors to that conversation agreed to convert their reflections into short pieces, without which this volume would not have been possible. My heartfelt thanks to them all for agreeing to continue on this journey. Robert Byron at Manchester University Press combined a rare combination of patience and enthusiasm through the life of this project, as did David Appleyard, Lucy Burns and others. Jonathan de Peyer's encouragement at the start of this project was crucial to its eventual success. Editorial work on this volume was supported by funding from the Department of Politics at University of York.

Introduction: Passionate politics in India today

Indrajit Roy

The world waited with bated breath for 23 May 2019. The results of India's seventeenth general election were expected, with a mix of anticipation and apprehension. But all those expecting a nail-biting finish – and that included most of us – were disappointed. The outcome was known within hours after counting of votes began. Defying predictions and punditry on all sides of the political spectrum, India's prime minister Narendra Modi led his Hindu nationalist Bharatiya Janata Party (BJP) to a resounding victory. Not only did the BJP increase its tally of seats in India's Lok Sabha (lower house of Parliament) it also bettered its vote share: no mean feat given the array of opposition forces Modi faced. When the final results were declared by India's Election Commission, the BJP had won a total of 303 seats in the 545-member Lok Sabha, up from the 270-odd seats it held in the previous parliament. The results showed that 45% of all Indians had put their faith in the Prime Minister and his coalition partners in the National Democratic Alliance (NDA), the highest percentage in thirty-five years. Sixty-seven per cent of all registered voters cast their ballots, surpassing voter turnout in an industrialised democracy such as the United States (2016 turnout: 56%). For an election that had been billed as 'The Battle for India's Soul', the verdict was decisive indeed.

The 2019 Indian general election is considered the most presidential among Indian elections in recent memory. The 45% vote share Modi and his allies mustered approaches the vote shares commanded by winners of presidential elections in contemporary democracies. For example, a 48% vote share brought Donald Trump to power as President of the United States of America. Brazil's Jair Bolsonaro won the presidential election with the support of 55% of his country's voters. In Turkey, Recep Erdoğan won the presidency on the back of 52% of his voters. Modi's majority in a parliamentary election is quite an achievement given the formidable array of opponents he faced in India's vibrant multiparty democracy.[1]

Emotions matter

How do we interpret the scale of Modi's win? Electoral support of this sort could barely have been cobbled together overnight. It is likely that Modi's perceived toughness on terror swung some support in his favour. Rajinder Singh, the 40 year-old gentleman who drove me from Delhi airport to my home on 9 May 2019, certainly believed Modi was a stronger prime minister than 'anyone after Indira Gandhi', while recalling his retaliation against the February terrorist attack in Pulwama. A resident of a *jhuggi* (slum) in Mehrauli, on the southern edge of Delhi, he was convinced that 'there was a 90% chance of Modi being re-elected'. But even if there had been no Pulwama, or Modi had not retaliated as he supposedly did, Rajinder told me in no uncertain terms, he would have still voted for Modi. 'Modi [using his last name] is hardworking', was Rajinder's constant refrain during our 40-minute taxi ride. He then added for good measure, 'We love him.'

If Rajinder loved the Prime Minister, Arati, my mother's cook, adored his party for the welfare services they had provided while in office. 'They have provided us with a house and a toilet', she declared. Arati wanted leave to return to her village in rural Bengal so she could cast her vote. She would travel with other women from her village who, like her, cooked food, washed clothes and swept floors in middle-class homes across Delhi. 'There is no way we're voting for anyone else', she was emphatic. 'We'll tell people we are voting for someone else, but we'll all quietly vote for the lotus', she whispered, with her finger across her lips. 'They care for us.'

A close friend, a successful IT professional who graduated from the prestigious Indian Institute of Technology, was even more emphatic about Modi's importance to safeguarding India's Hindus. 'Islamists are overrunning India', he feared, as his wife nodded anxiously. 'We will be reduced to minorities in our own country in the blink of an eye, and the *liberalandu* [a portmanteau of liberal and the Hindi word for a***hole] will be twiddling their thumbs.' Modi was the only thing that stood between the India and Islamisation, he fretted.

Feeling politics

Love, care and fear were of course not the only emotions on display. There was no dearth of passions, which frequently spilled over from the political arena into drawing room conversations, WhatsApp groups of families and friends, morning walks, and worship communities. From senior management professionals with IIM (Indian Institute of Management) degrees earned way back in the 1970s to ragpickers foraging in the neighbourhood garbage dump, and everyone in between – the portly owner of the kiosk in Chandni Chowk's Paranthe wali Gali or the bald butcher who sliced and gleaned *keema* in the corner meat shop near Greater Kailash; the posh old businessman who imported cosmetics from Paris or the posher and younger designer who sourced textiles from the rural hinterland; the itinerant vegetable vendor and the migrant construction worker – it was impossible not to eavesdrop. Everyone was passionate about politics. Anger, fear, hatred and panic wove together with adoration, admiration, hope and enjoyment. Passions were nourished by controversies, such as the row over malfunctioning electronic voting machines or the exchange of personal barbs between Prime Minister Modi and Rahul Gandhi, the president of the largest opposition party the Indian National Congress Party.

Most analysts of the BJP's stupendous victory are overwhelmingly focused on Prime Minister Modi's persona. In their accounts, Modi emerges as some sort of a sorcerer, a peddler of dreams, a weaver of yarns. Supporters point to his oration and erudition, while critics paint him as a bluff-master at best and a hawker of hate at worst. Academic accounts have labelled him a populist to refer to his ability to connect with the masses, bypassing his party organisation.[2]

Other analysts have emphasised the role of the BJP's superior party organisation. Party president Amit Shah's organisational acumen is celebrated or bewailed, depending on the analysts' own political predilections. The BJP's higher levels of financial endowments have been the subject of many articles. In this vein, people's identification with the BJP as a party is now becoming the subject of well-deserved attention. Researchers crunching data at the well-respected Lokniti deduced from their surveys that Modi was the excuse, rather than the reason, that people supported the BJP (see also Verma and Gupta, 2018). They would have supported the BJP anyway, it's just that Modi provided them with adequate justification to do so.

Our reflections in this volume follow the insights offered by exciting recent literature on emotions in South Asia.[3] Historian Margrit Pernau (2021a: 113) suggests that emotions matter at three different levels. First, they impact the way humans experience the world around them. Second, they shape the process through which individuals (and social groups) endow their experiences with meaning and understand the world. Third, emotions provide the motivation to transform the interpretation of the world into acting in the world. Such an understanding of emotions cautions against creating a dichotomy between emotional and rational analysis and between passion and reason. Indeed, just as the pursuit of rational interests is never emotionally neutral, passions often inhere their own rationalities.

That emotions offer a legitimate entry point to understanding society and politics is now well established. Emotions are not 'non-rational' (Calhoun and Solomon, 1984: 31). By definition, emotions suppose events or situations that are 'appraised as harmful or beneficial' (Aranguren, 2015). As neuroscientists have demonstrated, emotions support rationality, providing it with salience and goals (Elster, 1999). Furthermore, emotions are intrinsically social, embedded as they are in social interactions (Blom and Lama-Rewal, 2021).

In their insightful introduction to a fascinating volume on the politics of emotions in South Asia, anthropologists Amélie Blom and Stéphanie Tawa Lama-Rewal (2021: 12) distinguish between (i) the representation of emotion (ii) its expression, and (iii) the ways in which it is experienced. Representation of emotions describe how people's emotions are represented by others. The expression of emotions draws on verbal and non-verbal markers, including self-reporting of how respondents feel. The experience of emotions relates to the emotions people actually feel. Where the contributors to this book dwell on emotions, they reflect on the *expressed* rather than the representational or experiential dimension of emotion.

Emotions in electoral politics

Emotions matter. And so do the broader social, economic and political structures within which they are embedded. As sociologist Jack Barbalet reminds us, 'emotions must be understood in the context of the structural relations of power and status that elicit them' (Barbalet, 1998: 26). Feelings and ideas, and affect and cognition are not mutually exclusive, and certainly not opposed to one another, as sociologist, historian and writer Colin Barker reminds us (Barker, 2001). Feelings are best understood as an ensemble of political dispositions,[4] thus making it imperative to study them in the context of the social structures in which they are embedded.

The present volume offers new directions to the study of political feelings by focusing on them in the context of elections. The contributions thus contribute to overcoming the tendency of directing analytic attention to politicised emotions only in the context of social movements, cataclysmic events and other disruptive episodes. Such studies in turn reduce feelings to resources that were mobilised by political actors (McAdam et al., 1996; Aminzade et al., 2001; Goodwin et al., 2001) or suggest that feelings can be subsumed under the cultural production of identity (Melucci, 1980; Offe, 1985; Tambiah, 1996). We do not deny these possibilities, but rather recognise, with psychosociologist Simon Clarke and his colleagues, the 'interpenetration of reason and passion, thought and feeling' that characterise affective politics during elections (Clarke et al., 2006: 9).

The focus on feelings during elections mainstreams the study of political emotions in institutional and procedural contexts. Such an approach overcomes the prevailing tendency to limit attention on political emotions to such categories as the 'masses', the 'poor', 'social movements', 'popular politics' and other extra-institutional actors. In such literatures, emotions are subordinated to understandings of institutional politics and considered pathological, thereby rendered irrelevant to 'normal' politics. Under the circumstances, Jack Barbalet, the sociologist referred to above, challenges us to 'demonstrate the centrality of emotion to the routine functioning of non-deviant structures of social interaction. In doing so', he continues, 'it is sufficient to stick to normal not extreme expression of emotion' (Barbalet, 1998: 3). While recognising that the 2019 Indian general election was unlike any 'normal' election, the focus on feelings provoked by this election urges us to take emotions seriously even in banal, everyday circumstances.[5]

Our focus on passionate politics in the context of elections in India distinguishes the volume from the emerging body of work on emotions in South Asian politics. Indeed, after a period of relative neglect, there is now welcome attention to the politics of emotions in the regions, as historians, anthropologists and others offer us rich and granular perspectives. However, much of this fascinating work focuses on social movements (Blom and Lama-Rewal, 2021), community formation (Pernau, 2017) and collective action – including protests (Ahmed et al., 2017); riots (Mitchell, 2009; Pernau, 2021b); and displays of outrage (Blom and Jaoul, 2008), hurt (Ramdev et al., 2016) and militancy (Roy, 2011; Parashar, 2015). We have some excellent studies of emotions in the context of pride (Michelutti, 2004), humiliation (Guru, 2011) and nationalism (Benei, 2008). However, the role of emotions in studies around elections has tended to be neglected. The present book fills this crucial gap.

The neglect of emotions in electoral politics has led social scientists to ignore the importance of emotions in a key pillar of India's democracy: elections. While we have a growing understanding of emotions in the context of protest politics, social movements and riots, we have been left with the erroneous assumption that emotions are unimportant to electoral politics. Meanwhile, the increasingly sophisticated academic analysis of elections could do more to integrate the study of emotions. This book makes a preliminary contribution towards that end.

The passionate politics of Hindu nationalist welfarism

While the importance of Narendra Modi's persona and the BJP's organisational and financial prowess to the electoral outcomes cannot be ignored, the emotions that diffused through supporters need better understanding. Such emotions are shaped by the manner in which the BJP blended nationalism with Hindutva and welfarism over the past five years under Modi's watch.

Modi's resounding victory is an endorsement of his muscular nationalism and aggressive stance against neighbours Pakistan and China, significant in the wake of terror attacks on military personnel in February 2019. The attack killed forty soldiers. India retaliated through much-publicised attacks on alleged terror camps in Pakistan-controlled territory of Balakot, and claimed to have killed 300 terrorists affiliated with the dreaded Jaish-e-Mohammed group. Modi's approval ratings soared by as much as 7% (*Times of India*, 2019)[6] after these events, suggesting that nationalist fervour may have contributed to his emphatic win (Vaishnav, 2019).[7]

If nationalism resulted in a surge of support for Modi, Hindutva – the political ideology which puts forward that Hinduism, India's majority faith, ought to be the bedrock of Indian nationalism – provided much of the bedrock for the support in the first place. Results from the National Election Survey, conducted among a random sample of 24,236 voters as they left the polling stations in 211 parliamentary constituencies (National Election Studies, 2019),[8] suggests an unprecedented degree of Hindu consolidation behind the BJP and its allies: for the first time ever, over half of all Hindus reported voting for the BJP or its alliance partners, while the majority of Muslims reported voting for opposition parties (Sardesai and Attri, 2019).[9] During election speeches the Prime Minister himself invoked 'Hindu anger' against the opposition parties who had once accused Hindu radicals of fomenting terror (*Telegraph Online*, 2019),[10] while carefully crafting a Hindu persona (Khare, 2019) and assiduously courting the Hindu vote.[11] The BJP fielded a Hindu radical accused of plotting terror attacks on Muslims, promised to implement the National Register of Citizens that threatened (albeit obliquely) Muslims and Christians with detention and deportation and pledged to build a temple to honour Rama in the disputed northern Indian city of Ayodhya where right-wing activists had demolished a sixteenth-century mosque back in 1992 under the party's leadership. Even though the evidence that Hindu consolidation resulted from anti-Muslim sentiment remains mixed,[12] a rightward shift towards Hindu majoritarianism in India's political discourse is unmistakable.[13]

Blending nationalist fervour and emotions fomented by Hindutva, the BJP and its allies appear to have benefited from the feelings of care generated by the welfare programmes promised and implemented by the central government since 2014. One flagship programme announced by the government midway through its first tenure was the Ujjwala scheme, which promised to provide free liquefied petroleum gas to poor women. Analysts working with diverse sorts of data confirmed that the popularity of this scheme was a major reason for the BJP's ability to breach votes from the poor, a constituency with which it had always struggled.[14] Modi is widely seen as having delivered on promises of welfare, centred on providing welfare to the poor, such as homes, toilets, cooking gas and financial credit. Although the quality of these provisions remains vigorously debated – and many schemes have just been launched, so a full examination of their coverage and quality will only be possible in subsequent years – voters appear to trust Modi's ability to deliver on his pledges.[15] They have been willing to ignore the inconvenience caused to them by such controversial decisions as demonetisation of high-currency notes and the introduction of a unified Goods and Service Tax across India.

Recovering passions in electoral politics

Any claim that the passionate politics generated by Hindu nationalist welfarism in the run-up to the 2019 general election is unprecedented in India's political history will surely – and justifiably – invite swift rebuttals. The landscape of Indian politics is dotted with moments when passions, feelings and emotions were on full display. Nevertheless, attention to passions has tended to focus on cataclysmic events such as India's Partition and the communal violence that has blemished India's record as a democracy, mass movements such as the cow protection campaigns, agitations against the implementation of affirmative action, and collective protests against atrocities on women, children and members of oppressed social groups. Therefore, we make no claims about recovering passions in politics per se. Rather, what we hope to achieve in this volume is to direct attention to the passions that underpin such *routine aspects* of procedural democracy as elections.

Indeed, previous elections in India surely presented such opportunities to researchers. Modi's landslide re-election pales in comparison with another key moment in India's electoral politics. The 45% vote share he picked up was far lower than the 49% vote share the Congress Party mustered back in 1984. But those elections were held in the aftermath of then Prime Minister Indira Gandhi's assassination by her own bodyguards. Voters sympathised with her son Rajiv Gandhi who was contesting the 1984 election to carry forward his mother's mantle. There were no national-level opposition parties to speak of. The election had been held in the wake of ghastly anti-Sikh violence in Delhi and elsewhere in northern India. Passions were high as anger, fear and grief entwined to hand the Congress Party the largest ever mandate in postcolonial India.

In its heyday as India's dominant party, the Congress Party may well have benefited from such passionate politics. In the first ever general election after becoming a republic, held in 1951–52, the Congress Party under first Prime Minister Jawaharlal Nehru won 45% of the vote and 364 of 489 parliamentary seats. In the second general election, the Congress Party improved its vote share (47%) as well as seat share (371). In 1971, Mrs Gandhi commanded 43% of the vote and 352 seats out of 543, successfully translating a smaller vote share than Modi into larger seat-shares than he just did. Surely passions among voters translated into their thumping support for the Congress Party in all three cases. The theoretical and methodological opportunities provided by an analysis of passionate politics could help uncover the 'structures of feeling' that underpinned those electoral victories for interested researchers.

In that sense, we build on the pathways innovated by anthropologist Mukulika Banerjee in her fascinating ethnography of India's 2009 general election. Titled *Why India Votes*, the book focuses on 'ordinary Indians' experience of elections, and on what elections mean to them' (Banerjee, 2013: 4). The 'expressive acts of voting' to which Banerjee's accounts direct our attention emerge indeed from their feelings and emotions towards issues and politicians that journalists, academics and activists might find far less interesting than Modi or Hindu nationalism. Our volume broadens the dialogues initiated in *Why India Votes* to include conversations between political scientists, economists, sociologists and anthropologists to begin understanding the passionate politics which underpin electoral democracy.

The political passions on display during the 2019 general election provide us with a unique opportunity to do so. We hope that social scientists will continue these conversations around elections that may be considerably less interesting. As they do so, we may be offered ever richer and nuanced understandings of such practices as democracy and development.

Democracy and development in India

India is not only the world's largest democracy but also defies the conventional wisdom that development is a prerequisite for democracy. When India became independent in 1947, few people expected the impoverished country to survive. Nevertheless, Indians introduced universal adult suffrage soon after obtaining independence and adopted a republican constitution in 1950, a full fifteen years before economic superpowers such as the US lifted literacy and tax qualifications for voting.

Throughout the 1950s and 1960s international observers remained sceptical of India surviving as a democracy, given its huge levels of poverty and illiteracy. Yet, India not only survived but also emerged – warts and all – as one of the world's most thriving democracies. The country presents a very moving story of the ways in which some of the poorest people on the planet have sought to construct and sustain democracy against enormous odds. Free and fair elections were held as scheduled. Dissent was not only permitted but also celebrated. The national parliament and provincial legislative assemblies were becoming more and more representative of the population. The 2019 election results threaten those very substantial achievements.

India poignantly illustrates the global challenges posed to democracy by the rise of nationalism and populism. Indians are faced with an idea of nationalism that seeks to exclude significant sections of their own population from its ambit. And they have borne the brunt of right-wing populism, as shown by the growth of cow-protection squads administering vigilante justice over the last few years. Identity politics, or a politics that focuses on people's particular social identities, permeates political narratives in India as elsewhere in the world in 2019. Social identity provides the basis of political mobilisation. India today faces these challenges alongside countries such as Brazil, Turkey, the US and various European countries.

Indeed, Modi joins a galaxy of strongmen politicians such as Brazil's Jair Bolsonaro, Turkey's Recep Tayyip Erdoğan, the US's

Donald Trump and Hungary's Viktor Orbán, accused of rolling back the substantial democratic achievements of the last few decades. But let us not forget that these men are symptoms, not the cause, of supremacism, hyper-nationalism and right-wing populism. They are the product of broader economic, social and cultural processes that have been entwined with the democratic deepening witnessed across the world, including in India, since 1990.

This book and its contributions

The contributors to this volume share the belief that studying broader economic, social and cultural processes help us understand the results of the 2019 general election. After all, elections provide a window onto the hopes harboured by citizens, the anxieties they confront and the possibilities they imagine. The narratives that emerge prior to, during, and immediately after any elections offer unique insights into ongoing processes of social change. During the 2019 general election these processes generated a passionate politics that few other elections had. By directing attention to these processes, we add to the corpus of knowledge about an election that was widely billed as 'The Battle for India's Soul' (Tharoor, 2019).[16] That is our first contribution.

Appreciating these processes and the emotions they spawned requires a new approach that departs from conventional political science concepts such as populism, party machinery and vote buying. A genuine understanding of these processes needs conversations across academic disciplines, between economists, sociologists, anthropologists, and of course political scientists. Accordingly, the contributors to this volume delve social, economic and political structures within which India's voters are embedded, rather than the minutiae of the electoral process or the machinations of the different political parties. Through our conversations, we hope to unpack for you, our readers, the manifold passions that comprised the politics of the election in 2019. While sophisticated accounts and analysis of the election abound, we believe our interdisciplinary approach sheds new light on the economic, social and cultural dimensions of a significant political moment in India. This book's interdisciplinary approach is our second contribution.

The third contribution of this volume lies in our collective reflection on how passions infuse such routine aspects of politics as elections. The passionate politics described in this volume is thus distinct from passions that are produced during spectacular episodes as protests, riots and social movements. Some chapters explicitly analyse the passions on display during, prior to and following the elections. Others contextualise these passions. Together, the chapters assemble disparate expressions of emotions to help us make sense of the 2019 general election. This focus on a single empirical case furthers a theoretical contribution on the study of passions in politics: that emotion is entwined with reason, thereby contributing to render untenable the false dichotomy that is often drawn between the emotional and the rational.

The reflections in Part I weave together the feelings of fear and love that permeated politics during the 2019 elections. If the 2014 general election was heralded as India's social media election, the one in 2019 was most certainly a WhatsApp election (Murgia et al., 2019). The 300 million Indians on WhatsApp make the country the app's biggest market. Already in Brazil the app had gained notoriety (or popularity, take your pick). Jair Bolsonaro won the presidency riding high on a WhatsApp wave fuelled by rumours and misinformation. In India, the BJP ran the world's largest digital campaign to reach out to committed and floating voters with a plethora of targeted messages. Others were using the app too, to fuel fear of and anger against imagined others (Chapter 1), as well as love for the supreme leader, his Hindu nationalist credentials and the idea of India as a Hindu nation (Chapter 2). The section closes with thoughts on how these emotions are embedded in the anxieties spawned by India's transforming political economy (Chapter 3).

In Part II, our reflections turn to hopes harboured by many Indians for a social and political order guided by Hindutva, or Hindu-ness. These reflections alert us to the ways in which hopes for Hindutva entwined with anger against its opponents enmeshed with a moral panic that the Hindu way of life was somehow endangered, particularly with the slow but steady dissolution of caste hierarchies. The passions generated on social media were marshalled in favour of a century-old offline ideal that vowed to establish the Hindus as a political community (Chapter 1). This ideal was not only embraced by the self-styled 'upper castes' across class (Chapter 5) but also by members of historically oppressed Dalits for whom Hindutva appeared as more civil than popular Hinduism (Chapter 6).

If Hindus are envisaged as a unified political community under Hindutva, the Indian nation is imagined as a monolith. The Hindutva imagination challenges the special provisions extended by the Indian constitution to the State of Jammu and Kashmir. Our reflections in Part III meditate on the political circumstances of the state's troubled history (Chapter 7) that have generated the desires and resentments which place Kashmiris at odds with other Indians (Chapter 9). Tensions in Kashmir and the role of neighbouring Pakistan in fomenting them of course bear significantly on the Indian elections (Chapter 8): in February, a suicide bomber killed forty-odd Indian paramilitary troops, provoking a swift retaliation by India. Modi's ratings soared thereafter, effectively blending together angry Indians' love for their country with adoration bordering on exaltation for a strong and powerful leader who had taught the enemy a lesson.

Contributors to Part IV continue the reflections on love and anger, protection and panic with a focus on women in Indian society. They discuss the profound changes that are reshaping gender norms and relationships in India today, intersecting with changes in caste and class hierarchies, political institutions and religious traditions. We are offered a glimpse into the lives of young women living in hostels (Chapter 11) and the moral panics generated by freer intermingling of women and men (Chapter 10), enabling us to appreciate the significance of the emotions that permeate gender roles in contemporary India.

These reflections are carried forward in Part V in which our contributors discuss young Indian's aspirations and anxieties. On the one hand, a crumbling caste hierarchy and promise of economic opportunities following India's economic liberalisation foment unprecedented aspirations among young people in the country (Chapter 12). On the other hand, inadequate jobs restrict youth employment in careers of their choice. Many young women face additional limitations of social expectations that curb their aspirations even further (Chapter 11). The peculiar confluence of aspiration and anxiety certainly explains some of the enthusiastic support that 71 year-old Narendra Modi enjoys among young people in India today.

Passions do not exist in an economic vacuum. Our reflections in Part VI remind us of the economic basis of the emotions that politicians generate, manipulate and harness. The contributors discuss both the anxieties and hopes generated by the Modi government's demonetisation of high-denomination currency notes and the introduction of the Goods and Services Tax (Chapter 15). Feelings of being cared for and protected permeate the wide-ranging provision of welfare schemes, including houses and toilets, as well as financial inclusion of the rural poor (Chapter 16). Side by side, agrarian distress, growing joblessness and widening inequalities aggravate worries and apprehensions about the future (Chapter 14). Nevertheless, if the electoral campaign and election results are any indication, disgruntlement with the present regime did not translate into its dislodgement.

Our concluding section, Part VII, reflects on the implications of the elections for India and Indians. The overwhelmingly majority enjoyed by the BJP is likely to further the government's authoritarian tendencies (Chapter 17). Meanwhile, the fate of India's largest religious minority, the Muslims, hangs in the balance, given that they have been explicitly identified and targeted by the Hindutva ideals promoted by the BJP (Chapter 18). The section circles back to the ways in which emotion and reason are entwined by meditating on the reasoning of emotional politics (Chapter 19).

As a collective of social scientists who study politics, economics and society in India (often in comparative perspective), we do not discount the role of money, media and Modi in ensuring the results of 2019. Rather, we want to situate the electoral results within the political, economic and social *processes* that have shaped twenty-first century India. It is obviously not our contention that all such trends inevitably led to the BJP's massive electoral majority. But we do believe that a closer understanding of these processes is key to understanding the passionate politics that has produced the crushing legislative dominance that the Modi-led BJP commands.

It is imperative to distinguish what this book aims to do from what it does not. As an ensemble of conversations that arose out of a podcast series curated for *The Conversation*,[17] the book is *exploratory* rather than explanatory. We piece together different facets of passionate politics that entwined with broader economic, social and political processes leading up to the 2019 general election without claiming that these disparate pieces explain the puzzle of the BJP's stupendous victory. We are also mindful that the book does not aim to theorise passions in politics – that is a task for scholars affiliated with the growing field of 'emotion studies': rather, our more modest aim is to reflect on the ways in which *emotions entwined with reason* during the 2019 general election. Finally, the book refrains from delving into the minutiae of the elections, as we already have several excellent studies by renowned specialists on that topic already. Rather, as we add to the corpus of knowledge on an election widely billed as the 'Battle for India's Soul', we believe our *interdisciplinary approach* sheds new light on the economic, social and cultural dimensions of a significant political moment in India.

Notes

1 For context, consider the BJP's victory in comparison with the Conservative Party's landslide in the UK election of December 2019. Both parties/alliances won 45% of the vote. The difference is that India's election saw at least a hundred serious contenders while only about ten parties competed in the UK election.

2 A very readable account remains the political scientist Ajay Gudavarthy's 2018 book *India after Modi*. Another succinct account is provided in an academic paper by political scientists Christophe Jaffrelot and Louise Tillin (2017) in the magisterial *Oxford Handbook of Populism*. More descriptions of Modi as a populist are offered by Catarina Kinnvall (2019), Priya Chacko (2018), Christophe Jaffrelot and Louise Tillin (2017) and Paula Chakravarthy and Srirupa Roy (2015).

3 We are blessed with a rich, and growing, literature on emotions and feelings in South Asia. These include Orsini (2006), Blom and Jaoul (2008), Khan (2015), Pernau (2017), Chatterjee et al. (2017), Ali and Flatt (2017), Rajamani et al. (2018), and Blom and Lama-Rewal (2021). See also the contributions by Ali (2021), Pauwels (2021), Tandon (2021), Schofield (2021), Kulkarni (2021), Tignol (2021), Pernau (2021b), Maqsood (2021), Binder (2021), Stille (2021), Lee (2021), and Gandhi (2021) in the Special Issue of the journal *South Asian History and Culture*. Pernau's (2021a) introduction to that collection offers an extremely useful overview of the literature in the South Asian context.

4 This insight has been made explicit in the work of the sociologist Jeff Goodwin, James Jasper and Francesca Poletta in the introduction to their edited volume titled *Passionate Politics: Emotions and social movements* (Goodwin et al., 2001).

5 Social scientists disagree among themselves on how emotions differ from feelings. One distinction that might be made is this: emotions are neurophysiological reactions unleashed by a stimulus, whereas feelings are a self-perception of specific emotions, a subjective expression of emotions. While emotions are physical, feelings are mental. Traïni (2010) suggests that emotion describes 'the activity, undertaken by a reflective conscience, of selecting and transforming the information received from feelings while feelings relate to vague impressions and non-reflexive perceptions'. This subtle distinction, while important, is not centrally relevant to the present volume.

6 During polls conducted in January, Modi enjoyed an approval rating of 45% against 30% garnered by opposition leader Rahul Gandhi. Polls conducted in February, after the attack, suggest Modi's approval ratings increased to 52%.

7 Commentator Milan Vaishnav (2019) went on to assert that nationalism would be the biggest theme in the Indian elections. See the full interview at: https://carnegieendowment.org/2019/02/11/nationalism-not-hindutva-will-be-big-theme-for-2019-pub-78344 (accessed 9 May 2022).

8 For full details of the survey methodology, see www.lokniti.org/media/PDF-upload/1565073104_34386100_method_pdf_file.pdf (accessed 9 May 2022).

9 An elegant analysis of the available data is presented by Sardesai and Attri (2019).

10 See this article by the Indian newspaper the *Telegraph*: www.telegraphindia.com/india/modi-utters-hindu-13-times-in-one-speech/cid/1687994 (accessed 9 May 2022).

11 In an op-ed soon after the election results were announced, renowned historian Zoya Hasan (2019) succinctly argued that the results showed the Hindu vote bank had been 'consolidated, consecrated and sanctified'. Other commentators considered that the victory marked the emergence of a Hindu nation (Bal, 2019), the rigging of the Hindu mind (Apoorvanand, 2019), the successful allure of Hindutva for Hindus (Ashraf, 2019; Arora, 2019) and the tried and tested demonisation of religious minorities, especially Muslims (Ayyub, 2019; George, 2019).

12 See the nuanced discussion of the evidence in Sardesai (2019).

13 Insightful commentaries by political observer Suhas Palshikar (2019) and activist Yogendra Yadav (2017) suggest as much.

14 Political scientist Rajeswari Deshpande and her colleagues mined the National Election Survey for data and found some evidence to suggest that the Ujjwala scheme resonated with poor voters, especially women (Deshpande et al., 2019). Reporting for *The Hindustan Times*, journalist

Zia Haq (2019) also found that the BJP garnered unprecedented support from the poor in these elections, which could be credited to the welfare schemes.

15 A stark contrast is provided by voters' attitudes towards the Congress Party's promise of universal basic income. Although 56% of voters had heard about it, only a third had any faith that the party would be able to deliver (Deshpande et al., 2019).

16 This was the title of a commentary on the eve of the elections in April 2019 by Congress politician and former UN diplomat Shashi Tharoor for a piece he published with Project Syndicate (Tharoor, 2019). *New York Times* journalist Rana Ayyub also followed suit with a similar description in an April piece she wrote for Al Jazeera: www.aljazeera.com/indepth/opinion/high-stakes-battle-india-soul-190410110402766.html (accessed 9 May 2022). Another piece with the same title was published in *Foreign Affairs* by Carnegie expert Milan Vaishnav as the elections were taking place: www.foreignaffairs.com/articles/india/2019-05-06/battle-indias-soul (accessed 9 May 2022).

17 See the trailer for the six episodes of the podcast at: https://theconversation.com/india-tomorrow-podcast-series-from-the-anthill-trailer-114641 (accessed 9 May 2022).

References

Ahmed, S., Jaidka, K. and Cho, J. (2017). 'Tweeting India's Nirbhaya protest: A study of emotional dynamics in an online social movement', *Social Movement Studies*, 16(4): 447–465. doi:10.1080/14742837.2016.1192457.

Ali, D. (2021). 'Towards a history of courtly emotions in early medieval India, c. 300–700 CE', *South Asian History and Culture*, 12(2–3): 129–145.

Ali, D. and Flatt, E., eds (2017). 'Friendship in pre-modern South Asia', *Studies in History*, 33(1): 1–116.

Aminzade, R. R., Goldstone, J. A., McAdam, D., Perry, E. J., Sewell, W. H., Tarrow, S. and Tilley, C. (2001). *Silence and Voice in the Study of Contentious Politics* (Cambridge: Cambridge University Press).

Apoorvanand (2019). 'More than EVMs, it is "the Hindu mind" which has been effectively rigged', The Wire, 21 May. Available at: https://thewire.in/religion/rigging-of-the-hindu-mind-bjp-religion (accessed 21 December 2021).

Aranguren, M. (2015). 'Emotional mechanisms of social (re)production', *Social Science Information*, 54(4): 543–563.

Arora, N. (2019). 'A collective madness', *Himal Southasian*, 27 May. Available at: www.himalmag.com/a-collective-madness-india-elecions-modi-namit-arora-2019/ (accessed 21 December 2021).

Ashraf, A. (2019). 'Why Hindutva's dark fantasy about India's Muslims could become real', The Wire, 2 June. Available at: https://thewire.in/rights/muslims-india-modi-victory-hindutva (accessed 21 December 2021).

Ayyub, R. (2019). 'I've reported on Modi for over a decade: His Hindu nationalist ideas will be even more dangerous now', *Time*, 24 May. Available at: https://time.com/5595576/modi-victory-hindu-nationalism/ (accessed 21 December 2021).

Bal, H. S. (2019). 'The Hindtuva nation and its discontents', *The Caravan*, 23 May.

Banerjee, M. (2013). *Why India Votes?* (Delhi: Routledge).

Barbalet, J. (1998). *Emotion, Social Theory, and Social Structure: A Macrosociological Approach* (Cambridge: Cambridge University Press).

Barker, C. (2001). 'Fear, laughter, and collective power: The making of solidarity at the Lenin shipyard in Gdansk, Poland, August 1980' in J. Goodwin, J. M. Jasper and F. Polletta (eds) *Passionate Politics: Emotions and Social Movements* (Chicago: University of Chicago Press), 175–194.

Benei, V. (2008). *Schooling Passions: Nation, History, and Language in Contemporary Western India* (Stanford, CA: Stanford University Press).

Binder, S. (2021). 'Feeling religious, feeling secular? Emotional style as a diacritical category', *South Asian History and Culture*, 12(2–3): 278–294.

Blom, A. and Jaoul, N. (eds) (2008). 'Outrages Communities: Comparative Perspectives on the Politicization of Emotions in South Asia,' *SAMAJ* (online). Available at: https://journals.openedition.org/samaj/234 (accessed 23 May 2022).

Blom, A. and Lama-Rewal, S. T. (eds) (2021). *Emotions, Mobilizations and South Asian Politics* (London: Routledge).

Calhoun, C. and Solomon, R. C. (eds) (1984). *What is an Emotion? Classic Readings in Philosophical Psychology* (New York: Oxford University Press).

Chacko, P. (2018). 'The right turn in India: Authoritarianism, populism and neoliberalisation', *Journal of Contemporary Asia*, 48(4): 541–565.

Chakravarthy, P. and Roy, S. (2015). 'Mr Modi goes to Delhi: Mediated populism and the 2014 Indian elections', *Television and New Media*, 16(4): 311–322.

Chatterjee, E., Krishnan, S. and Robb, M. E. (eds) (2017). 'Feeling modern: The history of emotions in urban South Asia', *Journal of the Royal Asiatic Society*, 27(4): 539–557.

Clarke, S., Hoggett, P. and Thompson, S. (2006). *Emotion, Politics and Society* (London: Palgrave Macmillan).

Deshpande, R., Tillin, L. and Kailash, K. K. (2019). 'The BJP's welfare schemes: Did they make a difference in the 2019 elections?', *Studies in Indian Politics*, 7(2): 219–233.

Elster, J. (1999). *Alchemies of the Mind: Rationality and the Emotions* (Cambridge: Cambridge University Press).

Gandhi, A. (2021). 'Shock and awe: The embodied politics of force in India', *South Asian History and Culture*, 12(2–3): 328–344.

George, V. K. (2019). 'The Gujarat model, nationally', *The Hindu*, 17 June. Available at: www.thehindu.com/opinion/lead/the-gujarat-model-nationally/article27957832.ece (accessed 21 December 2021).

Goodwin, J., Jasper, J. M. and Polletta, F. (eds) (2001). *Passionate Politics: Emotions and Social Movements* (Chicago: University of Chicago Press).

Gudavarthy, A. (2018). *India after Modi: Populism and the Right* (Delhi: Bloomsbury).

Guru, Gopal (ed.) (2011). *Humiliation: Claims and Context* (New York: Oxford University Press).

Haq, Z. (2019). 'BJP gets the lion's share of vote in the poorest districts', *Hindustan Times*, 27 May. Available at: https://www.hindustantimes.com/india-news/bjp-gets-the-lion-s-share-of-vote-in-the-poorest-districts/story-pyuICdH368SujpHaG0WL7K.html (accessed 10 June 2022).

Hasan, Z. (2019). 'This is a landslide: India is now a majoritarian democracy', *The Citizen*, 23 May.

Jaffrelot, C. and Tillin, L. (2017). 'Populism in India' in C. R. Kaltwasser, P. Taggart, P. O. Espejo and P. Ostiguy (eds) *The Oxford Handbook of Populism* (Oxford: Oxford University Press), 179–194.

Khan, R. (ed.) (2015). 'Space and emotions in South Asian history', *Journal of the Economic and Social History of the Orient*, 58(5): 611–755.

Khare, H. (2019). 'An intoxicating verdict', *The Hindu*, 24 May.

Kinnvall, C. (2019). 'Populism, ontological insecurity and Hindutva: Modi and the masculinization of Indian politics', *Cambridge Review of International Affairs*, 32(3): 283–302.

Kulkarni, K. A. (2021). 'Performing intimacy: Slavery and the woman's voice in eighteenth-century Marathi lavani', *South Asian History and Culture*, 12(2–3): 206–221.

Lee, J. (2021). 'Disgust and untouchability: Towards an affective theory of caste', *South Asian History and Culture*, 12(2–3): 310–327.

Maqsood, A. (2021). 'Love in liminality: The modes and spaces of intimacy in middle-class Pakistan', *South Asian History and Culture*, 12(2–3): 261–277.

McAdam, D., McCarthy, J. D. and Zald, M. N. (1996). *Comparative Perspectives on Social Movements: Political Opportunities, Mobilising*

Structures and Cultural Framings (Cambridge: Cambridge University Press).

Melucci, A. (1980). 'The new social movements: A theoretical approach', *Social Science Information*, 19(2): 199–226.

Michelutti, L. (2004). '"We (Yadavs) are a caste of politicians": Caste and modern politics in a North Indian town', *Contributions to Indian Sociology*, 38(1–2): 43–71.

Mitchell, L. (2009). *Language, Emotion, and Politics in South India: The Making of a Mother Tongue* (Bloomington, IN: Indiana University Press).

Murgia, M., Findlay, S. and Schipani, A. (2019). 'India: The WhatsApp election', *Financial Times*, 5 May. Available at: www.ft.com/content/9fe88fba-6c0d-11e9-a9a5-351eeaef6d84 (accessed 1 September 2019).

National Election Studies (2019). 'LokNiti-CSDS National Election Study Post-Poll 2019 Methodology'. Available at: www.lokniti.org/media/PDF-upload/1565073104_34386100_method_pdf_file.pdf (accessed 23 May 2022).

Offe, C. (1985). 'New social movements: Challenging the boundaries of institutional politics', *Social Research*, 52(4): 817–868.

Orsini, F. (ed.) (2006). *Love in South Asia: A Cultural History* (Cambridge: Cambridge University Press).

Palshikar, S. (2019). 'People's demand for a strong leader feeds into the BJP's majoritarian politics perfectly', *Indian Express*, 26 June.

Parashar, S. (2015). 'Anger, war and feminist storytelling' in L. Ahall and T. Gregory (eds) *Emotions, Politics and War* (Abingdon: Routledge), 71–85.

Pauwels, H. (2021). 'Cultivating emotion and the rise of the vernacular: The role of affect in "early Hindi-Urdu" song', *South Asian History and Culture*, 12(2–3): 146–165.

Pernau, M. (2017). 'Feeling communities: Introduction', *Indian Economic and Social History Review*, 54(1): 1–20.

Pernau, P. (2021a). 'Studying emotions in South Asia', *South Asian History and Culture*, 12(2–3): 111–128.

Pernau, M. (2021b). 'Riots, masculinity and the desire for passions: North India, 1917–1946', *South Asian History and Culture*, 12(2–3): 244–260.

Rajamani, I., Pernau, M. and Schofield, K. B. (eds) (2018). *Monsoon Feelings: A History of Emotions in the Rain* (Delhi: Niyogi Books).

Ramdev, R., Nambiar, S. D. and Bhattacharya, D. (eds) (2016). *Sentiment, Politics, Censorship: The State of Hurt* (New Delhi: Sage Publications).

Sardesai, S. (2019). 'The religious divide in voting preferences and attitudes in the 2019 election', *Studies in Indian Politics*, 7(2): 161–175.

Sardesai, S. and Attri, V. (2019). 'Post-poll survey: The 2019 verdict is a manifestation of the deepening religious divide in India', The Hindu, 30 May. Available at: https://www.thehindu.com/elections/lok-sabha-2019/

the-verdict-is-a-manifestation-of-the-deepening-religious-divide-in-india/article27297239.ece (accessed 9 May 2022).

Schofield, K. B. (2021). 'Emotion in Indian music history: Anxieties in late Mughal Hindustan', *South Asian History and Culture*, 12(2–3): 182–205.

Sinha Roy, M. (2011). *Gender and Radical Politics in India: Magic Moments of Naxalbari (1967–1975)* (Abingdon: Routledge).

Stille, M. (2021). 'Public piety and Islamic preaching in Bangladesh', *South Asian History and Culture*, 12(2–3): 295–309.

Tambiah, J. (1996). *Leveling Crowds: Ethnonationalist Conflicts and Collective Violence in South Asia* (Berkeley, CA: University of California).

Tandon, S. (2021). 'Friendship and the social life of merchants in South Asia: The articulation of homosocial intimacies in Banarasidas' *Ardhakathanaka*', *South Asian History and Culture*, 12(2–3): 166–181.

Tharoor, S. (2019) 'A battle for India's soul', *Project Syndicate*, 3 April. Available at: www.project-syndicate.org/commentary/lok-sabha-election-battle-for-india-soul-by-shashi-tharoor-2019-04 (accessed 11 January 2022).

Tignol, E. (2021). 'The language of shame: A study of emotion in an early-twentieth century Urdu children's periodical (*Phūl*)', *South Asian History and Culture*, 12(2–3): 222–243.

Times of India (2019). 'Post-Pulwama, PM Narendra Modi's ratings rise by 7% to 52%: Poll', *Times of India*, 11 March. Available at: https://timesofindia.indiatimes.com/india/post-pulwama-pm-narendra-modis-ratings-rise-by-7-to-52-poll/articleshow/68350217.cms (accessed 9 May 2022).

Traïni, C. (2010). 'From feelings to emotions (and back again): How does one become an animal rights activist?', *Revue française de science politique*, 60(2): 335–358.

Vaishnav, M. (2019). 'Nationalism, not Hindutva, will be the big theme for 2019', Carnegie Endowment for International Peace. Available at: https://carnegieendowment.org/2019/02/11/nationalism-not-hindutva-will-be-big-theme-for-2019-pub-78344 (accessed 21 December 2021).

Verma, R. and Gupta, P. (2018). 'Speculation about Modi losing in 2019 are driven by an old arithmetic', The Print, 25 February. Available at: https://theprint.in/opinion/speculation-modi-losing-in-2019-are-driven-by-old-arithmetic/37773/ (accessed 21 December 2021).

Yadav, Y. (2017). 'What is to be done?', *Seminar*, 699, November. Available at: www.india-seminar.com/2017/699/699_yogendra_yadav.htm (accessed 23 May 2022).

Part I

Fear, love and fake news

1

Ordinary conspiracy theories and everyday communalism: Hindutva on the Indian cyberspace

Amogh Dhar Sharma

From the 'social media election' to the 'WhatsApp election'

In recent years, the dramatic rise of right-wing populist leaders in different parts of the world has been coeval with an unprecedented circulation of 'fake news'[1] and conspiracy theories in the public sphere, especially through new media platforms. Well before Trump appeared as the paradigmatic example of this double-headed phenomenon, Indian politics had come to foreshadow not only the earliest signs of 'post-truth politics', but also some of the grislier consequences of this trend. This chapter reflects on the passions excited by, and expressed though, these new social media platforms.

The 2014 Indian general election, which brought the Narendra Modi-led Bharatiya Janata Party (BJP) to power, was widely feted as 'India's first social media election' (Khullar and Haridasani, 2014). During the election campaign, political parties in India, most notably the BJP, placed an unprecedented emphasis on using social networking sites such as Twitter, Facebook, and YouTube as a part of its voter mobilisation strategy. Although the BJP's success in the 2014 election cannot simply be reduced to the efficacy of its digital propaganda alone, the role of the latter can hardly be underestimated. In addition to Modi's ability to deftly use social media to establish a direct connection with voters, the seductive edge of BJP's digital campaign rested on a combination of deliberate misinformation and half-truths that were designed to bolster Modi's status as the harbinger of growth and development, thereby absolving him from his association with the more virulent strand of Hindutva politics. Thus, for instance, during the 2014 election campaign one frequently encountered Photoshopped images of the skyline in Guangzhou, China being circulated as evidence of 'development' in urban Gujarat under Modi. Similarly, cherry-picked statistics were used to make tall claims about the supposed virtues of the 'Gujarat model of development'.

However, in addition to this elaborate propaganda machinery erected for the explicit purpose of campaigning, BJP's campaign in 2014 was also bolstered by a diffuse army of pro-Hindutva social media users who began rallying together under the banner of 'Internet Hindus' in online forums.[2] Since 2010, 'Internet Hindu' has become a popular term of self-description for many social media users in India who proudly champion their pro-Hindutva and pro-BJP credentials on the internet. Central to the online persona of these users is a cantankerous, belligerent and argumentative disposition – not only do they actively participate in the dissemination of pro-Hindutva/pro-BJP content, they also engage in vicious abuse and intimidation ('trolling') of those who are seen to be critics of Hindu nationalism and/or the BJP. Particularly significant here is the loyalty and devotion of these self-proclaimed Internet Hindus to Narendra Modi, which is why they are often derisively referred to as '*bhakts*' (lit. disciples) in online forums and in popular parlance. While the use of the internet by the supporters of Hindu nationalism is nearly as old as the advent of commercial internet services in the Indian subcontinent itself, what marks out 'Internet Hindus' as distinctive is the newfound visibility that these users enjoy and the tacit legitimacy that has been accorded to them by the political dispensation represented by the Modi government.

By the time of the 2019 general election WhatsApp groups had displaced social networking sites as the most crucial forum for the dissemination of political propaganda. As a result, many commentators claimed that India's 'first social media election' in 2014 had paved the way for 'India's WhatsApp elections' in 2019 (see Arun, 2019; Murgia et al., 2019). But what remained common to both campaigns was a similar propaganda machinery that was built on the edifice of 'fake news' and run on the strength of a large number of sympathetic social media volunteers spread throughout the country. If the 2014 campaign was all about advertising the 'Gujarat model of development', then the 2019 campaign was built around 'spinning' the purported achievements of the five years of the Modi government – ranging from the ostensible benefits of demonetisation to the government's 'tough stand' in the wake of Uri and Pulwama attacks.

According to some commentators, the pro-BJP trolls found on social media are largely an army of digital mercenaries who have thrown their weight behind the BJP because they are driven by pecuniary interests. It is often claimed that the BJP offers such social media trolls a certain sum of money for each tweet or Facebook post shared by them that is part of the party's propaganda. There is undoubtedly some substance to this claim as evidenced by the slick 'IT departments' and 'social media cells' that have become a staple presence across all political parties in the country, and the professional staff employed by these party units (Sharma, 2019).

However, to understand the motivations of pro-BJP social media trolls as solely driven by financial self-interest is flawed and analytically problematic. One the one hand, such a criticism tends to discount the deeply ideological reasons that motivate many of these self-proclaimed Internet Hindus to defend the BJP on online forums. On the other hand, this view also overlooks the fact that the circulation of 'fake news' and conspiracy theories is quite independent from the election cycle. Internet Hindus (and other pro-BJP social media users) do not cease being vocal once the election campaign is over; rather, their willingness to intercede on behalf of the BJP has become a quotidian and banal practice. That large swathes of the population are willing to act as the digital foot soldiers in defence of the Hindutva ideology *suo moto* indicates the salience that Hindu nationalism has acquired in the public culture at large. It is here that the peculiar properties of social media technology – such as its ease of use, rapid dissemination of data, creation of echo chambers, and the possibility of anonymity – and the decades-long activism undertaken by the Sangh Parivar – to consolidate the Hindu community and challenge secularism as a legitimate political norm – dovetail together to buttress the rise of the 'Modi moment' in Indian politics.

While the link between BJP's thumping victory in the 2014 and 2019 elections and the blitzkrieg of digital propaganda is undeniably important, it is only a small part of the wider communalisation of society and the banality of violence that has come to characterise everyday social life in contemporary India. Emotions are easily polarised, although it is important to remember that they are entwined within emergent reasonings of political life.

In between elections: cow protection, lynchings and WhatsApp vigilantism

The communalisation of everyday life, and the extent to which media technology is implicated in this process, is clearly apparent in the numerous cases of bovine-related lynchings that have dotted the tenure of the Narendra Modi government since 2014. While the veneration of the cow as a sacred symbol of Hindu culture and demands for legislation against cow slaughter have been long-standing tropes employed by Hindu nationalists since the turn of the century (van der Veer, 1994), the present-day bovine-related lynchings are an entirely new phenomenon. In their execution and inspiration, these lynchings have less in common with the Hindu–Muslim conflagrations witnessed during the days of the cow-protection movement in colonial India, and are instead reminiscent of the lynching of African Americans in the United States during the Jim Crow era.

The schematic pattern of these lynchings has been eerily similar. WhatsApp messages of dubious provenance begin by accusing someone of possessing or consuming cow meat. Invariably, the individual or family in question tend to be from the Muslim or Dalit community. The message quickly gathers traction and is widely disseminated, which then galvanises members from the local community to attack the individual(s) in question. Another common pattern in such cases is the impunity enjoyed by the aggressors and the support they frequently receive from the local BJP leaders. The sheer scale of the problem can be understood by looking at the cold hard statistics available on these lynchings. According to a Human Rights Watch report, between May 2015 and December 2018 alone there were at least 100 incidents of bovine-related lynchings that resulted in 44 deaths and nearly 280 injured. Muslims and Dalits constituted nearly two-thirds of all recorded casualties (Human Rights Watch, 2019). Not only has there been a sharp spike in such incidents since Modi became prime minister in 2014, the majority of these incidents have taken place in BJP-ruled states.

That a single WhatsApp message can easily incite people to attack others shows the extent of polarisation lurking beneath the surface of India's social life. In addition to the long-term communalisation of society that has been championed by the various outfits within the Sangh Parivar, the problem has also been fuelled by the declining levels of trust in two key institutions: mainstream news media and the police administration. While declining trust in the former makes one more likely to repose faith in rumours and dubious news stories, a lack of trust in the latter tends to provoke individuals to take matters of law and order into their own hands. Indicative of this generalised lack of trust and anomie that has come to characterise social life is the fact that instances of public lynchings have taken place on seemingly non-communal themes as well – in particular, rumours about alleged 'child abductors' have served as an instigating factor for mobs to attack unsuspecting individuals falsely accused of the crime.

While much has been said about how digital technology allows for such rumours to spread rapidly, the impact of the medium in aggravating the problem actually runs much deeper. A perverse feature of these lynchings has been the fact that the mob that participates in the attack often tends to record the entire incident on their phones and subsequently freely shares the video on social networking platforms. Prima facie, such a practice seems irrational – why would anyone record and disseminate a video that later can be used as evidence to prove their culpability in a crime? The reason for such perverse occurrences can only be understood by analysing how the properties of media technology have incentivised individuals to self-fashion and publicly advertise themselves as the defenders of the *Hindu Rashtra* (Hindu nation). In an era when muscular nationalism is ascendant, such videos become part of a collective ritual through which individuals seek to signal their contribution and allegiance to the nation-state that is increasingly taking on an ethnicised dimension. The presence of a sympathetic BJP government provides an extra layer of legal impunity.

Whether it is angry Twitter users hurling abuse at their critics or vigilante mobs seeking to avenge crimes against the holy cow, digital technology in their hands is not merely an instrument to disseminate 'fake news' and 'conspiracy theories'. Rather, the possibility of self-promotion promised by new media technology is precisely what incentivises individuals to position themselves as the proud defenders of Hindu culture in the first place. While the role of such symbolic and psychic benefits in driving individual behaviour might seem irrational, it should not be dismissed offhand. On Twitter, one finds many Internet Hindus advertising 'Followed by PM Modi' as a badge of honour on their profiles. While Modi has often been criticised for his decision to follow certain abusive Twitter handles, for these social media users being followed by the prime minister becomes an honourable distinction par excellence; it becomes the ultimate recognition and proof of their digital activism on behalf of the BJP and the ideology of Hindutva.

Who becomes an Internet Hindu?

While little is known about the actual people who call themselves Internet Hindus, their online persona tends to give rise to a number of stereotypes about them. Given their bellicose disposition and recourse to coarse language, it is tempting to think that these social media users are drawn largely from the ranks of the unemployed, lumpenised urban youth. For example, one popular commentator believes that such right-wing Hindutva trolls are predominantly sexually frustrated men who have little command over the English language and who come from relatively humble socio-economic backgrounds (Bhagat, 2015). In other words, we are given to believe that these Internet Hindus must be some kind of 'mofussil incels'. Such characterisations are rarely based on actual research and are predicated on the commonplace assumption that frustrations emerging from one's personal circumstances spur anomic behaviour in public life. In the context of cow-related lynchings, Modi and other BJP leaders have also dismissed the vigilante *gau rakshaks* (the so-called 'cow protectors') as 'anti-social elements', petty criminals, and extortionists (Hasan, 2016). However, such stereotypes are gross generalisations insofar as they conceal the diversity that exists among those who rally behind the BJP and Hindu nationalism in online forums. More seriously, they also tend to obfuscate how even relatively privileged and seemingly respectable individuals actively participate in perpetuating communal propaganda, information chaos, trolling and deliberate misinformation online.

In early 2010, based on a casual Twitter survey, most Internet Hindus described themselves as very well-educated, high-earning, qualified young professionals, with considerable international exposure (Gupta, 2010). Notwithstanding the non-generalisability of such an online survey due to the problem of self-selection and social desirability bias, it still stands to reason that socio-economic privilege neither inoculates one against fake news, nor does it deter one from indulging in cyber-trolling and extreme speech.

After all, since the early 1990s the middle classes and upwardly mobile elites have been the biggest votaries of the BJP. Even today, BJP's propaganda, which stokes anxieties around the themes of economic growth, national security, 'foreign infiltrators' and cultural pride, tends to have the most resonance in the imaginaries of privileged social groups such as upper-caste Hindus. Seemingly innocuous family WhatsApp groups, Facebook communities and Twitter users are some of the most unwitting participants that help spread BJP's propaganda, which frequently takes the shape of harmless jokes, funny memes and political satire. Far from being solely a problem of poverty and illiteracy, susceptibility to 'fake news' is in fact a problem of privilege and cultural anxiety.

Conclusion

As we find ourselves deeply entrenched in this era of 'post-truth politics' the heady optimism associated with new media technology that was palpable in the wake of the 2011 Arab Spring protests has rapidly dissipated. Instead, concerns have been raised, and rightly so, about the extent to which disinformation and digital propaganda can distort electoral outcomes. Our ability to find solutions to such a problem depends crucially upon our capacity to fully understand the complexities at hand. Those who choose to focus exclusively on the 'social' dimension of the problem tend to see regulatory oversight, stringent laws against the deliberate propagation of misinformation, and social awareness campaigns against 'fake news' as possible solutions. Others who focus on the 'technological' dimension of the problem have reposed their faith in technical fixes (such as daily limits on forwarded messages on WhatsApp) and retaliatory 'fact-check' news portals.

In India, supporters of Hindu nationalism have made use of misinformation and conspiracy theories for many decades to galvanise support for their ideology. While digital platforms such as Twitter and WhatsApp did not create the problem of communal polarisation out of thin air, they have certainly aggravated the situation to an unprecedented scale. Reflecting upon the build-up to the 2019 election campaign in India, this chapter has tried to highlight how the communalisation of everyday life combines with the particular properties of new media technology in dangerous ways, and how the two tend to reinforce one another. Although the BJP's propaganda machinery has certainly piggybacked on this phenomenon for electoral benefit, the problem does not end once the last vote is cast. The passions they generate continue to permeate social life, polarising it even further.

Notes

1 Some scholars have discouraged the use of the term 'fake news' given its politically loaded connotations, preferring instead terms such as 'information chaos' or 'disinformation'. While I am sympathetic to such a critique, I prefer using 'fake news' in this chapter given its resonance in contemporary public debates and its familiarity among non-academic audiences.
2 The term 'Internet Hindu' was first used by journalist Sagarika Ghose on Twitter as a tongue-in-cheek jibe at pro-Hindutva internet trolls. Since then, however, the term has been reclaimed by Hindutva supporters as a term of self-description.

References

Arun, C. (2019). 'India may be witnessing the next "WhatsApp election" – and the stakes couldn't be higher', *Washington Post*, 25 April. Available at: www.washingtonpost.com/opinions/2019/04/25/india-could-see-next-whatsapp-election-stakes-couldnt-be-higher/ (accessed 1 September 2019).
Bhagat, C. (2015). 'Anatomy of an internet troll: How social media birthed a strange new phenomenon in India, the Bhakts', *Times of India*, 11 July. Available at: https://timesofindia.indiatimes.com/blogs/The-underage optimist/anatomy-of-an-internet-troll-how-social-media-birthed-a-strange-new-phenomenon-in-india-the-bhakts/ (accessed 1 September 2019).

Gupta, K. (2010). 'Don't block the 'Internet Hindus', *The Pioneer*, 8 March. Available at: http://kanchangupta.blogspot.com/2010/03/dont-block-internet-hindus.html (accessed 1 March 2015).

Hasan, I. (2016). 'PM Modi slams Gau Rakshaks, says anti-social elements hiding behind the mask', *India Today*, 6 August. Available at: www.indiatoday.in/india/story/narendra-modi-slams-gau-rakshaks-cow-vigilantism-dalits-333728-2016-08-06 (accessed 1 September 2019).

Human Rights Watch (2019). 'Violent cow protection in India: Vigilante groups attack minorities', Human Rights Watch. Available at: www.hrw.org/report/2019/02/18/violent-cow-protection-india/vigilante-groups-attack-minorities (accessed 1 September 2019).

Khullar, A. and Haridasani, A. (2014). 'Politicians slug it out in India's first social media election', CNN, 10 April. Available at: www.cnn.com/2014/04/09/world/asia/indias-first-social-media-election/index.html (accessed 1 September 2019).

Murgia, M., Findlay S. and Schipani, A. (2019). 'India: The WhatsApp election', *Financial Times*, 5 May. Available at: www.ft.com/content/9fe88fba-6c0d-11e9-a9a5-351eeaef6d84 (accessed 1 September 2019).

Sharma, A. D. (2019). 'How far can political parties in India be made accountable for their digital propaganda?', Scroll.in, 10 May. Available at: www.scroll.in/article/921340/how-far-can-political-parties-in-india-be-made-accountable-for-their-digital-propaganda (accessed 1 September 2019).

van der Veer, P. (1994). *Religious Nationalism: Hindus and Muslims in India* (Berkeley, CA: University of California Press).

2

People-led campaigns in the 2019 general election: A case study of #Academics4NaMo

Swadesh Singh

Even before he became prime minister in 2014, Narendra Modi attracted a large set of passionate followers who staunchly believed that concerted attempts had been made by the ruling party of the time to silence him. His political journey, therefore, became a template of struggle against establishment. In aligning with him and fighting social media battles on his behalf, people felt they too were doing their bit.

Modi's passionate following only increased in the run-up to the 2019 general election. This passionate support was entwined with a rationality that sought to prevent a rollback into regimes of nepotism and corruption. They believed that criticisms of him, despite his many achievements, were simply a battle of survival by those who had run out of favour due to the shift in power. Attempts at shaming and dismissing these passionate followers as 'bhakts', 'uneducated', 'right-wing trolls' did not help. These were the supporters who identified deeply with Modi and felt that they too were being hounded and humiliated by those who had power and resources. In this chapter, I draw on my experience as a convenor of the #Academics4NaMo campaign to reflect on the campaign and its message.

A people's prime minister

Such tensions had important and specific fallouts in terms of Modi's election campaign: this time it was not just Modi as the PM candidate and his party that was out campaigning – sundry groups and individuals too threw their weight into the melee. These groups used their social capital to push the Modi campaign both online and offline.

They often had no association with the party. In fact, many of them did not even agree with all aspects of BJP's politics. However, they felt that Modi was the right candidate and a prospective victory for him meant a victory of sorts for them. #Academics4NaMo was one such campaign where members of the academic fraternity and people belonging to educated and informed sectors joined the campaign battle and tried to create an environment in favour of Narendra Modi in their respective surroundings, especially college and university campuses.

The members of #Academics4NaMo worked within their area of influence. These were people in the profession of spreading information and knowledge as teachers, research scholars and authors. Many of them lectured students, colleagues in staff rooms, wrote articles and rebuttals in newspapers, and, of course, on social media. When required, many of them also campaigned on the streets. All this was completely voluntary work arising out of their passionate belief in Modi and their conviction that he was the right choice. This passion was also what set the 2019 election apart from others as it mobilised armchair intellectuals and middle-class society that is known to remain reticent during elections, even avoiding voting during unfavourable weather.

As the election drew near, Modi emerged as the sole agenda pushing everything else to the background. He, in effect, became representative of a narrative antithetical to the opposition parties. The BJP's key campaigns like #MainBhiChowkidar (I too am a watchman) were built around the cult of Modi and with the aim of building a connection with the common voters. Under this campaign, videos were released on social media, hoardings were installed, and finally Modi interacted with professional watchmen in more than five hundred Lok Sabha constituencies through video-conferencing (Mistra, 2019). Besides such organised party efforts, people-led campaigns sprung up in various parts of the country and among various social segments.

People-led campaign

People from different professions and sections of society also planned and executed their own campaigns. Nation With NaMo was one of the first campaigns in this category which had started almost a year ahead of election. The campaign had a website, Facebook page, Twitter handle and Instagram account where appeals were made for volunteers who later allocated work according to constituencies and were given merchandise for distribution.[1]

Similarly, the campaign #ModiOnceMore mobilised influencers online.[2] These influencers later met offline at walks and small meetings and distributed T-shirts among supporters. A campaign which focused primarily on professionals in south Indian states was #ProNamo. NRI for NaMo rallied non-residential Indians in support of Narendra Modi.[3] #Academics4NaMo began three months ahead of the election at a time when academic debate around policy, economy and society was gathering pace. This campaign brought together academics, research scholars, columnists and thought leaders who believed in the leadership of Narendra Modi.

Such campaigns mobilised people, formed groups and ran campaigns both online and offline. These were people-led campaigns where common voters mobilised others within their operational groups and stepped out to voice their opinion in favour of Modi. These people-led campaigns got a good response and made the task a little easier for Modi (Kumar, 2019). Traditionally, a large section of the Indian electorate is known to work as silent voters. However, in the 2019 election, a number of people chose to step out to speak in favour of their candidate – in this context Modi – and organise small campaigns. #Academics4NaMo was one such people-led campaign that was formed to mobilise the section of society that disseminates knowledge and information like professors, scholars, thinkers, authors, journalists and columnists.

Why the campaign #Academics4NaMo

In 2014, when the Bharatiya Janata Party won the election it was commonly referred to as a crushing defeat for Congress and a landslide victory for the BJP. The result was seen in terms of numbers, seats, vote share and margins. When it came to ideology, it was described in highly tainted terms of hate, communalism and religious polarisation. Clearly, though the BJP had delivered a massive political victory it was not seen as an ideological win because a major section of

India's elite, the English-speaking intelligentsia, felt the new government was inimical to larger interests of the country and saw the Modi government with an acute sense of 'otherness'. The 2019 general election became much more than a race to Parliament. It became a battle of narratives. On the one side, the Rahul Gandhi-led Congress positioned itself as a champion of 'secular' beliefs and rights that marked an 'old India' and marshalled statements of academics and public intellectuals to give the impression that the Modi government did not enjoy the confidence and approval of learned and educated members of society.[4] On the other side, Modi emerged as a champion of a 'new India' that took seriously governance, nationalism and security.

At this stage the role of academics, intellectuals and thought leaders who believed in Modi's idea of a 'new India' became important. A section of opinion makers came together under the campaign #Academics4NaMo to counter the propaganda, create a positive environment and spread the word about the achievements of the Modi government. The campaign #Academics4NaMo believed that the battle of 2019 was between two narratives: on one side was the gloom-and-doom end-of-days narrative of the opposition which led the country towards the politics of dynasts, corruption, instability and appeasement; on the other side stood the narrative of the 'new India' of Narendra Modi where everyone was seen as a partner in growth. This group took it upon itself to explain to the electorate the importance of this election and how it could decide the direction and pace of the country.[5]

The campaign

#Academics4NaMo campaign was launched in New Delhi in the first week of March 2019 by professors and research scholars from Jawaharlal Nehru University, Delhi University, the Indian Institute of Technology and other universities (Kaushika, 2019). A core committee was formed to steer the activities of the campaign. Website, content, editing, designing, media, social media, offline meetings and outreach were handled by different teams. The goal was to express and consolidate the passionate love felt by the academics for the prime minister.

The first stirrings of this initiative began with an online campaign. A website was launched to help people understand its goal.[6] Academics and other thought leaders from different parts of the country registered and subscribed to newsletters through the website. Over the next few weeks, the campaign garnered the support of hundreds of academics, thinkers, scholars and intellectuals and over 2,000 members of these groups from more than eighty cities registered on the website.

The social media platforms Twitter, Facebook, LinkedIn, Instagram and WhatsApp were used to reach out to academics across India and inform them about this campaign. Through Change.org, academics, opinion makers, scholars and thought leaders were urged to come together and speak out for a leadership that had made quantum changes in the country in the last five years.[7]

The campaign provided a platform to these scholars to write about the policies, programmes and schemes of Prime Minister Narendra Modi's government. A separate segment was created on their website to feature these articles. On social media platforms too, these articles received traction. The response from the academic fraternity was also tremendous. They regularly received and published articles on a range of issues related to the five years of Modi government.

They went on to organise an essay competition, in the third week of March 2019, to encourage young scholars. The suggested themes were 'Modi2.0', 'Idea of a New India' and 'A Policy of Modi Sarkar'. More than two hundred entries were received by 28 March, ten young scholars were awarded for their essays, and selected entries were published on the website. One of the winning entries on 'New India' stated:

> Sometimes, 'New India' is understood as a quantum change in Indian aspirations and high pursuit of socio-economic development goals so as to put India in league with top economies like the USA and China. At other times it is also understood in terms of the use of modern technologies for the growth and advancement of India. An important aspect of all these ideas is a dignified life for citizens in an inclusive society that will value the originality, culture, tradition and heritage of the country. In New India people will strive to fulfil not only their personal dreams but also the aspirations of the country as a whole.

Another winning entry on 'A Policy of Modi Sarkar' discussed the financial reforms introduced by the incumbent government:

It is important to understand that demonetisation was not an isolated event. It was rather a part of a long drawn out strategy. The first steps were to bring most of the population within the banking net and enhance digital infrastructure. Among these, Jan-Dhan Yojana successfully brought 92% population in banking net. Simultaneously, digital payments infrastructure was enhanced to reach 14% of the economic transactions within a year. On the other hand, a special investigation team was constituted to handle the foreign-parked black-money, which has helped in recovering approximately Rs. 1.2 Lakh [120,000] Crore by the end of 2018.

#Academics4NaMo was also in the news for bringing a unique perspective to the election campaign. This campaign successfully pushed back the signature campaigns used by the opposition to create the impression that academics and thought leaders opposed the incumbent government.[8] As a team, some of the members of this group also got together and wrote rebuttals from time to time to the narratives propped up by the intellectuals batting for the opposition. These rebuttals were published in mainstream media and helped to swing the debate. One such rebuttal published by popular online portal The Print took on the politics of signature campaigns over employment data:

> In deference to facts and contemporary pace, it is inaccurate to use one year's employment sample as representative of five years, and further use this to claim highest or lowest in 45 years. In statistical studies, the devil lies in the detail – sample size, year, time taken, comparative parameters – and in academia it is shocking to build arguments on a section of an unverified report. In this light, the said academics should have instead appealed to political parties and media personnel to read statistics holistically and not use partial or leaked reports to create an environment of uncertainty. (Mishra et al., 2019)

News about the campaign was also shared by the NaMo app of Prime Minister Narendra Modi on 24 March 2019. Taking the campaign to the next level, the team announced small offline meetings on 2 and 3 April 2019. Those who joined through websites and became part of this campaign were asked to hold small meetings in their hostels, campuses or neighbourhoods. Members were helped with talking points to ensure positive and meaningful engagement. Members across the country held meetings and actively shared pictures of such meetings online. Following this effort, #Academics4NaMo also helped in organising intellectual meets in Kanpur and Lucknow. The second round of small offline meetings was announced on 8 and 9 May 2019. This time teachers and research scholars were the focus of the campaign. Participants were provided with campaign T-shirts which were worn for these meetings. More than 200 small meetings of 10–15 people in 60 cities were organised on these dates. Besides Delhi-NCR, Kolkata, Chennai and Mumbai, members shared images of these meetings from Lucknow, Jodhpur, Jaisalmer, Dimapur, Chandigarh, Gorakhpur, Varanasi, Ahmedabad, Patna, Motihari, Bhopal, Gaya, Kanpur, Lucknow, Kolkata, Chennai, Palakkad, among others.

On social media too, #Academics4NaMo created ripples. It was among the top India trends on Twitter on 22 March and 18 May. Members regularly wrote through this campaign and provided feedback through the website and an active email account. A two-way communication was created through optimum use of social media and newsletters. A team of volunteers comprising teachers, students and research scholars worked round the clock reaching out to members, updating websites and social media handles, providing creatives and ensuring that Modi's message and vision reached as many people as possible.

The hidden faces

This campaign saw voluntary participation of people from across the country who galvanised simply to support Modi's candidature. Many of the participants were ordinary silent voters who did not have an explicit association with any party and also did not personally know the core members of the campaign. They came to know about the campaign either by virtue of being in the academic fraternity or through social media, and took the decision to become a part of the campaign. The campaign specifically created room for people who weren't regular party supporters and who might not be in complete agreement with its views on different issues. Modi was the single binding factor in this campaign, bringing together people who felt that he had done a good job and deserved a second term.

The general election of 2019 saw a highly charged environment with people on both sides passionately putting forward their views by using different channels of mainstream media and social media.

This was the first time that India saw strong people-led campaigns that targeted specific sections of society. With the ever-expanding persona of Modi, most of these campaigns were built around him as the leader, and easy access to media helped these campaigns gather support and momentum. It can therefore be said that clarity of vision, objective and message, along with well-oiled party machinery, can push past the threshold in terms of reach, to arrive at a point where people pick up the electoral message and create their own small, localised campaigns outside the party umbrella – as seen in the 2019 election.

Notes

1 Facebook page of Nation With NaMo: www.facebook.com/NationWithNaMo2019/ (accessed 18 October 2019).
2 Twitter handle of #ModiOnceMore: https://twitter.com/modioncemore (accessed 18 October 2019).
3 Website of NRI for NaMo: http://nri4namo.org/ (accessed 18 October 2019).
4 Tweet of Sam Pitroda endorsing teachers' condemnation of Narendra Modi: https://twitter.com/sampitroda/status/1125606517347057664?lang=en (accessed 18 October 2019).
5 www.academics4namo.com/about/ (accessed 6 September 2019).
6 www.academics4namo.com (accessed 6 September 2019).
7 #Academics4NaMo petition: www.change.org/p/academics-academics4namo-researchers-professors-and-thinkers-for-narendra-modi-in-2019-elections (accessed 21 December 2021).
8 'Intellectuals from DU, JNU and IIT supported Modi': https://aajtak.intoday.in/story/campaign-on-twitter-for-uniting-the-intellectual-community-to-support-narendra-modi-1-1070209.html (accessed 21 December 2021).

References

Kaushika, P. (2019). '300 academics from JNU, IIT, BHU & other universities launch campaign for Modi re-election', The Print, 8 March. Available at: https://theprint.in/politics/300-academics-from-jnu-iit-bhu-other-universities-launch-campaign-for-modi-re-election/202902/ (accessed 6 September 2019).

Kumar, M. (2019). 'Lok Sabha election campaign 2019', Inext Live, 31 May. Available at: www.inextlive.com/lok-sabha-election-campaign-2019-campaign-launched-by-bjp-phir-ek-baar-modi-sarkar-201905300027? fbclid=IwAR1-U7qyEr0uWtOUWICMlzd__UKl02mYVJejrMD-MlXavHT0PvQ4ght0–24 (accessed 21 December 2021).

Mishra, V., Abhinadan, N. and Singh, S. (2019). 'Rahul Gandhi using 108 scholars' dissent on data makes it political, not intellectual concern', The Print, 19 March. Available at: https://theprint.in/opinion/rahul-gandhi-using-108-scholars-dissent-on-data-makes-it-political-not-intellectual-concern/207616/ (accessed 21 December 2021).

Mistra, R. (2019). 'PM Narendra Modi to address nation through video conference', *India Today*, 31 March. Available at: www.indiatoday.in/mail-today/story/pm-narendra-modi-to-address-nation-through-video-conference-booths-set-up-at-500-locations-1490443-2019-03-31 (accessed 21 December 2021).

Part II

The emotive politics of Hindu nationalism

3

Neoliberalism and cultural majoritarianism in India

Ajay Gudavarthy

Across the globe, right-wing politics – by which I refer to a brand of politics that wishes to invoke categories such as tradition, reinforce social hierarchies, and arrange society around given ascriptive identities of caste and religion – has gained an unprecedented ascendance that few had expected, even a few years ago. We need more authentic explanations that do not merely offer a moral and political critique of the authoritarian elements intrinsic to the right. However, it needs to be understood that the right also represents a world view that people positively affirm: emotions are not opposed to reasoning but are essentially evaluative. Once we begin to understand that right-wing politics is not merely about brainwashing but is a way of making sense of social life within the limits of a social context they live in then we need to approach the hegemony of the right and its authoritarian elements differently from the existing left-liberal discourses that offer either structuralist analysis or reduce it to use of force and fake news (Patnaik, 2019).

Ascendance of the right partly emerges from the crisis of colonial and capitalist modernity in India (Arnold, 2015) that introduces modernist language of law, rights and individualism. Such a colonial-capitalist modernity could neither include everyone nor could it sustain those it included by offering better economic opportunities and social mobility. Modernity has opened up social differences in its quest for equality without actually knowing how to realise it or what that new utopia of 'equality, liberty and fraternity' actually looks like. In the process, modernity made social life complex, morally uncertain, socially unsettled and personally burdened without ever resolving the issues it has opened up for negotiation. Multiple floodgates of social dynamics were opened, from intimate sexual issues to impersonal issues of structural exclusion. It only offered ad hoc solutions that were fixing the problems as they emerged. Complexity without moral certainty can be emotionally draining and has the potential of raising larger questions of purpose of life, and set in anxiety and anomie (Mishra, 2016).

At another level, the modern principles of justice themselves became sources of exclusion, and sources of domination. Truth, reason, equality, freedom and deliberation were themselves under stress and scrutiny in terms of their ability to achieve what they promise. Even these were cited by those critical of the modernist project and its emphasis on 'progressivism' as vehicles of carrying the same domination that they promised to fight and vanquish. The project of a universal, inclusive justice was delegitimised by various progressive philosophies of the twentieth century. They rightly questioned, but without offering an alternative. Cultural sociologist Jeffrey Alexander, in his book on *The Dark Side of Modernity*, argues that 'Social theorists have struggled to comprehend the Janus-faces of modernity. Weber linked this-worldly asceticism to autonomy and domination, yet while conceptualizing flight, he saw no remedy to rationalization. Simmel pointed to the otherness haunting modernity, yet normalized the stranger' (Alexander, 2013: 4).

All political movements for justice carry within them the seeds of injustice. Movements for autonomy, such as those of Kashmir and Assam, could also be represented as movements representing closed worlds that are insular and chauvinistic. Demands for linguistic assertion could also be called out for being nativistic and narrow-minded. Demands for more freedom could be represented as being without fraternal bonding where the state was made to withdraw in the name of freedom, welfare was delegitimised in the name of efficiency, and the law and institutions were delegitimised in the name of regulation and control. What such a critique led to was a social vacuum. There were questions without any answers. Modern societies got caught in inextricable circularity, notwithstanding the gains and benefits they were bringing to marginalised communities. In other words, modernity is Janus-faced; it brings mobility from extreme forms of oppression and violence of traditional communities, and creates violence of its own kind.

The right is occupying this vacuum, and promises not only concrete answers but simple ones. Further, its utopia of the future is based on the certainty of the past. Societies of the past represent the nostalgia of a lost community that did not have this kind of endless complexity but more a self-assured mode of living and bonhomie of coexistence. Past is the only idealism and the only palpable utopia that looks not only real but also realisable. It promises to put breaks on the explosion of modern complexities and ethical uncertainty.

Further, the right is promising to preserve the social power that groups wield, and to undermine others who potentially threaten it. This mode of mobilisation speaks to social groups across class, caste and region. Every class, caste and region, however marginalised, also wields some power and authority that they wish to deploy to further consolidate their position. What progressive modernity promised made everyone's position uncertain, even as it promised collective emancipation. Regressive traditionalism of the right, in contrast, is unburdening social groups from the guilt of wielding power over others and pitching for it as a natural condition that cannot be ever fully overcome. Thus, Rashtriya Swayamsevak Sangh (RSS) argues for replacing the ideals of equality with those of *samarastha* – social harmony.[1]

To begin with, the myth of *samarastha* assures you of what you already have, even if it does not promise greater mobility. It replaces modernist ideals with those of discipline, control and security. Even for the most marginalised, for the time being, it brings a sense of certainty that progressive modernity could not promise with confidence. It is about controlling the complexity that had no direction, not about giving a new direction.

The neoliberal growth model has further contributed to this nostalgia of a 'return to the past'. Neoliberalism here refers to widescale market reforms, commercialisation and privatisation of basic public goods such as health and education, tax rebates to corporate firms that leads to economic inequalities and centralisation of resources, and unabated consumption. It thus supports extension of competitive markets into all areas of life, including social, political and cultural. The facelessness of the neoliberal model makes the assurances offered by the right appear more comforting and less unfair. Communities are terrorised by the homelessness wrought by neoliberalism and look to the right to deliver the wonderland of equality and justice. The expression of emotional care to which Roy's interlocutor refers in the introduction to this volume is warmly welcomed by social groups rent asunder by the onslaught of neoliberalism.

The new consent to the right has to be made sense of through this kind of compassionate prism, even as we are alert to the injustices and totalitarianism such consent will inevitable unleash. The moot question that needs to be addressed is what effective difference will a compassionate approach make to our current methods of countering the right. To begin with, we will have to address the legitimate anxieties that are pushing people towards the right, even if we do not necessarily agree with how those anxieties are being articulated by the right.

The culture of neoliberalism

The Indian political landscape is changing faster than we can grasp. Though inequality was generally considered unfair and unjustified only a few decades ago (Phillips, 1999), the transformation in the manner in which power and domination are perceived means that this is no longer the case. As a consequence, the freedoms for which individuals yearn have come to be found within the confines of neoliberalism and the fraternity necessary for social solidarity is experienced as cultural majoritarianism.

This new nexus between neoliberalism and majoritarianism has altered the conventional dynamic between the desire for security and the aspiration for freedom, the hope for autonomy and the compulsions of responsibility, the comfort of community and the rights of the individual.

The appeal of neoliberalism cannot be underestimated. Though it reduces citizens to mere consumers, it deploys the language of freedom and choice, giving individuals the opportunity to aspire to dignity and mobility by connecting them to the modern market.

Even as the idea of citizenship is hollowed out by neoliberalism, the majoritarianism operating alongside claims to foster a sense of community. Though majoritarianism curbs civil liberties, it does not impose limitations on the freedom to consume. In fact, cultural majoritarianism require neoliberal reforms precisely because they provide for political practices (that augment majoritarianism by moving away from the language of rights and entitlements; from citizen to consumer) to be redefined.

All this is evident in the manner in which the current regime is seeking to monetise and corporatise the economy through Jan Dhan, Mudra,[2] the opening of bank accounts, digitalisation and similar initiatives. It aims to link nationalism to the market through the Goods and Services Tax, which was promoted with the slogan 'one nation, one market'.[3]

However, it must be noted that even as absolute inequality has grown in India by many times since neoliberal reforms were launched in 1992,[4] they have also managed to push many Indians from abject poverty and absolute destitution to tenuous inclusion.[5] This has created a tiny elite in the most vulnerable of social groups. A recent International Monetary Fund report emphasised this, noting that the fastest intergenerational mobility today in India is not among the upper castes but among the Other Backward Classes (OBCs) (Bhattacharya et al., 2019).

Neoliberal reforms provide the mirage that economic opportunities are expanding and reinforce the idea that there is no alternative to this course of action, even if those opportunities are not immediately visible. This was evident in how the lack of jobs and the agrarian crisis did not hurt the Bharatiya Janata Party's electoral prospects in May 2019.[6]

At the same time, even as cultural majoritarian politics is breaking trust and dividing one group from another, it is laying emphasis on creating a united, stronger India. Majoritarianism creates a complex web of both inclusion and exclusion. As it excludes religious minorities from basic citizenship rights it provides an immediate sense of inclusion for the most deprived of Hindu caste groups. Even though Dalits are today experiencing a frontal assault on their rights and dignity (The Quint, n.d.), many feel more included in national life as members of a collective or the national. This holds true for Adivasis too, even though they might not be witnessing any major change in their social and economic position (Tewari and Mishra, 2018; Asher et al., 2019[7]). Cumulatively there is no major change, relatively they are better off than their previous generations were, and this makes a difference to their political subjectivity. Since this spread of inequality and crushing of fraternity is incremental and sporadic, it does not allow for any easy alternatives to emerge. While much of progressive-left politics in India correctly argues that neoliberalism leads to inequality and majoritarianism leads to masculine sectarianism, it somewhat falters in recognising the graded nature of the process.

The processes of relative mobility and incremental sectarianism are making it difficult for progressive-left politics to mobilise effective protest. Instead, anger against the State is being converted by cultural majoritarian politics into retributive politics between social groups. This phenomenon of targeting the less powerful can be seen in the growing intra-subaltern conflicts between various sub-castes within the Dalits and the OBCs. After all, it is easier for deprived groups among the Hindus to express their anger against disempowered Muslims than a nonresponsive state. It is infinitely more difficult for the marginalised castes to protest against powerful castes rather than gain acceptance into a majoritarian Hindu identity.

While it is clear, because of growing street violence, anger and hatred, that there is simmering discontent about the system, it is not inevitable that this anger will be articulated in terms of a transformative politics. In spite of neoliberalism and majoritarianism the progressive politics opposed to right-wing majoritarianism seem to be struggling to find clarity about how to respond to the complex web of inclusion–exclusion the system has created. They have ended up with a circular assertion of freedom within neoliberal constraints and fraternity and solidarity within a majoritarian celebration.

Notes

1 For the RSS idea of *samarastha*, see www.uniindia.com/caste-lang-and-sects-are-not-identity-of-hindus-dr-mohan-bhagwat/other/news/1040641.html (accessed 9 May 2022).
2 Jan Dhan and Mudra are schemes from the Modi government aimed at financial inclusion.
3 For a detailed analysis of social policy and its connection with the cultural majoritarian project, see Gudavarthy and Vijay (2020).
4 Chancel and Piketty (2019) show that the share of national income captured by the bottom half in both India and China after 1980 has been broadly similar. The big difference between the two countries is that the middle 40% in India got 23% of the increase in national income since

1980, while the same group in China got 43% – a massive gap of 20 percentage points. This 20% difference was largely captured by the top 1% in India.

5 The 2019 Global Multidimensional Poverty Index (MPI) report (MPI, 2019) stated that, between 2005 and 2016, India lifted 271 million people out of poverty and reduced deprivations.

6 One reason that inequality does not cause great anger is the fact that many caste and class groups have moved away from assessing equality in terms of absolute levels to adopting ideas of relative mobility: they compare themselves with social groups in their immediate proximity, and judge whether they are better off than their fathers and grandmothers.

7 See www.dartmouth.edu/~novosad/anr-india-mobility.pdf (accessed 2018).

References

Alexander, J. (2013). *The Dark Side of Modernity* (Cambridge and Malden, MA: Polity).

Arnold, D. (2015). *Everyday Technology: Machines and the Making of India's Modernity* (Chicago, IL: University of Chicago Press).

Asher, S., Matsuura, R., Lunt, T. and Novosad, P. (2019). *The Socioeconomic High-resolution Rural-Urban Geographic Dataset on India (SHRUG)*. Working paper, ref. C-89414-INC-1 (London: International Growth Centre).

Bhattacharya, S., Blomquist, J. and Murgai, R. (2019). 'Poverty to vulnerability: Rethinking social protection', *Indian Express*, 4 March. Available at: https://indianexpress.com/article/explained/poverty-social-development-per-capita-income-narendra-modi-gdp-5609326/ (accessed 9 May 2022).

Chancel, L. and Piketty, T. (2019). 'Indian income inequality, 1922–2015: From British Raj to billionaire raj?', *Review of Income and Wealth*, 65(S1): S33–S62. doi: 10.1111/roiw.12439.

Gudavarthy, A. and Vijay, G. (2020). 'Social policy and political mobilization in India: Producing hierarchical fraternity and polarized differences', *Development and Change*, 51(2): 463–484.

Mishra, P. (2016). *Age of Anger: A History of the Present* (London: Allen Lane).

MPI (2019). *Global Multidimensional Poverty Index 2019: Illuminating Inequalities* (UNDP and Oxford Poverty and Human Development Initiative).

Patnaik, P. (2019). 'This is as close to fascism as you can get', Sabrang, 28 May. Available at: www.sabrangindia.in/interview/close-fascism-you-can-get-prabhat-patnaik (accessed 9 May 2022).

Phillips, A. (1999). *Which Equalities Matter* (Cambridge and Malden, MA: Polity).

Tewari, R. and Mishra, A. (2019). 'Every second ST, every third Dalit & Muslim in India poor, not just financially: UN report', The Print, 12 July. Available at: https://theprint.in/india/every-second-st-every-third-dalit-muslim-in-india-poor-not-just-financially-un-report/262270/ (accessed 9 May 2022).

The Quint (n.d.). 'Hunted: India's lynch files'. Available at: www.thequint.com/quintlab/lynching-in-india/ (accessed 9 May 2022).

4

The BJP and the war on history

Shalini Sharma

In 2019 the BJP (Bharatiya Janata Party), led by Narendra Modi, won a huge victory in the Indian general election, increasing their tally of seats from 2014, and reducing their nearest rivals to an ineffectual rump. Commentators and political scientists can't agree on the reasons for Modi's success. Was it a result of effective campaigning and unchecked amounts of money thrown into the coffers of the BJP machine? Was it, as in 2014, the strength of Modi's individual appeal – the common man taking on entrenched elites? Or was it a peculiarly Indian form of authoritarian populism fuelled by Modi's aspiration to boost the country's status as a global power (Faleiro, 2019; Pong and Srikanth, 2019; Varadarajan, 2019). Populism and the personal appeal of Modi notwithstanding, this chapter argues that the 2019 general election revealed the ability of the BJP to claim that it was the truly national party of India. In other words, the BJP presented itself as the authentic custodian of Indian culture and history, a history that the BJP's main rivals, the Congress Party, had silenced since Independence in 1947. The BJP had championed this 'Hindutva' agenda in the 2014 election, but in 2019 it became much more emphatic. As Modi claimed at the official launch of the election campaign in March 2019, 'Our vision is of a new India that will be in tune with its glorious past … India's 1.3 billion people have already made up their minds' (Al Jazeera News, 2019). Narratives of an imagined past were effectively mobilised to anchor the passions that permeated politics leading up to and during the 2019 election.

This chapter surveys how and why the Hindutva version of Indian history became so prominent in the 2019 election. I focus on four main developments. First, the recent recovery by the BJP and its allies of the reputation of the early twentieth-century historian and ideologue of Hindu nationalism, Vinayak Damodar Savarkar (1883–1966). Secondly, I look at the continuing fallout from the 1992 destruction of the Babri Masjid mosque in Ayodhya (Uttar Pradesh). Then, thirdly, I examine some key recent BJP appointments in national history organisations, and also some of the 'history wars' that have surrounded school textbooks. Finally, I discuss how influential Hindutva commentators have cultivated the idea of Hindu victimhood as a problem in India's long history – namely 'Hinduphobia'. History is a powerful political tool which provides rationalities into which emotions are embedded. Narendra Modi's party has learnt this lesson with tremendous effect.

Sanitising Savarkar

An early signal of how history would feature in the forthcoming election came in early 2019, with the resurrection of the campaign to give the Bharat Ratna (India's highest civilian award) to Vinayak Damodar Savarkar. This was a controversial move. Savarkar has always been vaunted for producing in 1907 the first Indian account of the 1857 rising against the British. By the 1920s he was making the case for an independent 'Hindu nation' free of Christians and Muslims. He later flirted with fascism and Nazism, and was implicated in the assassination of Gandhi in 1948 (Sampath, 2019). For decades Savarkar occupied a relatively ambiguous position within the pantheon of Indian national heroes. All that changed rapidly during the election campaign. Giving its support to a posthumous honour for Savarkar – recognition that his own family descendants did not desire – the BJP asserted that Indians would have been unaware of the 1857 war of independence against the British, but for his 1907 book. By December 2018, Modi, already a fan of Savarkar, was openly declaring his own support, paying a visit of homage to the notorious Cellular Jail in the Andaman Islands, in which the British had incarcerated Savarkar in the early 1920s. Two months later, Dr Mohan Bhagwat, leader of Rashtriya Swayamsevak Sangh (RSS), added his own endorsement: 'If we come together leaving aside the traditional differences and divide, the dream of Swatantrya

Veer Savarkar of Hindu Rashtra could be realised. He projected a strong nation with Hindu culture which has a strong scientific base' (*Hitavada*, 2019). Five days after the election result was announced in May 2019, the BJP leadership joined in unison to mark Savarkar's birthday. He was an inspiration towards 'nation-building', noted Modi (*Outlook*, 2019).

Appropriating Ayodhya

As well as controversial historians such as Savarkar, contested historical sites featured in the 2019 election. At the beginning of the year, Modi promised that the construction of a Hindu temple would go ahead on the site of the Babri Masjid mosque in Ayodhya, which had been razed to the ground in 1992. The RSS seized on this. RSS leader Mohan Bhagwat declared that a Rama temple would go up in Ayodhya within four months of the election. Then, at the end of February, a group of Hindutva activists marched to Ayodhya to press the message home. In this way, a subject of communal tension and outrage that had simmered away for almost three decades was turned into political capital during the election. Hindutva ideologues had prepared the ground. After the destruction of the mosque in 1992, a study showed how popular, mass-produced tracts had perpetuated the myth that Rama, the Hindu deity, was born in Ayodhya (Basu et al., 1993). This same 'truth' about Rama's birthplace flourished in literature produced by the Vishwa Hindu Parishad (the Universal Hindu Council) and was also taught in RSS *shakhas* (schools) across the country, as well as in its sister organisations in the UK and USA (Pandey, 1994). These tracts claimed that the mosque was a symbol of Muslim oppression of Hindus, aligning with claims that secular Congress Party politicians were 'appeasing' the Muslim minority 'voting bloc' in contemporary India. Commentators have been slow to note the wide chasm that has opened up between on the one side the sort of history practised in universities, which broadly endorses India's post-1947 secular pluralism, and on the other, the explosion of communal propaganda reinterpreting in particular the Mughal and colonial periods of the Indian past.

The saffronisation of history

The insertion of Savarkar as well as the Babri Masjid mosque dispute into the 2019 election campaign points to a wider trend evident in contemporary Indian culture: the overt politicisation of some of the country's national history organisations. The BJP has previous form here. For example, in 2000 Murli Manohar Joshi, the Human Resource Development Minister in Atal Bihari Vajpayee's government, began to weaken the autonomy of national cultural institutions, such as the National Council of Educational Research and Training and the Central Board of Secondary Education which advised over textbook production, national heritage and historical research. The directors of these institutions were filled with BJP sympathisers who pursued Joshi's strategy of rewriting history to present a more Hindu-centric version of the past. References to the Hindu caste system were deleted (The Wire, 2016). *Towards Independence*, two volumes of a collection of primary materials documenting the run-up to 1947, one edited by Sumit Sarkar and one by K. N. Pannikar, were blocked because of the so-called Marxism of the editors (Ninan, 2000). Prominent commentators complained about the 'saffronisation' of education (Delhi Historians' Group, 2001).

Since 2014, Modi's government has been uncompromising in changing the composition of those all-India bodies charged with overseeing history education. As soon as Modi entered office in 2014 several university vice-chancellorships went to BJP sympathisers: at Ahmedabad, the Banaras Hindu University and at the Jawaharlal Nehru University (JNU) in Delhi. So too did national directorships of all-India bodies charged with overseeing education. For example, a relatively unknown scholar, Yellapragada Sudarshan Rao, who claimed that the epics *Ramayana* and *Mahabharata* were true accounts of ancient India and not mythology, was appointed to lead the prestigious Indian Council of Historical Research (*Outlook*, 2014). Under the leadership of Mahesh Sharma, the Minister of Culture and Tourism, a committee was set up to prove that the first Indians were indigenous 'Hindus', not migrants as previously demonstrated by archaeological evidence. The same committee was also directed to prove that Hindu scriptures are based on fact and not myth, in an effort to subsequently revise school textbooks (Jain and Lasseter, 2018).

Hinduphobia and history

It is not only within India that Hindutva ideology has tightened its control over the past since 2014. The rhetorical strategy of depicting the majority population of India as victims – 'Hinduphobia' – has emerged in the writings of a number of commentators outside India, for example through the publishing house Voice of India. These external commentators are important interlocutors in any understanding of the BJP election victory in 2019, not least because they interpret 'Hindutva' ideology for overseas Indians who are minorities in their adopted home countries, such as the UK, the EU, USA, Middle East, Southeast Asia and Australasia. They serve as loudspeakers for Modi, helping to deflect the common criticism (especially in the world media in 2014) that he is a crude nationalist who has never escaped his inconvenient Gujarat past.

For some time writers connected to the Voice of India publishing house, such as the US-based Rajeev Malhotra and David Frawley (aka Vamadeva Shastri), have been producing texts that question the legitimacy of Indian secularism, rejecting the 'unity in diversity' model that has been the dominant paradigm of Indian history since 1947. So too has the philosopher S. N. Balagangadhara, based, until recently, in Belgium (Gottlob, 2007; see also Sharma, 2017). Difficult aspects of Hinduism, such as the caste system or bodily pollution, were written off by these revisionist authors as mere constructions of colonial knowledge – that is to say, simple ideas foisted upon authentic Indians by outsiders whose main intention was, and still is, to Christianise or 'break up' India. For example, in his *Breaking India* (2011) Rajeev Malhotra claimed that a nexus of international Christian funding organisations was intent on destroying the tolerant Indian nation.

A tangible shift in the influence of these Hindutva commentators occurred after the BJP gained power in 2014. One of the first acts of Yellapragada Sudarshan Rao, as the new director of the Indian Council of Historical Research in 2014, was to invite Balagangadhara to deliver the annual Maulana Azad Memorial Lecture (Bidwai, 2014). A few days later Mohan Bhagwat was quoted as saying:

> [i]n the past 1,200 years our mindset has been polluted and influenced by the values of people and forces that attacked Bharat and ruled

over her. We need to wipe out this influence completely by decolonising our mindsets with sustained and consistent efforts. ... And that once this prerequisite was achieved [decolonising mindsets], only then we would be in a position to proceed to the second stage of introducing and establishing an education system based on our culture, life values and ethos. (*Organiser*, 2014)

The use of the phrase 'decolonising our mindsets' has a particular meaning to a Western audience, not least because of the recent Black Lives Matter campaigns in the UK and USA, yet here its inference points towards, not away from, a racist nationalism.

Similarly, the stock of Rajeev Malhotra has risen in India since 2014. He was appointed an honorary visiting professor in the Centre for Media Studies at JNU (traditionally the epicentre of anti-BJP sentiment). Malhotra's prolific publishing, social media presence and regular speaking engagements at academic conferences since 2014 mean that the charges of plagiarism levelled at him earlier have been easily forgotten. He has led the assault on 'academic Hinduphobia', most notably in his critique of Wendy Doniger, the eminent American Indologist. Malhotra was joined at JNU by another erstwhile 'luminary' of the Hindu-nationalist diaspora, Subash Kak, who was appointed Honorary Professor of Engineering. Kak, a computer scientist who had published on the Aryan invasion theory and regularly defended Vedantic myths as science long before the BJP were in power, also joined Modi's Science, Technology and Innovation Advisory Council (Somasekar, 2018). For his part, Frawley was presented with the Padma Bushan (the third-highest civilian award in the Republic of India) for services to literature and education in 2015. Since then his *Arise Arjuna: Hinduism Resurgent in a New Century* has been published in a new edition, and he has taken to social media, denouncing jihadis, the radical left and even Wikipedia for alleged Hinduphobia.

Although at the extreme end of Hindutva ideology, Malhotra et al. are the tail wagging the nationalist dog, providing a scholarly legitimacy to the alternative versions of Indian history propagated by the BJP and RSS. This plays well among the Indian diaspora, the some 28 million NRIs (non-resident Indians) and PIOs (persons of Indian origin). It has been well-documented in studies of diasporas that dominant groups within immigrant communities latch on to the most conservative elements of the country they leave behind, mythologising their home country as an idyll to which they long to return (Anderson and Longkumer, 2018; Dakshina Murthy, 2019). The BJP has successfully marketed itself in such communities as a link to India, a conduit through which immigrant children can learn Indian languages, a network through which businesses, friendships and temple development can grow side by side (Zavos, 2010). Modi has developed a celebrity-style rapport with these expatriates:18,000 filled Times Square in New York to hear him speak when he came over to address the UN in 2014; 60,000 filled Wembley Stadium when he came to London in 2015. Modi's political success in India is an affirmation of Hindus' status in their own host countries.

The Hindutva makeover of Indian history has continued apace since Modi's victory in 2019. 'Freedom fighter' Savarkar remains in line for a national award; in the meantime urban flyovers named after him have gone up in Bengaluru and Mangaluru. In November 2019, India's Supreme Court finally approved the plan to erect a new Hindu temple on the site of the Babri Masjid mosque. The objectivity and independence of the Indian Council of Historical Research becomes more circumscribed by the day. In September 2019, at the launch of a new Hindutva manifesto, *The RSS: Roadmaps for the 21st Century*, Mohan Bhagwat called on the Indian Council of Historical Research (ICHR) to 'shed light on Indian methodologies, to give currency to the works of genuine historians who have plodded through the facts. It should re-examine history writing that has been based on prejudices, distortions and manipulations' (Anand, 2019). More recently, the ICHR has been pressed into service by the Ministry of Defence to help write a history of India's borders (*New Indian Express*, 2019). Most significantly of all, Modi has turned up the volume on using history to demonise Indian Muslims, stressing that it is Hindus who need rescuing from the distortions pedalled by liberal and secular versions of the nation's past. Just ahead of visiting the USA in September 2019, Modi laid into Hinduphobia, telling an audience in Mathura that '[i]t is this country's misfortune that when some people hear the words "Om" and "Cow", they get triggered. They think the country has gone back to the 16th century' (Bhattacharjee, 2011). For a self-styled 'common man' without much formal education beyond high school, Modi has a subtle grasp on India's itchy history trigger and how it can anchor emotions.[1] So, in January 2020 when he defended the controversial Citizenship Amendment Act, claiming to offer protection to all Indian minorities except Muslims, he claimed that 'historical injustices' were being corrected (*Times of India*, 2020). He may well have been referring to Pakistan's treatment of minority Hindus, but to an Indian national audience impassioned by the relentless Hinduisation of history of the last few years, it was the enemy within to whom his words seemed directed.

Note

1 A seven-part series, *Modi: Journey of a Common Man*, directed by Umesh Shukla, was screened during April and May 2019. Modi gained a BA and masters degrees as a mature student.

References

Al Jazeera News (2019). 'Modi kicks off election campaign with promise of "new India"', Al Jazeera News, 28 March. Available at: www.aljazeera.com/news/2019/3/28/modi-kicks-off-election-campaign-with-promise-of-new-india (accessed 16 December 2019).

Anand, A. (2019). 'RSS roadmap for 21st century India – rewrite history, "Indianise" education, museum revamp', The Print, 30 September. Available at: https://theprint.in/politics/rss-roadmap-india-rewrite-history-indianise-education-museum-revamp/298828/ (accessed 17 March 2020).

Anderson, E. and Longkumer, A. (2018). '"Neo-Hindutva": Evolving forms, spaces, and expressions of Hindu nationalism', *Contemporary South Asia*, 26(4): 371–377.

Basu, T., Datta, P., Sarkar, S. and Sarkar, T. (1993). *Khaki Shorts and Saffron Flags: A Critique of the Hindu Right* (New Delhi: Orient Longman).

Bhattacharjee, K. (2011). 'As Narendra Modi's remarks on Hinduphobia show, liberals must get used to being shown the mirror', OpIndia, 11 September. Available at: www.opindia.com/2019/09/as-narendra-modis-remarks-on-hinduphobia-show-liberals-must-get-used-to-being-shown-the-mirror/ (accessed 23 June 2020).

Bidwai, P. (2014). 'How the Sangh Parivar is taking over education and culture institutions', Scroll.in, 25 December. Available at: https://scroll.in/article/695730/how-the-sangh-parivar-is-taking-over-education-and-culture-institutions (accessed 13 April 2017).

Dakshina Murthy, K. S. (2019). 'Sense of "Hindu victimhood" triggers NRIs love for Modi', *The Federal*, 13 April. Available at: https://thefederal.com/opinion/why-nris-love-modi/ (accessed 31 January 2021).

Delhi Historians' Group (2001). *Communalisation of Education: The History Textbooks Controversy* (New Delhi: Delhi Historians' Group). Available at: www.friendsofsouthasia.org/textbook/NCERT_Delhi_Historians__Group.pdf (accessed 6 November 2019).

Faleiro, S. (2019). 'Absent opposition, Modi makes India his Hindu nation', *New York Review of Books*, 29 July. Available at: www.nybooks.com/daily/2019/07/29/absent-opposition-modi-makes-india-his-hindu-nation/ (accessed 10 May 2020).

Gottlob, M. (2007). 'India's unity in diversity as a question of historical perspective', *Economic & Political Weekly*, 42(9): 779–785.

Hitavada (2019). 'Savarkar's dream can be realised if we leave aside differences, divide: RSS chief', *Hitavada*, 27 February. Available at: https://link.gale.com/apps/doc/A578757330/STND?u=keele_tr&sid=bookmark-STND&xid=7c373df1 (accessed 24 May 2022).

Jain, R. and Lasseter, T. (2018). 'By rewriting history, Hindu nationalists aim to assert their dominance over India', Reuters Investigates, 6 March. Available at: www.reuters.com/investigates/special-report/india-modi-culture/ (accessed 6 November 2019).

New Indian Express (2019). 'Rajnath Singh initiates maiden attempt at writing history of country's borders', *New Indian Express*, 18 September. Available at: www.newindianexpress.com/nation/2019/sep/18/rajnath-singh-initiates-maiden-attempt-at-writing-history-of-countrys-borders-2035494.html (accessed 17 January 2020).

Ninan, A. (2000). 'INDIA: Righting or rewriting Hindu history', Inter Press Service, February. Available at: www.sacw.net/India_History/ann022000.html (accessed 7 November 2019).

Organiser (2014). 'Bharat has to provide new alternative of education to world – Mohan Bhagwat', *Organiser*, 1 December. Available at: https://organiser.org/2014/12/01/57845/general/r21d95f83/ (accessed 24 May 2022).

Outlook (2014). 'Ramayana, Mahabharata are true accounts of the period … not myths', *Outlook*, 21 July. Available at: https://magazine.outlookindia.com/story/ramayana-mahabharata-are-true-accounts-of-the-periodnot-myths/291363 (accessed 10 April 2019).

Outlook (2019). 'PM Modi, BJP leaders remember Veer Savarkar on birth anniversary', *Outlook*, 28 May. Available at: www.outlookindia.com/website/story/india-news-pm-modi-bjp-leaders-remember-veer-savarkar-on-birth-anniversary/331082 (accessed 6 November 2019).

Pandey, G. (1994). 'Modes of history writing: New Hindu history of Ayodhya', *Economic and Political Weekly*, 29(25): 1523–1528.

Pong, J. and Srikanth, S. (2019). 'India 2019 election results: Modi's landslide in charts', *Financial Times*, 24 May. Available at: www.ft.com/conten t/1a4ce784-7dce-11e9-81d2-f785092ab560 (accessed 31 January 2021).

Sampath, V. (2019). *Savarkar: Echoes from a Forgotten Past, 1883–1924* (New Delhi: Penguin/Random House).

Sharma, S. (2017). 'Hindutva and historical revisionism', *Histories of the Present*, 20 July. Available at: www.historyworkshop.org.uk/hindutva-and-historical-revisionism/ (accessed 31 January 2021).

Somasekar, M. (2018). 'New committee formed to advise PM on science, tech-related policy issues', *Hindu Business Line*, 28 August. Available at: www.thehindubusinessline.com/news/new-committee-formed-to-advise-pm-on-science-tech-related-policy-matters/article24799809.ece (accessed 31 January 2021).

The Wire (2016). 'Interview: The Modi government's recipe for historical writing and research', The Wire, 16 May. Available at: https://thewire.in/history/interview-the-modi-governments-recipe-for-historical-writing-and-research (accessed 9 April 2019).

Times of India (2020). 'CAA to fulfill old promises to religious minorities in neighbouring countries: Modi', *Times of India*, 28 January. Available at: https://timesofindia.indiatimes.com/india/caa-to-fulfill-old-promises-to-religious-minorities-in-neighbouring-countries-modi/articleshow/73693318.cms (accessed 20 June 2020).

Varadarajan, S. (2019). 'Vijaya Modi? Yes. Vijayi Bharat? Not on your life', The Wire, 23 May. Available at: https://thewire.in/politics/election-results-2019-narendra-modi-wins (accessed 3 May 2020).

Zavos, J. (2010). 'Situating Hindu nationalism in the UK: Vishwa Hindu Parishad and the development of British Hindu identity', *Commonwealth and Comparative Politics*, 48(1): 2–22.

5

The passionate politics of the Savarna poor

Indrajit Roy

A much-remarked feature of the 2019 Indian general election was the unprecedented support garnered by the BJP among poorer voters. Analysing data from the National Election Survey, the growing vote share for the BJP among the poor has been noted (Jaffrelot, 2019: 151). Journalistic accounts have explained such support by dwelling on the resonance of social welfare schemes with poor voters. Taking a more historical perspective, some analysts have illustrated the role of welfare provisioning by the BJP's fraternal organisations in consolidating the party's support among the Adivasi poor (Thachil, 2014), whereas others have shown that support for the BJP surged among the poor from the self-styled 'upper castes' after the introduction of reservations for Other Backward Classes (OBCs) in 1990 threatened their status (Suryanarayan, 2018).

Drawing on these perspectives, this chapter urges attention to the surging support for the BJP among members of certain caste communities within the poor, compared to others. It furthers reflects on the ways in which such passionate support entwined with specific political, social and economic rationalities, which in turn underscore the rationality of emotions in politics. Support for the BJP-led National Democratic Alliance (NDA) among poor people of 'upper caste' or Savarna communities was considerably higher than among either OBCs or Dalit communities, whose members have been historically oppressed as 'lower caste' and 'untouchable' respectively. The thumping support for the BJP among the Savarna poor, despite the economic difficulties posed by several policies of Modi's first government, may be explained by the affirmative action for 'economically weaker sections' instituted a few months prior to the election. This chapter reflects on the political emotions that led to the institution of affirmative action for this social class. It first discusses the class basis of the BJP's re-election. Next, it highlights the caste differentiation of the class vote for the NDA. Third, it discusses the importance of affirmative action in attracting Modi, the BJP and the NDA to the Savarna poor, a social class whose members found themselves with a precarious privilege. The chapter concludes by reflecting on agendas beyond the BJP's Hindu nationalist welfarism that continue to motivate members of poor people from other castes.

The BJP's consolidation of power: a changing politics of the poor

Narendra Modi dedicated the BJP's electoral landslide to India's unorganised workers, the homeless, households without toilets and the law-abiding tax-paying middle classes. 'Only two castes exist', he thundered, 'the poor and those who work for the poor.' Laced with claims that his previous government had enhanced the dignity of the poor, Modi's speech may well have been made by a politician with a leftist tag. His speech craftily elided the contribution of the country's rich to the BJP's electoral success. Table 5.1 summarises the class basis of the BJP's support, drawing on political scientist Christophe Jaffrelot's (2019) useful presentation of data from the National Election Survey. The data suggests that support for the BJP among the poor has been rising over the past decade. Although richer voters' support for the BJP outstripped that of the poor, the lower and the middle classes by almost 8 percentage points, the *increase* in support for the party among the poor was remarkable. While the BJP's return to power was fuelled primarily by the rich, poor voters increased their support for the BJP by almost 12 percentage points between 2014 and 2019. Support for the party among poor voters more than doubled over the decade between 2009 and 2019.

The caste-differentiated analysis of the class vote presented in Table 5.2 suggests that support for the BJP among poor people of Savarna communities, such as Brahmins and Rajputs, was crucial to the party retaining government. Among Brahmin voters, the BJP

Table 5.1 Class voting for the NDA, 2014 and 2019

	2019	2014	2009
Poor	36	24	16
Lower	36	31	19
Middle	38	32	22
Upper	44	38	25
Total	38	31	19

Source: Based on Jaffrelot (2019: Table 2).

Table 5.2 Caste-disaggregated class vote for the BJP, 2019

Community	Poor	Lower	Middle	Rich
Dalit	34	32	27	30.5
OBC	39	36	37	44
Rajput	71	72	68	68
Brahmin	67	62	66	67
Total	36	36	38	44

Source: Based on Jaffrelot (2019: Tables 7, 10, 11 and 12).

drew support almost equally from the two ends of the class spectrum. Among Rajput voters, support for the BJP among the poor and lower classes in fact outstripped that of their richer co-ethnics.

Indeed, poor people's electoral support for the BJP varied considerably across caste. Contrasted to the Brahmin poor and the Rajput poor, enthusiasm for the BJP among the Dalit poor and the OBC poor was considerably more muted. While 67% of poor Brahmin voters and 71% of poor Rajput voters claimed to have cast their vote for the BJP and its allies, those levels of support plummeted among poor OBC voters (39%) and poor Dalit voters (34%). If poor people's politics could be credited (or blamed) for fuelling Modi's return to power, it was important to consider a politics of the poor not in an abstract caste-blind sense, but a politics of the Savarna poor.

What explains the overwhelming support for the NDA among the Savarna poor? Idioms of care were inherent in much-publicised welfare schemes such as Ujjwala might explain a general support among the poor (but see Deshpande et al. (2019) for the limitations of such an approach), but explanations more specific to the Savarna poor are required to make sense of their crushing enthusiasm for the NDA. Despite economic hardships caused by such measures as demonetisation, the introduction of the centralised Goods and Services Tax and unprecedented levels of unemployment, the passionate support for the BJP among the Savarna poor might suggest an irrational commitment to its agenda not seen among poor people of other caste groups. However, such an approach obscures the political reasoning of the Savarna poor, which drew succour from the affirmative action policy introduced by the Modi government a few months prior to the election.

Affirmative action for the Savarna poor

Modi's cabinet ratified affirmative action for the Savarna poor on 7 January 2019. Ten per cent of all jobs in public institutions were 'reserved' for the clunkily titled 'economically weaker sections' among so-called 'General Castes', the official term to refer to members of Savarna communities. Distinguishing poor people of Savarna backgrounds from poor people of Dalit, Adivasi and OBC backgrounds by noting affirmative action schemes for the latter groups, the Union Cabinet extended an idiom of care towards a social class it identified as having been neglected by all previous governments.

In doing so, the Cabinet Note[1] that justified the policy was drawing on the resentments prevailing among the Savarna poor against the perception that existing affirmative action policies had benefited members of other communities, such as Dalits, Adivasis, OBCs and even Muslims and Christians who were covered under State-specific protective discriminations from time to time. Such resentments are exacerbated by the palpable fear that Savarna communities are losing the superior social status they enjoyed vis-à-vis members of other communities considered ritually and socially subordinate in the caste hierarchy. The emergence of vibrant anti-caste movements over the twentieth century shook up this hierarchy. The establishment of state governments headed by politicians of backgrounds stigmatised as 'lower caste' in the populous northern states at the dawn of the twenty-first century threatened to destroy this hierarchy altogether. The Prevention of Atrocities against Scheduled Castes and Scheduled Tribes Act (hereafter the Atrocities Act) gave legal foundation to the social and political movements against caste hierarchies. Highlighting the provisions made for Dalits, Adivasis and OBCs, the Cabinet Note proceeded to 'make a strong case' in favour of affirmative action for the former.

It took a mere twenty days for affirmative action for the Savarna poor to go from the drawing board to the book of law. What explains the uncharacteristic speed? The Atrocities Act appeared to be particularly contentious. Not only did it prohibit crimes against members of Dalit and Adivasi communities, the Act also identified concrete action against criminals. For one, it established fast-track courts for the trial of offences against Dalits and Adivasis. It outlined steps for the rehabilitation of victims. Persons accused of atrocities against Dalits and Adivasis were not permitted anticipatory bail. The Atrocities Act was thus resented in rural India. Early in 2018, India's Supreme Court ordered a dilution of the Act by insisting that arrests be contingent on approvals and enquiries conducted by local police officers. The court order sparked anxieties among Dalits, Adivasis and progressives among other communities across India that the Atrocities Act would be significantly diluted. Fearing the loss of newly cultivated Dalit and Adivasi electors, the government acted swiftly to negate any dilution of the Atrocities Act.

Anger, betrayal, anxiety: sustaining a precarious privilege

The reassurances to Dalits and Adivasis angered Savarna voters. They staged widespread protests on streets in Delhi and across the central and western Indian states that headed for legislative assembly polls in December 2018. Analysing the protests, an editorial in the *Forward Press*, an online publication that self-consciously offers a subaltern view of society and politics in India, presciently argued that the protestors felt betrayed by the modest safeguards for protecting the rights of historically oppressed communities taken during Modi's first term in office.[2] Placards proclaiming 'Narendra Modi,

Liar Modi' illustrated these feelings of betrayal, as did the slogan 'Black days have come', a play on the BJP's promise of ushering in 'Good days' on Modi's ascension to power back in 2014. In the central Indian State of Madhya Pradesh, Brahmin protestors minced no words about the political fallout of their anger. Women and men prominently held up yellow banners with bold text in red that flared the open threat 'When the Brahmin thunders, thrones are toppled'. Another banner declared, 'Only those who safeguard Brahmin interests will rule the country'.

Such street protests were complemented by scathing campaigns on social media. One particularly provocative post compared Modi with the notorious colonial official Sidney Rowlatt. Rowlatt was notorious for instituting the Anarchical and Revolutionary Crimes Act of 1919, widely referred to as the Rowlatt Act. The Act allowed police to arrest anyone suspected of revolutionary activity without a warrant and incarcerate them indefinitely. The post juxtaposed an image of Rowlatt alongside an image of Modi and made a point-by-point comparison of the Rowlatt Act and the Atrocity Act, which Modi now came to be associated with as a defender. These alleged similarities included:

> *Both allow Indians to be arrested without having committed a crime*
> *Both allow Indians to be arrested without a warrant*
> *Both allow Indians to be detained in prison indefinitely*
> *Both destroy the lives of young people by foisting criminal cases on them*
> *Both impose tyranny on Indians in the name of the law*

Such comparisons between draconian colonial-era laws designed to suppress a subjugated population and progressive democratic laws designed to counter continued discrimination of historically oppressed populations were of course entirely unjustified. Nevertheless, the purported parallels clearly conveyed the indignation harboured by Savarnas against Modi's defence, reluctant though it was, of the Atrocities Act.

Another post added insult to injury by comparing Modi with former prime minister Vishwanath Pratap Singh whose advocacy of affirmative action for Other Backward Classes in 1989 earned him the undying hatred of Savarnas across India. The organiser of a little-known group that styled itself as Bharatiya Vikas Manch Arakshan Virodhi Sangathan (which translates into Indian Development Forum Anti-Reservation Organisation) declared that 'After VP Singh, Narendra Modi is the second Prime Minister who will be remembered for conspiring against Savarnas.' Of aristocratic lineage himself, Singh's espousal of affirmative action during his short-lived tenure as PM sparked widespread protests among Savarna youth. Several such young men had immolated themselves to express their anger against a policy they believed would extinguish their opportunities, careers and social status. While feted by OBCs, Singh faced opprobrium from fellow Savarnas for the remainder of his political career for having betrayed their hopes. Modi now faced a similar future, the post threatened.

The affirmative action for the Savarna poor hastily implemented by the Modi government needs to be understood against the backdrop of such a heady cocktail of passions. Finding their social status and caste privileged threatened by an ineluctably changing social order, the Savarna poor worried that the BJP under Modi was buckling to the very groups they held responsible for their present predicament. These anxieties are unjustified: as economist Nitin Bharti's (2018: 13) analysis of data from the India Human Development Survey shows, the mean values of income, wealth and consumption among Savarnas is much higher than any other social group.[3] However, Bharti's analysis also alerts us to the fact that *within-caste inequality* within Savarnas is highest across all caste groups. While the Savarna poor are socially privileged vis-à-vis members of other communities, their marginalisation *within* their caste group is much higher than the within-caste marginalisation of poor people in other caste groups.[4] On the one hand, the Savarna poor face marginalisation within their caste communities. On the other hand, they confront the spectre of ever-diminishing social status as members of Dalit, Adivasi and OBC communities appear to benefit from favourable policies (that the latter groups do not actually benefit as much as they are perceived to is clear from the data cited at the start of this paragraph). Such a contradiction lies at the heart of the precarious status of the Savarna poor. The introduction of affirmative actions for them following their public demonstrations of anger, betrayal and anxiety suggested that Modi's government cared for them and listened to them. Its swift initiation played no small role in reconciling them to the NDA.

The many politics of the poor: imaginations beyond the BJP and the Congress Party

The overwhelming emphasis in this chapter on the political support to the NDA by the Savarna poor should not blind us to the politics of poor people of other castes. After all, as economists Sabina Alkire and her colleagues have shown,[5] the Savarna poor comprise less than a quarter of poor people in India. Their consolidation around Modi, the BJP and its allies cannot be subsumed under the general rubric of 'the poor'. Certainly, even as the levels of support for the BJP among poor voters of Dalit and OBC castes has leapt over the previous electoral cycle, it is still far behind that of Savarna voters across all classes. Indeed, as Table 5.3 illustrates, their support for parties *beyond* the BJP and its national rival the Congress Party outstrips their votes for either of these parties. Large sections of the poor from among these castes refuse to be framed within the BJP/ Congress binary that frames much of the narrative around Indian elections.

The divergent perspectives of poor people from different caste groups were evident from ethnographic research on citizenship I conducted under the aegis of the Economic and Social Research Council (ESRC, grant number ES/L009676/1). Atul Anand, one of the ethnographers on that project, reported an exchange between a vegetable vendor (of the Dalit Raidas community – we call him Bhullan) and a headloader (of the Brahmin community – we call him Om Prakash) employed in one of the city's hundreds of flour mills. Om Prakash insisted that the BJP was the only party that could govern India since the alternative, Congress, was incompetent. While Bhullan did not deny the Congress' incompetence, he vehemently disagreed that the BJP is the only alternative. Elsewhere, Bhullan noted the continuing relevance of other leaders such as the Rashtriya Janata Dal politician Lalu Prasad Yadav and the Bahujan Samaj Party chief Ms Mayawati. The political imagination of Dalit voters such as Bhullan signal the diverse possibilities entertained by poor people from historically oppressed communities. Such possibilities take us

Table 5.3 Class/caste voting for BJP, Congress and others, 2019 (%)

Community	Poor			Lower			Middle			Rich		
	BJP	Cong	Others	BJP	Cong	Others	BJP	Cong	Others	BJP	Cong	Others
Dalit	34	14	52	32	22	46	27	26	47	30.5	24	44.5
OBC	39	14	47	36	21	43	37	18	45	44	19	37
Rajput	71	15	14	72	15	13	68	18	14	68	18	14
Brahmin	67	9	24	62	13	25	66	12	12	67	10	23
Total	36	17	47	36	21	43	38	21	41	44	20	36

Source: Based on Jaffrelot (2019: Tables 7, 10, 11 and 12). The vote shares for 'Beyond' were deduced by subtracting the sum of Congress and BJP vote shares from 100.

beyond binary narratives that hinge on the Hindutva welfarism offered by Modi or the secular welfarist alternatives of the Congress Party.

Conclusion

Scholars of passions in politics are increasingly reflecting on the ways in which emotions are entwined with reason. Emotions are not autonomous of reason. Neither are they determined by reason: why else would affirmative action generate such passion among the Savarna poor when it impacts a mere handful of jobs in India's *shrinking* public sector? Faced with growing marginalisation within the Savarna communities and mounting challenges by Dalits, Adivasis and OBCs to a social order that traditionally privileged them, the Savarna poor found their fears assuaged by a policy that demonstrated the government's care for them. At the same time, the chapter also urges against the temptation of subsuming the poor under a single rubric. Instead, it points to the ways in which we may appreciate the many politics of the poor beyond the binaries posed by the BJP and Congress.

Notes

1 The confidential Cabinet Note was accessed by The Wire under a Right to Information Act and is freely available at: https://thewire.in/government/ews-quota-consultation-law-ministry (accessed 9 May 2022).
2 For example, Modi backed affirmative action policies in promotions rather than limiting these to appointments. His government accorded constitutional status to a government commission dedicated to the advancement of Other Backward Classes. The undermining of the Supreme Court's dilution of the Atrocities Act proved the proverbial last straw. The full analysis is available at: www.forwardpress.in/2018/08/why-are-the-upper-castes-angry-with-narendra-modi/ (accessed 9 May 2022).
3 For example, the annual household income of Brahmins was INR 167,013. For non-Brahmin Savarnas it was INR 164,633. For OBCs, Scheduled Castes and Scheduled Tribes it was INR 104,099, INR 89,356, and INR 75,216 respectively. For Muslims, the figure was INR 105,538.
4 Bharti's (2018: 25) data is illuminating. The top 10% of Savarnas owned 60% of total Savarna wealth in 2012. This was higher than the top 10%

wealth shares among OBCs (52%), Dalits (47%) and Adivasis (51%). His analysis of the bottom 10% and 50% within each caste group reveals, unsurprisingly, that the steepest decline between 2002 and 2012 in wealth shares has occurred among Savarnas (Bharti, 2018: 26).

5 See Table 8 of their working paper for the United Nations University's WIDER programme, freely available at: www.ophi.org.uk/wp-content/uploads/OPHIRP54a_vs2.pdf (accessed 9 May 2022). They suggest that Dalits, Adivasis and OBCs comprised 21%, 9% and 43% respectively of the poor in India. Other castes, which include Savarnas and Muslims, constituted 22.7% of the poor. We can safely infer that the Savarna poor are thus far less a share of the total population of the poor. A fuller version of that paper is now available as Alkire et al. (2021).

References

Alkire, S., Oldiges, C. and Kanagaratnam, U. (2021). 'Examining multi-dimensional poverty reduction in India, 2005/6–2015/6: Insights and oversights of the headcount ratio', *World Development*, 142: 1–25. doi.org/10.1016/j.worlddev.2021.105454.

Bharti, N. K. (2018). 'Wealth inequality, class and caste in India: 1961–2012', World Inequality Database Working Paper 2018/14. Available at: https://wid.world/document/n-k-bharti-wealth-inequality-class-and-caste-in-india-1961-2012/ (accessed 23 May 2022).

Deshpande, R., Tillin, L. and Kailash, K. K. (2019). 'The BJP's welfare schemes: Did they make a difference in the 2019 elections?', *Studies in Indian Politics*, 7(2): 219–233.

Jaffrelot, C. (2019). 'Class and caste in the 2019 Indian elections: Why have so many poor started voting for Modi?', *Studies in Indian Politics*, 7(2): 149–160. doi: 10.1177/2321023019874890.

Suryanarayan, P. (2018). 'When do the poor vote for the right wing and why: Status hierarchy and vote choice in the Indian states', *Comparative Political Studies*, 52(2): 209–245. doi:10.1177/0010414018758752.

Thachil, T. (2014). *Elite Parties, Poor Voters: How Social Services Win Votes in India* (Cambridge: Cambridge University Press).

6

Seeking humanist Hinduism: Education and new Gurukul coaching models of Hindutva

Suryakant Waghmore

On 15 August 2018, Mohan Bhagwat, the Rashtriya Swayamsevak Sangh (RSS) chief, visited an English-medium school run by Rashtrotthana in Bengaluru. As the chief guest for the Independence Day celebrations, he unfurled the national flag and called for responsibility, sacrifice, world progress and peace – evoking ideas from Buddha and the Preamble to the Indian constitution.[1] Rashtrotthana is part of the Sangh Parivar, and Mohan Bhagwat's speech was in line with his Vijaya Dashami speech in 2015 in Nagpur, where he evoked a (new) *dharma* with universal claims based on diverse but certain essential elements of *sewa* and compassion. This included recognition of caste discrimination and Ambedkar's politics of compassion.

> In Shri Guruji's [second chief of the RSS] words, Ambedkar's talent was a confluence of *Acharya Shankar's* sharp intellect and *Tathagat Buddha's* unbounded compassion [...] Let us all Hindus unite! Do not compromise with any discrimination. Let us set an example of human brotherhood to the world afflicted by sorrow.[2]

Ambedkar, however, is depoliticised and peripheral in the praxis of the RSS. Caste is not frequently mentioned as a great ethical past, and discrimination on its basis is increasingly recognised as a problem to be dealt with. As Ambedkarite and Mandal movements revolve around the repertoire of caste as structural inequality, I argue that Hindutva constructs Hinduism as a civil religion, not necessarily bound by caste anymore, but as a step towards mobilising various castes in favour of nationalist Hinduism.

Hinduism as civil religion

Civil religion need not impinge on private religion and it is not always invoked in favour of worthy causes (Bellah, 1967). I draw on Robert Bellah, who used the idea of American civil religion to refer to 'a set of beliefs, symbols, and rituals that exist alongside of, and rather clearly differentiated from, the churches'. While Hinduism in its popular practice lacks the universal salvation philosophy of solidarity and may seem more like a collection of castes that occasionally unite for political and ritual purposes, Hindutva seeks to actively unite the divided and hierarchically ordered castes under the rubric of Hindu unity. The fear of the 'other' (Muslims and Christians) mostly dominates the repertoires of such mobilisation, along with cow protection and localised communal conflicts.

Despite its growth, Hindutva has limited cultural and ideological resources to unite Hindus, and prominent repertoires (include othering of Muslims and the construction of a golden past) face the challenge of popular Hinduism as it continues to be embedded in multiple hierarchies of class, gender and caste (Waghmore, 2018). Further, new urbanism promotes individualism and newer freedoms that may not want to be embedded in either caste or group-driven religious solidarity (Waghmore, 2019). Caste association and politics create competitive groups and cultures that are not always conducive to constructing a nationalist Hindu identity. In the newer context of mobility, urbanism, incipient individualism and rampant caste competition, Hindutva works towards constructing Hinduism as a civil religion, which is open to science, education, equality, world peace and, more importantly, driven by the ethic of sacrifice. All of these are evoked as part of a glorious past. Based on the case of Rashtrotthana and its recent initiative – Tapas – I will elaborate on how Hindutva wears an increasingly accommodative, futuristic and compassionate coat. It continues to be anti-West (Christianity) and anti-Islam (Muslims), but a new discourse of equality and humanism works towards constructing Hinduism as a civil religion.

Locating caste and Rashtrotthana in Karnataka

Rashtrotthana was formed in 1965 out of volunteerism (*sewa*) of the RSS. It was founded by M. C. Jayadev (1932–2017), a Lingayat, who led the organisation until the mid-1990s. Jayadev joined the RSS during his college days. He resigned from his job as a manager at Hindustan Garage Motors to devote himself fully to the RSS (and later Rashtrotthana) and the larger project of nation-building. He was a very important Lingayat voice in the RSS and is said to have been a strong supporter of the BJP leader and fellow caste-man B. S. Yediyurappa. In 2011, when Yediyurappa was in competition with a Brahmin worker of the Sangh for the Chief Minister post, Jayadev stood by him – dividing the RSS along caste lines (Shankar, 2011). Caste is latent in the daily workings of Rashtrotthana and the RSS, and it manifests in divisive form among the workers and leaders mostly because of politics-induced caste polarisation. However, Jayadev's voluntary spirit and selflessness for the cause of the Sangh and nation till the end of his life are sources of inspiration for workers in Karnataka and beyond, including Prime Minister Narendra Modi.

Rashtrotthana grew significantly under M. C. Jayadev and is now one of the most important social organisations in Karnataka. Though the RSS and affiliated organisations are largely controlled and run by Brahmins, non-Brahmin workers like Jayadev too have contributed significantly to the RSS over the years. The increased support among Lingayats for the BJP during the past two decades may undermine the role the RSS has played in enrolling non-Brahmins, particularly Lingayats, into the Hindutva fold.

Presently, Rashtrotthana runs several projects that broadly cover health, education, livelihood and culture, and religious nationalism is the ideological force behind all its initiatives. While Rashtrotthana initially began as a movement to produce literature for Hindu awareness and unity, over the years it has emerged as a major social, educational and cultural organisation in Karnataka. This has been achieved with significant support from successive governments, corporate and individual donations, and the ideological commitment of the RSS workers. In Bengaluru alone, Rashtrotthana has two major English-medium schools (there are twenty-five schools in Karnataka and most of these are Kannada-medium schools), a major blood bank and thalassemia day-care and dialysis centre,[3] a goshala (shelter for Indigenous cows), a yogic sciences and research institute, and a well-equipped publishing house that publishes books and booklets[4] on important Hindu personalities[5] who embodied the ethic of sacrifice for the nation.

The impressive infrastructure is mobilised through donations. For instance, the blood centre is built on land (currently estimated to be over INR 250 million) donated by Jayantilal Nagarlal Shah and the land for the Central Board of Secondary Education school at Thanisandra was donated by M. C. Modi. Modi was a Gandhian and eye surgeon in Bangalore known for his exhaustive free eye surgeries. When in power, 'individuals' within Congress too have extended state support over time (the yoga building in 1972 gained from such support, and similarly land was provided for the Nandagokula[6] orphanage). Over the years, Rashtrotthana has built networks with corporate bodies and generous individuals who have supported its cultural and social endeavours.

Education is one of the main areas of Rashtrotthana's interventions. In Karnataka, the Lingayats and the Vokkaligas extend their economic and political influence into the academic sphere, founding and controlling several educational societies and institutions – other castes have also followed this pattern. However, Vokkaligas in southern Karnataka and Lingayats in northern Karnataka dominate the academic sphere (Patil, 2007). Rashtrotthana thus is a small player as compared to the Lingayat and Vokkaliga networks. However, it seeks to compete with several other institutions and market forces that undermine the (Hindu) tradition and culture. Rashtrotthana counters its marginal position through repertoire and strategies that weave together a discourse of economic justice, recovery of Hindu heritage, compassionate and sacrificial ethics – broadly framing and consolidating Hinduism as a civil religion. Below I discuss the case of Tapas to elaborate.

Tapas – inclusive Gurukul

Indian Institutes of Technology (IITs) are considered premier institutes of engineering education in India, and admission to them is sought by the new and old middle classes. Admission to the undergraduate programmes is through the national competitive Joint Entrance Examination. Success in this exam, however, is more a function of coaching, and coaching companies charge anywhere between 400,000 and 600,000 rupees annually. Coaching begins as early as seventh or eighth grade and is well beyond families with limited means and income. Workers and founders of Tapas maintained that the Tapas project is aimed at reaching out to the most meritorious among the poor in Karnataka and making coaching available to them.

The term 'Tapas' draws from '*tapasya*',[7] and its motto was decided in keeping with the NGO-ised discourses, 'reaching the unreached'. Founders emphasise the need for providing quality education to the poor, irrespective of caste and religious considerations.[8] The idea was borrowed from Super 30, an educational coaching programme for the poor run by Anand Kumar in Bihar. Super 30 is known for its exceptional success, and Anand Kumar has received several national and international awards. A Bollywood movie was also made about his story. In 2010, he was awarded the Yashwantrao Yuva Puraskar by Akhil Bharatiya Vidyarthi Parishad (ABVP) in Bangalore. Drawing from Kumar's intervention, Dinesh Hegde (CEO of Rashtrotthana) and M. P. Kumar[9] pursued the idea to create Tapas. As compared to Super 30, Tapas was to have better standards of residence, food and infrastructure for its students, while being rooted in Hindu culture. While there is a class basis for providing education to the poorer students so that they can make it to the elite IITs, it was also coupled with the idea that the poor could preserve culture and contribute to nation-building better, as opposed to the well-off who study at IITs and mostly leave the country. Gajanan Lokhande,[10] who works in the corporate sector, volunteers actively and coordinates administrative and intellectual endeavours of *Parivar* (Sangh) on education, explained:

> Our main idea is to uplift, reach the unreached – the children who are highly talented but who cannot afford the education of highest form. Most of the children are from rural and humble backgrounds … We are transforming three generations. By getting one child here, we are transforming the student's life, parents' life. We bring the marginalised into the mainstream and our hope is that they will contribute to nation-building … Almost 95% of IIT graduates go abroad. They indirectly help, of course. We want these students to directly help in nation-building. Bring people who are not in the current education system, bring them in [mainstream], transform them and put them into nation-building activity.

While Gajanan believed that quality education should be made available to all free of charge, and education at Rashtrotthana was in accordance with UNESCO's ideal of rooting education in culture and the Panchamukhi Shikshana of old, Gurukul form was therefore relevant (physical, emotional, psychological, intellectual, and spiritual development).

Besides education, culture is also taught to the students at Tapas. The economically well-to-do urbanised were seen as more inclined to Western values – almost beyond redemption. Advertisements for state-wide tests and admission eligibility to Tapas are mailed to major government schools and posted online, as well as published in some selected newspapers. Only those with an annual income level below INR 150,000 are eligible to apply. Following the state-wide screening test, workers of Rashtrotthana pay home visits to shortlisted candidates to ensure that their income levels are indeed below INR 150,000.

Coaching with samskara

Tapas annually admits around thirty students for pre-university college. Of the students who joined between 2017 and 2019, 50% were from the high castes, followed by 41.3% from Other Backward Castes (OBCs) and 8.7% Scheduled Castes (SCs). None were from the Scheduled Tribes. The selected students are put through a ten-day test to see if they can survive the rigorous *dinachari* (daily schedule based on Ayurveda) that is central to life at Tapas. The *dinachari* is engraved on the walls of the Tapas building.

The daily schedule is organised to provide an environment of 'discipline' and 'purity' as such a sociocultural environment is considered necessary for academic achievement. The nationalist monk Swami Vivekananda's ideals of renunciation and service to the nation further provide the foundations for the coaching education at Tapas. The *dinachari* begins at 4.30 am and involves yoga, *bhajans* and prayer, along with studies. Activities like yoga, *bhajans*, celebrations of Hindu festivals, and *desi* [Indigenous] games are said to provide and strengthen the foundation of *sewa* (service to motherland) among the students of Tapas. The ideal of nationalist voluntary service is also cultivated through the occasional RSS *shakhas* at Tapas.

Following a generous grant from the public sector Oil and Natural Gas Corporation, Tapas moved to a new building at Banashankari campus. Tapas is now well equipped with a library, labs, study rooms, classrooms, a dining room, kitchen, and shared living facilities for students. Pictures of Goddess Saraswati, *Bharat Mata* and *Om* adorn the classroom walls and pictures of Indian scientists and national heroes adorn the corridors. At the entrance is a large picture of Swami Vivekananda and on the side is a tree of success with photos of students of Tapas who have made it to IITs – thus constructing Tapas as a space of scientific education and simultaneously a reservoir for nationalist Hinduism.

Students on the campus follow 'Tapasya' in actuality. They have limited contact with their families and the outside world and have no access to the internet or smartphones. Trips outside are limited to those planned for exposure (including IITs and a goshala run by Rashtrotthana). *Shakha* meetings (RSS assembly) are organised weekly or fortnightly and constitute critical sociocultural engagement for students. Students shared that the *shakhas* help them appreciate and live as a Hindu collective through games, lectures, worship, slogans and songs. Successful past students and other personalities with Hindutva orientation regularly visit Tapas to motivate students and emphasise the need for culture and *sewa*. Along with coaching, students imbibe knowledge about the cultural heritage, military power and past economic might of the Hindu nation.

Despite its focus on providing coaching, Tapas is organised more on the *gurukul* (residential) form of education. Instead of a warden, Tapas has Rukmini (aged 50) as *Mataji* (mother), who used to be an active member of the ABVP in her undergraduate years and served as secretary of the *Vidyarthini* section. Rukmini has a mother-like relation with all students of Tapas, and she follows up on their lives and careers both during and after Tapas, helping them in educational and familial matters. The thick social network of Rashtrotthana with other social organisations is used to help students in all possible forms.

Rukmini is from the Vokkaliga caste and is a paid employee. She explained the need to inculcate *samskara* among students along with formal (Western) education: 'Flower is education, the smell of the flower is *sansakar* … both are integrated … you would not like a smell-less flower … no one in society would like a person without *sansakaras* … learning is important and with learning *sassakaras* is most important.'

Sanskara, in actual terms, involves singing *bhajans* and prayers in the morning and evening, along with practising meditation and yoga.

Bhajans are sung twice a day. Students also pray before every meal. The prayers include *Mathruvandana*, *Brahmanada*, meditation and *shanti* mantra, which are said to relax the mind and help improve concentration, attention, devotional feeling and respect towards (our) tradition and culture. Singing of *Vande Mataram* is also a routine at Tapas. For students, it evokes happiness and a sense of patriotism. Gowtham R, a first-year student at Tapas shared:

> Singing *Vande Mataram* makes me feel very patriotic and happy. It makes a shiver run down my body. I feel an immense source of happiness and pride when I sing it. I am so happy to be here in Tapas because it helps me love my country more than I could till now.

Sanskara also means respecting elders at home and senior workers at Tapas. It is common for the alumni and present students to touch the feet of workers at Tapas. The embodiment of these daily rituals contributes to taking pride in the history and culture of Hindu India and a political consciousness about invasion of India – both medieval and colonial India – that caused the decay of Indian (Hindu) society and culture. Rudip, a student from the Vokkaliga caste, completed his education at Tapas and now studies at one of the prestigious IITs. He recalled how *karyakartas* (RSS workers) would talk about the nation, 'our' duties towards it, patriotism, and the impact it had on him:

> Earlier [before joining Tapas] I used to celebrate festivals, but now I know why we celebrate festivals. Earlier history was only Mahatma Gandhi and Jawaharlal Nehru – now I know Shivaji and Chandrashekar Azad … Before joining Tapas, when there were surgical strikes [against Pakistan in 2016], I simply read that in the newspaper and left it at that. But the air strikes [Balakot in 2019], we used to read every detail in the newspaper.

After joining Tapas, practising yoga and singing *bhajans* helped Rudip build a spiritual self, and the attack on Pakistan became a matter of nationalist pride and excitement for him. Hinduism had become a national and nationalist religion that was part of the banal and everyday. The most memorable days at Tapas for him were also celebrating festivals like Ganesh Chaturthi, for the collective effort that was put into decorating and cooking by students. Hinduism had been turned into a national civil religion with a heightened sense of political and religious consciousness coupled with Hindu unity. Rudip had discovered Hinduism afresh; it involved preserving the old but also giving up the old – a sublated Hinduism.[11]

Sublated Hinduism: from Hinduism of caste to Hinduism as a civil religion

Sublation in Hegelian dialectic is both negation and preservation of an earlier form, and it is neither synthesis nor irony (Palm, 2009). The evolving of Hinduism into a civil religion in Hindutva discourses is thus part of the dialectic within Hinduism. As suggested earlier the citizenship discourses and anti-caste politics in Phule-Ambedkarite movements frame Hinduism of caste as one opposed to freedom and citizenship rights of marginal groups, and this discourse has now spread from southwest to northwest India. The making of Hinduism into a civil religion in Hindutva discourse is thus a necessity both for local politics and global cosmopolitan claims.

In the everyday functioning of Rashtrotthana, and more particularly Tapas, the hierarchy of caste is replaced with the hierarchy of respect, seniority and submission to authority within the movement and the historical narratives it is based on. None of the present students that I talked to from marginal castes complained of discrimination along caste lines. This is decidedly different from popular Hinduism. Such a version of inclusion is indeed not egalitarianism; it is rather an alternative version of hierarchy that promises a reversal of estrangement embedded for non-pure castes in popular Hinduism.

Hinduism as a civil religion is a nationalised religion, one where the territory of India and a 'thin' and abstracted notion of Hinduism are merged to create a new common space that can mediate between the localised communities of sects and castes. Hinduism is reconstructed as an accommodative and civil religion for all Hindus, and Hindu *Manushyata* (humanism) is evoked to counter westernisation and internal 'divisions'.

The making of Hinduism as a civil religion also points to a new Hindu consciousness among the lower and marginal castes, which counters the estrangement popular Hinduism creates. While liberal Hindus hope to use Hinduism to counter Hindutva, Hindutva is slowly countering the ills of the Hindu religion by framing and promoting Hinduism as a national civil religion. Caste, however, is not just localised but integral to the metaphysics of Hinduism, and Hinduism as a civil religion continues to find it difficult to overcome caste.

Notes

1 Speech accessed from: www.youtube.com/watch?v=IfICIgMg4As (accessed 13 August 2020).
2 Full transcribed speech accessed from: https://samvada.org/2015/news/mohan-bhagwats-rssvijayadashami-speech-2015/ (accessed 12 December 2020).
3 On the day of my visit, I observed several Muslim patients. The head of Rashtrotthana informed me that close to 40% of beneficiaries at the Thalassemia Centre were Muslims.
4 These include people like Bala Gandharva, Ramana Maharishi, Obavva, Tulsidas and several others.
5 This is not the standard range of north Indian eminent Hindus who represent the RSS's idea of national self-sacrifice and includes some local personalities like Bala Gandharva, Ramana Maharishi and Obavva.
6 As per Hindu mythology, Krishna and his brother Balram were brought up by King Nanda in Gokul as their lives were at risk from their evil uncle, Kansa. The name of the orphanage (Nanda-Gokul) symbolizes a foster home.
7 Tapasya refers to the meditation, austerity and self-discipline that monks resort to for *moksha*. The students too are expected to achieve a similar focus and self-discipline towards their goal of making it into IITs.
8 Only one Muslim student has studied at Tapas; he is now pursuing engineering at the National Institute of Technology, Suratkal.
9 Names of some respondents in this paper have been changed. M. P. Kumar is the founder and CEO of Global Edge Software. A former member of ABVP, though not a full-time worker, he volunteers considerable time planning and supporting the activities of Rashtrotthana. His company also provides an annual donation of around INR 2 million for the everyday operational costs of Rashtrotthana.
10 Personal interview.
11 I thank Thomas Blom Hansen for helping me build on Hegelian dialectic and its analytical utility in theorising nationalist Hinduism as a civil religion.

References

Bellah, R. N. (1967). 'Civil religion in America', *Daedalus*, 96(1): 1–21.

Palm, R. (2009). 'Hegel's concept of sublation', PhD thesis, Institute of Philosophy, Katholieke Universiteit Leuven, Leuven.

Patil, S. H. (2007). 'Impact of modernisation and democratisation on a dominant community: A case study of Lingayat Community in Karnataka', *Indian Journal of Political Science*, 68(4): 665–684.

Shankar, B. V. S. (2011). 'Now caste politics takes centre stage', *Mid-day*, 15 April. Available at: www.mid-day.com/news/india-news/article/Now-caste-politics-takes-centre-stage–118770?button=next (accessed 28 August 2019).

Waghmore, S. (2018). 'From hierarchy to Hindu politeness', in S. Jodhka and J. Manor (eds) *Waning Hierarchies, Persisting Inequalities: Caste and Power in 21st Century India* (Delhi: Orient Blackswan), 113–139.

Waghmore, S. (2019). 'Community, not humanity: Caste associations and Hindu cosmopolitanism in contemporary Mumbai', *South Asia: Journal of South Asian Studies*, 42(2): 375–393.

Part III

Love, hate and Kashmir

7

The historical roots of conflict over/in Kashmir

Sarah Ansari

Kashmir is a region with a long and distinct history today straddling the border between India and Pakistan; it is divided between the two states, but claimed in full by both, although many Kashmiris would prefer to be independent. Such tensions have generated considerable political emotion not only in the Kashmir region but across the nation-states of India and Pakistan, which continue to resonate. To understand the historical roots of the Kashmir conflict and the passions it stirs in India (and Pakistan), we need to go back to the 1940s and in particular to the violence, bloodshed and accompanying heartache of what is known as Partition – namely, the sudden (and cataclysmic) division of Britain's Indian empire into two new but separate independent states – India and Pakistan – in the summer of 1947. The impact of this division and its implications for the princely state of Jammu and Kashmir set in motion the conflict that is now embedded in the region.

The road to Independence and Partition, 1939–47

The speed with which the end of empire took place in South Asia had a great deal to do with the changed position of Britain after the Second World War, both in the region itself and in relation to Britain's wider geopolitical standing.[1] When in 1939 Britain took the 'jewel' in their imperial 'crown' into the war without first consulting Indians, the leading nationalist organisation – the Indian National Congress – opposed it; widespread nationalist protests ensued, culminating in the 1942 Quit India movement, a mass movement against British rule. For their opposition, key nationalist leaders including M. K. Gandhi and Jawaharlal Nehru, together with thousands of ordinary Congress workers, were imprisoned until 1945. Meanwhile, Britain's wartime requirement for local allies gave the Muslim League, a party that claimed to speak for Indian Muslims and led by Muhammad Ali Jinnah, an opening to offer its cooperation in exchange for future political safeguards. In March 1940, the Muslim League's Lahore resolution (which has later been viewed as the moment when the demand for 'Pakistan' was triggered) called for the creation of 'separate states' – plural, not singular – to accommodate Indian Muslims in the future, whom it argued constituted a separate 'nation'. Historians are still divided on whether this rather vague demand was purely a bargaining counter or a firm objective. But while it may have been intended to solve the minority issue, it ended up aggravating it instead. [2]

After the war had ended, Attlee's Labour government in London recognised that Britain's devastated economy could not cope with the cost of its overextended empire. A Cabinet Mission was dispatched to India in early 1946, and Attlee described its purpose in ambitious terms: 'My colleagues are going to India with the intention of using their utmost endeavours to help her to attain her freedom as speedily and fully as possible. What form of government is to replace the present regime is for India to decide; but our desire is to help her to set up forthwith the machinery for making that decision.' [3]

The decision to accept Indian demands for independence was finally agreed in February 1947, with the proposed British departure set for June 1948. However, following the arrival of a new viceroy, Lord Louis Mountbatten, and in view of the inability of the main interests involved – the British, the Congress and the Muslim League – to reach a compromise solution that would keep India united at Independence, an announcement was made on 3 June 1947 to speed up the process considerably; the date for Independence was brought forward to 14/15 August 1947 and it would be accompanied by Partition. Decisions with huge and long-lasting consequences were therefore made extremely quickly. This speed also applied to the process of deciding on where the new dividing line between the two countries would run. A British judge, Sir Cyril Radcliffe, with no prior experience of India, was brought out to draw up the boundary, but he was given only five weeks in which to identify and secure agreement from all sides. And as Radcliffe later admitted, he had relied on out-of-date maps and census materials. The result was that two key provinces, the Punjab and Bengal, were each split in two.[4]

Religious concerns certainly contributed to why Independence was accompanied by Partition, and what happened afterwards, both in the short and longer term. By 1947, large numbers of Indian Muslims felt genuinely concerned about what the future political arrangements in independent India would mean for them as a perpetual minority within this new political unit (Muslims overall represented around a quarter of India's total population). And it was this concern that the Muslim League was able to tap into and win support for in its negotiations with the British and the Congress over the shape of these future political arrangements. However, it is important not to assume that all Muslims in India before August 1947 supported the idea of Partition (Qasmi and Robb, 2017). And it was only very late in the day that the Muslim League was able to win meaningful electoral support in the provinces of British India that possessed Muslim majorities (such as the Punjab and Bengal). Eventually, many Muslims chose not to migrate at all to Pakistan, which is why today they make up such a substantial minority (about 14%) of India's population, according to the 2011 census.

Partition may have broken the stalemate in terms of political negotiations, but it generated a huge amount of uncertainty and violence in a summer marked by intense confusion and human suffering, triggering as it did riots, mass casualties and a colossal wave of migration. Millions of people moved to what they hoped would be safer territory, with Muslims heading towards 'Pakistan', and Hindus and Sikhs in the direction of 'India'. As many as 14–16 million people may have been eventually displaced, travelling on foot, in bullock carts and by train. Estimates of the death toll post-Partition range from 200,000 to two million. Many of these people were killed by members of other communities and sometimes their own families, as well as by contagious diseases that swept through refugee camps. Women were often targeted as symbols of community honour, with up to 100,000 raped or abducted.[5] Thus Partition introduced bitterness into the relationship between India and Pakistan from the outset, and hugely complicated reactions to the political events that unfolded in Kashmir. The frequent (and often violent) expression of passions around Kashmir (on both sides of the border) testifies to the emotional dimension of Partition.

The impact of Independence and Partition on Kashmir

In 1947, Jammu and Kashmir was one of around 584 princely states (also called 'native states') that together covered about 60% of the subcontinent's territory.[6] Like the others, it was not formally part of British India in 1947 but instead subject to subsidiary alliances laid down over the previous two centuries, which meant that it was effectively under indirect rule (Ramusack, 2008). According to the plans drawn up by the British in the run-up to Independence, princely states would initially have the right to remain independent, or to join India or Pakistan. It was up to each ruler to decide the future of their territory and its people. In the main, this proved relatively unproblematic, especially where there was a clear geographic compulsion, or where the wishes of the ruler and his subjects were straightforwardly aligned in terms of religious identity. In the end, however, those princely states that had perhaps considered remaining independent found it impossible in practice to do so. Accordingly, the vast majority of princely states acceded to either India or to Pakistan by the agreed deadline, signing the Instrument of Accession, as the official treaty was known. According to the basic tenets of the treaty, the governments of India and Pakistan would control only foreign affairs, defence and communications, leaving all internal issues to be administered by the states. Having signed, states would then be represented in the Constituent Assembly of India, thus becoming an active participant in framing the new constitution. But problems arose where or when the ruler and his subjects disagreed. Jammu and Kashmir was one of a small number of princely states where this proved to be the case (Copland, 2002).

Its ruler at the time, Maharajah Hari Singh, was a Hindu whose Dogra Rajput ancestors had purchased the greater part of the territory from the East India Company in 1846, but the population of Jammu and Kashmir had an overall Muslim majority (Huttenback, 1961). In the British census of India of 1941, Kashmir registered a population made up of 77% Muslims and 20% Hindus, with Buddhists and Sikhs comprising the remaining 3%, while the proportion of Muslims in Jammu stood at 53%.[7] It was Hari Singh's belief that his state could exercise its right to stay independent, and in taking this stance he was backed by Sheikh Abdullah, the leader of Kashmir's largest political party, the National Conference, that sympathised with the INC. The other main local party at this time was the Muslim Conference which favoured the option of joining Pakistan (Snedden, 2012: 22). In July 1947, Mountbatten's political advisor, V. P. Menon, recognising that Kashmir 'presents some difficulty', was still suggesting that it was 'possible that a predominantly Muslim State like Kashmir cannot be kept away from Pakistan for long' and the matter be left 'to find its natural solution'.[8]

In the months preceding Partition Hari Singh initially chose the option of remaining independent, signing what was called a 'standstill agreement', at least with the future Pakistani authorities. But because his administration did not manage to do the same thing with India, the process was effectively paused until a final decision could be made. The knock-on effects of communal violence now spread to the region. Large numbers of Hindus and Sikhs from towns and cities that seemed likely to be included in Pakistan, such as Rawalpindi and Sialkot, had started arriving in Jammu from March 1947. After 14/15 August, communal tension in the state increased.

Conflict over/in Kashmir, 1947–48

The first sign of trouble occurred in Poonch, a district in southwest Kashmir, where local Muslims (led by ex-soldiers) demonstrated in favour of joining Pakistan. Their protests then spilled over into 'open revolt', which resulted in the establishment of an 'Azad Kashmir' government, headed up by Sardar Mohammed Ibrahim, in the districts of Poonch and Mirpur. Elsewhere in the Maharaja's territories, local Muslims came under pressure to migrate to Pakistan, with some 100,000 moving during these uncertain weeks in the direction of Sialkot alone (Snedden, 2012: 27–32, 41–47).

Meanwhile, Pakistani-imposed blockades of fuel and other essential commodities resulted in the Maharajah sending his prime minister, Justice Mehr Chand Mahajan (a notable lawyer in pre-Independence Punjab, Mahajan had been appointed a judge of the Punjab High Court in 1943 and also a member of the Radcliffe Commission that had demarcated the new boundary between India and Pakistan) to Delhi where Mahajan requested assistance from the Indian government on 19 September. This request seemed to signal a change of heart on the part of the Maharaja with respect to joining India. However, Nehru, in response, set as a precondition that Sheikh Abdullah first be released from prison and involved in the state government. The Maharaja accordingly released Sheikh Abdullah on 29 September. But before any further action could be taken, on 22 October a *lashkar* of Tribal militias from the Frontier Tribal Areas adjoining the North-West Frontier Province – some five thousand strong and with the backing of the authorities in Pakistan – crossed the border into the Kashmir valley where they came within miles of the Maharaja's summer capital, Srinagar (Ankit, 2016).

India now offered military assistance to the Kashmir authorities conditional on the Maharaja signing the Instrument of Accession in India's favour. What happened next remains controversial because there is still disagreement over whether the Maharajah signed the Instrument of Accession to join with India *before* or *after* India had sent in its troops. Either way, following the accession of the state to India on 26 October 1947, Indian troops were airlifted to Srinagar. They proceeded to secure Jammu, Srinagar and the valley itself, but the onset of winter made much of the state impassable and fighting flagged. Meanwhile, on 1 November 1947, Mountbatten flew to Lahore for a conference with Jinnah, proposing that, in all the princely states where the ruler did not accede to a dominion corresponding to the majority population (which would have included other states such as Junagadh and Hyderabad), the accession should be decided by an 'impartial reference to the will of the people'. But Jinnah rejected the offer. Nehru, for his part, took the legal position that Kashmir represented Indian territory, and so India would conduct a plebiscite, were one to take place (Schofield, 2010).

In January 1948, Nehru, recognising the degree of negative international attention that the dispute was attracting and in the face of criticism from fellow Congress politicians such as Sardar Patel who regarded it as a bilateral issue, referred the Kashmir issue to the UN Security Council, accusing Pakistan of assisting in an assault on Indian sovereignty, while Pakistan responded with counter charges that India had acquired Kashmir by 'fraud and violence'. In April 1948 the Security Council passed a resolution that – by requiring the withdrawal of tribesmen and Pakistani nationals as well as a reduction in Indian troops – failed to satisfy either India or Pakistan. The UN also passed a resolution in favour of a plebiscite to decide matters, and it sent out a commission (the United Nations Commission for India and Pakistan or UNCIP) three times over the course of 1948–49 to negotiate the withdrawal arrangements in line with this proposed solution (Schofield, 2010: 67–70; Shankar, 2016).

By this time, however, Pakistani regular troops had been openly sent into Kashmir, where they confronted an Indian army, which – like their own – was headed by a British officer (Field Marshal Sir Claude Auchinleck was India's supreme commander 1943–48, while Frank Messervy and Douglas Gracy were Pakistan's commander-in-chief from 1947–48 and 1948–51 respectively). Over the course of 1948, the conflict gradually solidified; and at one minute to midnight on 31 December 1948 a ceasefire along what came to be known as the 'Line of Control' was agreed with effect from 1 January 1949. In the end, no withdrawal was ever carried out by either side: India wanted Pakistan to withdraw first, while Pakistan contended that there was no guarantee that India would withdraw afterwards.[9]

Divided Kashmir, 1949 to the present

The longer-term outcome of the conflict was that the western portions of the Maharaja's territory – today known as Azad Kashmir, and also Gilgit-Baltistan – came under permanent Pakistani control. The remainder was reconstituted as the Jammu and Kashmir state (J&K) within the Indian framework. While India cites the 1951-elected Constituent assembly of Jammu and Kashmir, which voted in favour of confirming accession to India, Pakistan claims that India has shown disregard to the UN by failing to hold a referendum to determine the future of the state. Importantly, between 1950 and 2019, J&K remained the only state in India which enjoyed special autonomy under Article 370 of the constitution of India, according to which all laws enacted by the Parliament of India, except for those in the field of defence, communication and foreign policy, had to be ratified by the J&K state legislature before they could be applied there.[10] In October 2019, the BJP Indian government led by Modi formally revoked J&K's semi-autonomous status, splitting it into two separate federal territories in an move to integrate it fully into India (Ellis-Petersen et al., 2019).

The fact that India and Pakistan found themselves fighting a war over Kashmir so soon after Independence had significant long-term consequences for both countries. From the get-go, they were on a war footing. Right from the outset Pakistan spent a huge proportion of its GDP on military-related development which undoubtedly hindered all sorts of other necessary state-building programmes. The Kashmir conflict also added to the number of displaced people who had to be accommodated and rehabilitated in both countries, but whose status was regarded as distinct from the earlier Partition-related refugees.[11] The political upheaval caused by those events continue to shape political emotions, which in turn underpin nationalist rationalities, to the present day.

Notes

1 See Khan (2015) for a clear overview of the impact of the conflict on life and politics in British India. For a more military assessment of the Second World War's impact on the region, see Raghaven (2019).

2 Reasons explaining the growth of support for the Muslim League from the late 1930s onwards have generated huge debate among historians and political scientists. Key contributions include those by Jalal (1985), Devji (2013) and Dhulipala (2015).

3 'India: statement by the Cabinet Mission'. Hansard, Lords Debate, 16 May 1946, Vol. 141, cc. 271–287. Available at https://api.parliament.uk/historic-hansard/lords/1946/may/16/india-statement-by-the-cabinet-mission (accessed August 2020).

4 For a detailed assessment of Britain's 'hasty, ill-planned and extremely bloody' exit from India (p. 4), and Radcliffe's role more generally, see Chester (2009).

5 The literature on Partition is voluminous. For useful overviews of its causes and impact, see Khan (2007), Talbot and Singh (2009) and White-Spunner (2018).

6 For an exploration of developments that shaped Kashmir's regional identity in precolonial and colonial times, see Zutshi (2004).

7 It should be noted that this percentage excludes Poonch – unfortunately it has not been possible to track down data that includes the whole of Jammu at that time.

8 V. P. Menon to C. P. Scott, 17 July 1947, R/3/1/166, ff. 11–12, Document 151, in Mansergh and Moon (1983: 213–214).
9 For documentary insights into the developments of this period, see Carter (2018).
10 For a critical assessment of the 'special status' of J&K over time, see Noorani (2014). For details on Indian policy towards Kashmir, see Kanjwal (2018).
11 For more discussion of the subsequent Indo-Pakistan tension regarding Kashmir, see Ganguly (2001) and Jacob (2019).

References

Ankit, R. (2016). *The Kashmir Conflict: From Empire to the Cold War, 1945–66* (London: Routledge).

Carter, L. (ed.) (2018). *Towards a Ceasefire in Kashmir: British Official Reports from South Asia, 18 September–31 December 1948* (London: Routledge).

Chester, L. (2009). *Borders and Conflict in South Asia: The Radcliffe Boundary Commission and the Partition of Punjab* (Manchester: Manchester University Press).

Copland, I. (2002). *Princes of India in the Endgame of Empire, 1917–1947* (Cambridge: Cambridge University Press).

Devji, F. (2013). *Muslim Zion: Pakistan as a Political Idea* (London: Hurst & Co).

Dhulipala, V. (2015). *Creating a New Medina: State Power, Islam, and the Quest for Pakistan in Late Colonial North India* (New York: Cambridge University Press).

Ellis-Petersen, H., and a reporter in Sringar (2019). 'India strips Kashmir of special status and divides it in two', *Guardian*, 31 October. Available at: www.theguardian.com/world/2019/oct/31/india-strips-kashmir-of-special-status-and-divides-it-in-two (accessed 11 May 2022).

Ganguly, S. (2001). *Conflict Unending: India–Pakistan Tensions since 1947* (New York: Columbia University Press).

Huttenback, R. A. (1961). 'Gulab Singh and the creation of the Dogra state of Jammu, Kashmir, and Ladakh', *Journal of Asian Studies*, 20(4): 477–488.

Jacob, H. (2019). *Line on Fire: Ceasefire Violations and India–Pakistan Escalation Dynamics* (New Delhi: Oxford University Press).

Jalal, A. (1985). *The Sole Spokesman: Jinnah, the Muslim League and the Demand for Pakistan* (Cambridge: Cambridge University Press).

Kanjwal, H. (2018). 'Building a new Kashmir: Bakshi Ghulam Muhammad and the politics of state-formation in a disputed territory (1953–1963)', PhD dissertation, University of Michigan.

Khan, Y. (2007). *The Great Partition: The Making of India and Pakistan* (London: Yale University Press).

Khan, Y. (2015). *The Raj at War: A People's History of India's Second World War* (London: Bodley Head).

Mansergh, N. and Moon, P. (eds) (1983). *The Transfer of Power 1942–7*, Vol. XII: *The Mountbatten Viceroyalty. Princes, Partition and Independence 8 July–15 August 1947* (London: Her Majesty's Stationery Office).

Noorani, A. G. (2014). *Article 370: A Constitutional History of Jammu and Kashmir* (2nd ed., New Delhi: Oxford University Press).

Qasmi, A. U. and Robb, M. E. (eds) (2017). *Muslims against the Muslim League: Critiques of the Idea of Pakistan* (Cambridge: Cambridge University Press).

Raghaven, S. (2019). 'Building the sinews of power: India in the Second World War', *Journal of Strategic Studies*, 42(5): 577–599.

Ramusack, B. N. (2008). *The Indian Princes and their States* (Cambridge: Cambridge University Press).

Schofield, V. (2010). *Kashmir in Conflict: India, Pakistan and the Unending War* (3rd ed., London: IB Tauris).

Shankar, M. (2016). 'Nehru's legacy: Why a plebiscite never happened', *India Review*, 15(1): 1–21.

Snedden, C. (2012). *The Untold Story of the People of Azad Kashmir* (London: Hurst & Co).

Talbot, I. and Singh, G. (2009). *The Partition of India* (Cambridge: Cambridge University Press).

White-Spunner, B. (2018). *Partition: The Story of Indian Independence and the Creation of Pakistan in 1947* (London: Simon & Schuster).

Zutshi, C. (2004). *Languages of Belonging: Islam, Regional Identity and the Making of Kashmir* (New York: Oxford University Press).

8

This side of paradise: The rise, fall and decimation of regional politics in Kashmir

Shaswati Das

In the post-Independence era, the arc of Kashmir's participation in broader Indian politics can, at best, be described as erratic and volatile. Since 1999, the rise of the Islamist jihadist group Jaish-e-Mohammad has reshaped Kashmir's political evolution. India has witnessed five general elections since 1999. While the country's overall voter turnout was pegged between a healthy 58% in 1999 and 67.1% in 2019, Kashmir's contribution remained negligible. Across Anantnag, Baramulla and Srinagar, voter turnouts in 1999 stood at 14.3%, 27.8% and 11.9%. Turnouts changed only marginally in 2019, to 9.7%, 38.9% and 15.6%, respectively – a year, when India boasted of its highest ever voter turnout at 67.11%.[1] If the largely dominant Hindu (and Kashmiri Pandit) belt of Jammu is excluded, then the Kashmir region itself comprises the three parliamentary constituencies of Anantnag, Baramulla and its capital city of Srinagar. For the sake of clarity, this chapter discusses political behaviours and outcomes solely in the Kashmir region. While voter turnout across all three constituencies changed only marginally (Figure 8.1), all three witnessed their highest ever turnouts in 2009, at 27.1%, 41.8% and 25.6%, respectively. Both 1999 and 2019, however, bookended a period of electoral, political and military upheaval with the lowest voter turnouts at both ends of the spectrum.

Each election was followed by an almost triumphant declaration by the Central leadership about the region's electorate having chosen wisely at the ballot box over a Kalashnikov, regardless of the turnout. Such declarations betrayed a linear observation of subnational

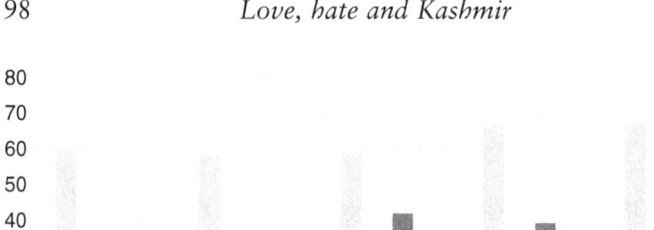

Figure 8.1 India and Kashmir: comparative voter turnouts (%)

electoral behaviour. In fact, an examination of democracy is a delicate, micro-level conversation. In reflecting on attitudes towards political process in Kashmir, such a conversation must necessarily consider the two major political players – the National Conference (NC) and the People's Democratic Party (PDP). The NC styles itself as a secular socialist formation. The PDP is proudly ethnonationalist. Both formations are underscored by the presence of Islamist freedom fighters who are declared militants or terrorists by the Indian state.

This chapter recognises the use of the term jihadists – or individuals rooted in Islamic extremism, dedicated to a struggle according to laws enshrined in the Qur'an (Mehdi, 2020) – in tandem with the beliefs and perception among local Kashmiris. The two-decade period from 1999 to 2019 often found the NC and the PDP in the crosshairs of its electorate. Consequently, the narrative of jihadism and collective violence as a political recourse found greater resonance among an electorate whose impatience and disenchantment with its legitimate political representation had given way to apparent apathy. A new-found sense of pride and loyalty in the 'freedom fighters,' or jihadists, upstaged any last vestiges of faith in a democratic political process, giving way instead to a sense of betrayal, anger and indignation at having been left out in the cold.

Humanism, democracy, amity

In the period after 1947, the National Conference largely enjoyed a monopolistic reign over Kashmir, on occasion joining forces with the Indian National Congress. By the late 1980s however – and in the run-up to the outbreak of separatism and Islamic jihadism in the region – the NC was mired in controversy and allegations of electoral fraud. And with the turn of the decade, in 1990, Kashmir's demographic fabric split as the region's Kashmiri Pandit population was driven out in the wake of unrelenting, polarising violence (Essa, 2011). Rising on the heels of that turmoil was the People's Democratic Party, led by Mufti Mohammad Sayeed and his daughter, Mehbooba Mufti. While the NC continued to make renewed efforts at scrambling back to power, the PDP had begun to build its legacy – cognisant of the people's festering grievances and the influence that the separatist movement wielded over the civilian population. Over the course of the decade, by 2005, as the NC lost ground, the PDP was looked upon by the then Manmohan Singh-led United Progressive Alliance (UPA) government, the region's civilians, and separatists, as an instrument of fostering an integration of regional and national identities (Ali, 2009). The transition of power was complete (Wani, 2014).

Essentially, federalism ought to have established sovereignty that would have been shared and negotiated with the state apparatus in Kashmir (Rudolph and Rudolph, 2010). Juxtaposed with this transition of power in Kashmir, an earnest attempt at national integration came from India's then prime minister Atal Bihari Vajpayee, in April 2003. Having extended the olive branch to geopolitical arch-rival Pakistan, Vajpayee recognised the need to roll out economic and communications infrastructure projects in the region, to address rampant unemployment in the state. Vajpayee's three-point plan of *insaniyat* (humanism), *jamhooriyat* (democracy) and *kashmiriyat* (Kashmir's cultural amity) was critical to staunching jihadism in the region (Parthasarathy, 2018). In the years that followed, jihadist factions of the Hizbul Mujahideen and the ethnonationalist group, the Hurriyat Conference, remained divided (Shah, 2018). However, with Vajpayee's electoral loss in the general election of 2004, political mobilisation in the region eventually came to a standstill.

If Kashmir is to be examined from the prism of 'neo-modern militarism' in the post-1990 decade, dissonance occurred when the mobilisation of identities and allegiances clashed with the mobilisation of military power (Duschinski, 2009). In so doing, the region's secular political fabric unravelled. To maintain its stranglehold over the region, successive national governments attempted to bulldoze the region with development – an exercise that further spurred political mobilisation, as a more politically conscious younger generation began to actively seek alternate avenues of expression (Ganguly, 1996). By 2008, Vajpayee's vision of integration and dialogue had fallen through, and a resurgent Hurriyat and Hizbul Mujahideen stepped in. The once colossal NC, whose legitimacy had come under question across the region, could do little. With the general election of 2014, the political narrative in the country and in Kashmir, changed. The central political dispensation underwent a radical facelift with the Bharatiya Janata Party (BJP)'s landslide victory, catapulting Prime Minister Narendra Modi to the top job. Meanwhile, in Kashmir, the cracks within the PDP had become apparent. Once popular, the party's self-serving dynastic politics had embittered its local electorate (Naseem, 2017), which now believed that it was no different than its predecessor, the National Conference. The mistrust became ever more glaring when, in the ensuing assembly elections of 2014 in Kashmir, there appeared no clear mandate, locking the region in a political deadlock for months on end.

In 2015, PDP leader Mufti Mohammad Sayeed made a herculean, albeit controversial, attempt to tide over this political impasse brought on by a hung verdict in the 2014 assembly polls. Much to the horror of its electorate, Sayeed, and the BJP, which had opposed Kashmir's autonomy by demanding the state's full integration into India, formed an alliance that set the ball rolling for the eventual collapse of the region's political, social and demographic structure. The PDP's association with the BJP came across not just as tone-deaf, but one that made it amply clear to the population that the party was oblivious to the region's political realities. With Sayeed's passing in 2016, and his daughter Mehbooba Mufti's ascension as the state's first woman chief minister, the alliance began to sour. This was, however, just the tip of the iceberg. An intelligence tip in July 2016 set in motion a series of actions that culminated in the killing of prominent jihadist Burhan Wani in an encounter (Bhat, 2019). Civilian discontent swept the valley and the PDP–BJP faultlines became glaring. For the next two years, Mufti tried to placate a population that had been left smarting in the wake of the alliance, exacerbated further by Wani's encounter. By now, with the general election of 2019 on the anvil, the BJP-led Centre had begun to estimate its losses. Determined to go ahead with its policy of increased militarisation in the region, and to secure a landslide victory in India, it severed ties with the PDP in June 2018.

The war of attrition

The complete collapse of even symbolic political and governmental representation in 2018 spelt pandemonium for Kashmir. The dominant sentiment of anger, resentment and hate that had been brewing since Wani's death in 2016, manifested in an all-out clash of security forces with the region's civilians and jihadist factions. In the wake of Wani's killing, funerals were held – in absentia – across Kashmir, and the region was peppered with violent clashes between civilians and security forces, ceasefire violations along the India–Pakistan border and an even louder, resounding chant for 'freedom' (Bukhari, 2016). The Centre went by its textbook method of clamping down on communication networks in the valley, placing the region's separatist leadership under house arrest and stepping up security presence across the region (Gabel et al., 2020). The situation in Kashmir plummeted rapidly. The violence that broke out in the wake of Wani's death was testament to his popularity and the passions of the Kashmiri population, of which he had been representative. With no political dispensation left to trust, collective violence seemed like the only recourse to addressing aggravated grievances.

By 2018, the situation had become ever more unyielding. That year, a total of 452 people were killed in the region – 271 jihadists, 95 security personnel and 86 civilians – and there were 1,458 incidents of stone pelting (SATP, 2010). Politically, Kashmir remained under the governor's rule, devoid of any democratically elected government. Militarily, however, alarm bells had begun to ring in New Delhi. Security forces, and intelligence units in Jammu and Kashmir (J&K) conveyed to New Delhi that the situation was fast regressing. Rates of recruitment among jihadists continued steadily into 2019, with the year recording 2,007 cases of stone pelting and 135 fatal attacks. Consequently, in its report in 2019, the Office of the UN High Commissioner for Human Rights (OHCHR) also raised serious concerns about excesses by both Indian security forces and armed jihadist factions across the Indian- and Pakistan-held regions of Kashmir. While the report pointed out India's aggressive military response towards civilians by way of pellet guns, it mentioned that jihadist groups were responsible for extensive human rights abuses, kidnappings, killings of civilians who were perceived as informants, sexual abuse, recruitment of children for jihadist activities, and attacks on people associated with the region's political organisations (OHCHR, 2019).

Meanwhile in Pakistan, jihadists belonging to Jaish-e-Mohammad set about putting together facilitators, logistical and vehicular support towards executing a mission in Pulwama. A young boy from Kashmir's Pulwama district would be trained specifically for a mission that would alter Kashmir's political history. Just two months into 2019, that well-laid plan was put into action. On the afternoon of 14 February 2019, Adil Ahmad Dar – a school dropout from Pulwama's Gundibagh village in south Kashmir – drove an explosives-laden vehicle into a Central Reserve Police Force convoy, killing forty security personnel. In the days that followed, sentiments ran high among both the security forces and the average Kashmiri. Dar, however, was a cog in the wheel. In interviews I conducted across north and south Kashmir (Das, 2019), groups of local youth across Pulwama, Shopian, Srinagar and Budgam claimed they were proud of their aspirations of joining jihadist groups in the region. Furthermore, even as security forces in the region alternated between coercive and non-coercive methods of counterterrorism, urging families to recall their sons from jihadist activities, Dar's father remained obdurate. For him, the remorse at the loss of lives paled in comparison to the pride they felt at what their sons did. As a stark reminder of the Sisyphean task that any security or political establishment was up against, he reiterated that children in the valley, especially sons, were taught how to use pistols from a young age, following which they underwent rudimentary training on their induction into jihadist groups, before being sent on their missions. Burhan Wani, he said, had inspired generations to fight for the state, including his own son. The resentment against India had run deep enough for the local people to shun any political overtures made by the regional or national establishment and settle for alternate mechanisms of grievance redressal.

The decisive polls of 2019

The Pulwama blast had three fallouts. First, the Centre decided to tighten its grip. Second, both the NC and the PDP knew exactly how the Centre would react and decided to scramble, once again, to regain lost political control. And third, the local people now knew for certain that there would be little to no legitimate political choice for them – a sentiment which was underscored further by 2,007 cases of stone pelting against security forces.

My fieldwork in Kashmir at the time suggested as much. Local youth, who were eligible to vote, had left their homes to undergo 'training' that would enable them to make a difference, and effect change in a region that had been short-changed by its political leadership.[2] In the period between the Pulwama blast and the general election, field interviews with families of the youth[3] revealed that as soon as the region's youth completed basic schooling they had begun to turn to the path of *mujahid* (Islamists who fight on behalf of the community) to right the wrongs of the region's political dispensation.

An uneasy calm settled on Kashmir over the next two months as India went to the polls. India's general election of 2019 recorded the highest ever voter turnout at 67.11% across 542 parliamentary constituencies in the country, catapulting the BJP to power yet again. However, for Mufti and her party it was near decimation, as the PDP lost across Baramulla and Srinagar, and Mufti's former seat of Anantnag, replaced by a candidate from the National Conference (Yasir, 2019). While jihadist and separatist factions in this conflict zone had always announced a poll boycott, voter indignation and solidarity with the boycott led the former state of Jammu and Kashmir to record the country's lowest voter turnout at 44.97% (including Jammu region). Accentuating the people's political disillusionment was the voter turnout across the three parliamentary constituencies in Kashmir, with Baramulla at 31.76%, Srinagar at 14.43% and Anantnag at 8.98% (Election Commission of India, 2019). Burhan Wani's execution may have expedited the collapse of local politics, but there was no greater indicator of fraught voter sentiments than the fact that Kashmir itself accounted for the country's lowest turnout – even lower than its own record in the previous years.

Notes

1 Statistics derived from www.indiavotes.com/ (accessed 13 September 2021).
2 Ghulam Hassan Dar, interviewed by the author, Pulwama, February 2019.
3 Anonymous families, interviewed by the author, Shopian and Awantipora, February 2019.

References

Ali, N. (2009). 'The making of Kashmiri identity', *South Asian Diaspora*, 1(2): 181–192. https://doi.org/10.1080/19438190903109545.

Bhat, S. A. (2019). 'The Kashmir conflict and human rights', *Race Relations*, 61(1): 77–86. https://doi.org/10.1177/0306396819850988.

Bukhari, S. (2016). 'Why the death of militant Burhan Wani has Kashmiris up in arms', BBC News, 11 July. Available at: www.bbc.co.uk/news/world-asia-india-36762043 (accessed 1 September 2021).

Das, S. (2019). 'Kashmir on the edge as terror rears its ugly head again in valley', Mint, 25 February. Available at: www.livemint.com/news/india/kashmir-on-the-edge-as-terror-rears-its-ugly-head-again-in-valley-1551029616147.html (accessed 2 September 2021).

Duschinski, H. (2009). "Destiny effects: Militarization, state power, and punitive containment in Kashmir valley', *Anthropological Quarterly*, 82(3): 691–717.

Election Commission of India (2019). *Statistical Report of General Election 2019 – Including Vellore PC where Election was held in August 2019*. Available at: https://eci.gov.in/files/category/1551-general-election-2019-including-vellore-pc/ (accessed 13 September 2021).

Essa, A. (2011). 'Kashmiri Pandits: Why we never fled Kashmir', Al Jazeera, 2 August. Available at: www.aljazeera.com/news/2011/8/2/kashmiri-pandits-why-we-never-fled-kashmir (accessed 13 September 2021).

Gabel, S., Reichert, L. and Reuter, C. (2020). 'Discussing conflict in social media: The use of Twitter in the Jammu and Kashmir conflict', *Media, War & Conflict*, 1–26. https://doi.org/10.1177/1750635220970997.

Ganguly, S. (1996). 'Explaining the Kashmir insurgency: Political mobilization and institutional decay', *International Security*, 21(2): 76–107. https://doi.org/10.2307/2539071.

Mehdi, S. E. (2020). 'Serving the militant's cause: The role of Indo-Pak state policies in sustaining militancy in Kashmir', *Journal of Asian Security and International Affairs*, 7(2): 244–255. https://doi.org/10.1177/2347797020939012.

Naseem, I. (2017). 'Political nepotism rife in Kashmir: After Mehbooba's "re-Election" as PDP President, her brother set to be inducted into state ministry', Firstpost, 14 December. Available at: www.firstpost.com/india/political-nepotism-rife-in-kashmir-after-mehboobas-re-election-as-pdp-president-her-brother-set-to-be-inducted-into-state-ministry-4258597.html (accessed 13 September 2021).

Office of the United Nations High Commissioner for Human Rights (OHCHR) (2019). *Update of the Situation of Human Rights in Indian-Administered Kashmir and Pakistan-Administered Kashmir from May 2018 to April 2019* (UNHCR).

Parthasarathy, G. (2018). 'Vajpayee and the value of Kashmiriyat', *The Hindu* Business Line, 9 March. Available at: www.thehindubusinessline.com/opinion/columns/g-parthasarathy/vajpayee-and-the-value-of-kashmiriyat/article21678033.ece1 (accessed 13 September 2021).

Rudolph, L. I. and Rudolph, S. H. (2010). 'Federalism as state formation in India: A theory of shared and negotiated sovereignty', *International Political Science Review*, 31(5): 553–572. https://doi.org/10.1177/0192512110388634.

Shah, K. (2018). 'Vajpayee's Kashmir policy was more than a slogan', Observer Research Foundation, 20 August. Available at: www.orfonline.org/expert-speak/43479-vajpayee-kashmir-policy-more-than-slogan/ (accessed 13 September 2021).

South Asia Terrorism Portal (SATP) (2010). 'Datasheet-terrorism-related-incidents-data' 2010. Available at: www.satp.org/datasheet-terrorist-attack/incidents-data/india-jammukashmir (accessed 26 September 2021).

Wani, G. (2014). 'Sub-regional conflicts and selective autonomy in J&K: Hill councils in power', *Race & Class*, 56(2): 81–92. https://doi.org/10.1177/0306396814542919.

Yasir, S. (2019). 'Mehbooba Mufti loses Anantnag for massive crackdown on protesters after Burhan Wani's death and PDP alliance with BJP', Firstpost, 24 May. Available at: www.firstpost.com/politics/mehbooba-mufti-loses-anantnag-for-massive-crackdown-on-protesters-after-burhani-wanis-death-and-pdp-alliance-with-bjp-6692791.html (accessed 31 August 2021).

9

The fear of Indian settler colonialism and the battle for Kashmir's soul

Ather Zia

The siege of Kashmir

On 5 August 2019, the Bharatiya Janata Party (BJP) government delivered on one of its long-held election promises – the removal of Kashmir's special autonomous status under Articles 370 and 35-A of the Indian constitution. The BJP government's disregard for India's own constitutional promises is nothing new for Kashmiris. Only, their method has been somewhat different in being the ultimate spectacle of military and constitutional re-annexation. The plan for the evisceration of Kashmir's special status has been pursued as a matter of Indian national policy since its inception. In 1963, Jawaharlal Nehru, India's first prime minister stated that the gradual erosion of Kashmir's autonomy was underway and would be gone in time (Noorani, 2010; Raghavan, 2014). A minister from the Indian National Congress, Nehru's party, recently reiterated this claim boasting that, unlike the BJP, the Congress had diluted Article 370 twelve times without any controversy (*Times of India*, 2019). Indeed, Congress had used deft political and juridical engineering by deploying Kashmiri client politicians and collaborators and did not rely solely on military might or broad tampering with the constitution.

It is no surprise that, except for disagreements on the execution, there has been across-the-board consensus for the removal of Article 370 from Indian political parties that otherwise oppose the BJP. Not only was Kashmir's autonomy removed but the state was demoted to a union territory and bifurcated. All this was done without consulting the Kashmiris or their legislature, which is currently dismissed.

This move has been called unconstitutional, deceitful and undemocratic (Deshmane 2019). The BJP indeed completed an important part of the Indian neocolonial expansionist policy in Kashmir. This chapter illustrates that Kashmiris have stood for autonomy less as loyalty to the Indian federation and more to protect their territorial sovereignty from a demographic onslaught and settler colonialism. However, Article 370 was a symbol of Kashmir's historical sovereignty and served to underwrite the demand of self-determination by the Kashmiri people. This chapter concludes that very little will change on the ground vis-à-vis the resistance shown by Kashmiri people as the threat of Indian settler colonialism becomes a reality. It thus outlines the rationality of territorial sovereignty within which the passionate politics of resistance is enmeshed in Kashmir.

In 1949, a number of Kashmiri politicians who favoured India negotiated the inclusion of Article 370, which was contrary to the plebiscite clause. The Article allowed Kashmir to retain autonomy in all matters, except defence, currency and foreign affairs. Another Article, 35-A, was included which barred non-Kashmiris from attaining property and franchise, thus ensuring Kashmiris retained their permanent residency, called the 'state subject'. All the provisions of the Indian constitution were not applicable in Kashmir, and required consensus from the local legislature. To remove Article 370, the concurrence of constituent assembly of the state of Jammu and Kashmir was needed, but this was disbanded in 1956. According to many legal experts this made Kashmir's special status iron-clad. However, most Kashmiris saw the special status as an unjust ruse to thwart the plebiscite and one of the first sly moves by India to usurp the territory.

In time it was clear that Article 370 was a Trojan horse designed to eviscerate Kashmiri autonomy. In 1954, the Indian government extended Indian citizenship and the fundamental rights charter to Kashmir (Bose, 1997). The Indian fundamental rights charter permits preventive detention to curb threats on national sovereignty or public order and was used to punish Kashmiri dissenters and steadily criminalise the movement for independence and plebiscite (Noorani, 2011). The Indian government's policy of legal incorporation of the region, termed occupational constitutionalism, 'became sedimented through the work of the courts across time' (Duschinski and Ghosh, 2017: 34).

In 2019, the first signs that the Indian government was preparing to remove Kashmir's autonomy began in late July with the deployment of approximately 48,000 extra troops in the state. This is in addition to over 700,000 Indian forces already occupying the region (see OHCHR, 2018). The Amarnath Yatra, an annual Hindu pilgrimage, was suspended; pilgrims, tourists and non-local students were taken out of the region. Kashmiris panicked, but the government downplayed any concerns as fake news. A curfew was imposed, and a massive communication blackout was enforced that included shutting down the internet, mobile phones, basic cable and landlines.

Kashmiris are not new to living under siege, but this lockdown was unprecedented because all forms of communication were banned. A large number of Kashmiri resistance leaders, civil society activists – even India's own collaborators and client politicians – were put under arrest. Mass arrests continued, and at one point more than 13,000 young boys had been detained and many imprisoned in jails outside Kashmir.[1] Kashmiri journalists were barred from reporting and newspapers ran out of newsprint. Foreign reporters initially covered the situation, but were later banned.[2] The Indian government has been continuously projecting that the situation on the ground is normal.

As months passed the siege became a humanitarian crisis (*Lancet*, 2019). The lack of communication exacerbated the scarcity of essential supplies, medicines and healthcare.[3] Caged yet restive, Kashmir erupted in more than 300 incidents of stone pelting at the Indian forces (*New Indian Express*, 2019). Historically, Kashmiris have used a form of resistance called the *hartal*, a civil boycott, which Kashmiris deployed during this siege as well to express their disapproval of the Indian regime's policies and highlight their demands for self-determination and independence. Even after restrictions were partially lifted, for months businesses remained close, roads deserted – the sullenness of people becomes a mark of disdain when their voices are repressed.[4]

The BJP government has been domestically and internationally projecting that the removal of Kashmir's autonomy is needed to pave the way for *vikas* (development) and rooting out nepotism and 'terrorism'. Yet India's own analysts have shown that the development indices for Kashmir are already high or have shown improvement (Rajalakshmi, 2019). Arguments about how the removal of Article 370 will allow the implementation of corruption-free governance and a host of fundamental rights – such as the right to education, a minimum wage, minority rights, and social reservations – have been contested as misleading, disingenuous, false and a 'strawman'.[5] It is reasonable to ask that if this decision is about Kashmir's development, why were the Kashmiris caged and subsequently suffering a double lockdown as the Covid-19 crisis unfolded? Even though, in early 2020, bans on some mobile phone services and landlines were lifted, the digital apartheid continues with partial restrictions on the internet and telephone services, even during the pandemic.[6]

Threat of settler colonialism

Often called an open-air prison, Kashmir is one of the most militarised zones in the world. In 1991, to suppress a popular Kashmiri armed movement, India imposed the Armed Forces Special Forces Act which gives its armed forces unlimited powers to act with impunity. Gross human rights violations effected by government forces include the killing of more than 70,000 people, over 10,000 enforced disappearances, rape used a weapon of war, mass incarcerations and injuries like the world's first mass blindings (Zia, 2019).

In 2014, in the election manifesto for Kashmir's state assembly, the BJP promised to provide land at cheap rates for the establishment of colonies for retired soldiers. In July that year, the Goods and Services Tax, which is a single tax system across India, was finally imposed on Kashmir, much to the fear and resistance of people and constitutional experts who declared that the state's fiscal autonomy had essentially ended. In 2015, the Rashtriya Swayamsevak Sangh (RSS), a Hindu supremacist organisation and the ideologue of the BJP, backed a public interest litigation in the Supreme Court seeking to repeal Article 35-A.

In 2008, the fear of an Indian settler influx had been renewed by the fear of 'land grab' or what has been termed 'demographic terrorism' (Hussain, n.d.). That year, the Kashmir government agreed to transfer forty hectares of forestland to the Amarnath Yatra pilgrimage site. Kashmiris took to streets fearing establishment of separate settlements, triggering what has been termed 'Kashmiri Intifada'. The resistance leaders called the move establishing a state within a state. Parallels were drawn with the Israel Land Authority's new constructions in Har Homa, East Jerusalem, in 2005. Hindu fundamentalist parties continue to fan nationalistic flames to this day, heavily infusing politics with religion. Hindu pilgrims are mobilised to visit Hindu holy sites in Kashmir more as a patriotic duty than for spiritual salvation. In 1963, about 4,000 pilgrims visited Amarnath; in 2015, the number has grown to about 200,000 (Zia, 2020). The fear of settler colonialism in Kashmir remains palpable.

In 2015, the Kashmiri High Court passed a historic judgment stating that Article 370 was 'permanent' and the Indian Supreme Court declared that only the Parliament could remove the article. Nevertheless, the BJP weaponised several arguments for removal of Article 370. It alleged the article was discriminatory to Kashmiri women who married men not holding a permanent residency of the state. In 2002, the Kashmir High Court had given a ruling that Kashmiri women who married non-Kashmiris would not lose their permanent residency. The only caveat was that the rights of their heirs were not specified and needed to be adjudicated on a case-by-case basis. Nonetheless, a committee had already been appointed by the subsequent administration to devise a lasting solution for this lacuna. The BJP also used the plight of the Valmikis and West Pakistan refugees. The Valmikis are Hindus belonging to the repressed Dalit caste. In the 1950s, when the municipality workers had gone on strike, the Kashmiri government had brought in two hundred Valmiki families from Punjab to work as cleaners. Even though the Valmikis were employed by the government, given residential land and retained their rights as Indian citizens, they did not get the status of permanent residents of Kashmir. The younger Valmiki generation, who had received education, lacked access to local political or professional opportunities (Bhandari, 2019). Kashmir had passed the Manual Scavenging Prohibition Act in 2010, but its implementation was slow. Other laws safeguarding the scheduled castes and scheduled tribes had been passed, but the historical contentions around demography had put the hapless Valmikis at a disadvantage. Another minority the BJP weaponised were the 4,000 families who migrated from West Pakistan in 1947. They established communities on the frontiers and received Indian citizenship and franchise for the parliamentary elections. But even though successive Kashmiri governments tried to ameliorate their financial situation, they were not made permanent residents of Kashmir.

While raising the issue of these two communities, on the other hand, the BJP government repealed Kashmir's own minority act that enabled the transfer of ownership rights of state land to its occupants against a set remuneration. These occupants were often from the Indigenous community of Gujjars and Bakerwal, a pastoral nomadic people who are dominantly Muslim and live between the provinces of Kashmir and Jammu, the third province of the former state. The last decade had seen increasing strife between the Muslim Gujjar and Bakerwals and the local Hindus in Jammu. This came to a head when, in 2018, an 8 year-old Gujjar and Bakerwal girl was gang-raped and murdered.[7] The accused were all from the Hindu community. The BJP openly supported the perpetrators and everyone who came out in their support. They did not even allow the dead child's body to be buried in the village. The pastoralist community now fears returning to the grazing grounds. The threat of demographic shifts has added to the fears of Muslims in the region, bringing back memories of the massacre of Muslims in Jammu in 1947 (Thapar, 2019).

Before 1947, Muslims comprised 61% of the population of Jammu (Aslam, 2020). Estimates suggest that Hindu mobs killed between 200,000 and 500,000 Muslim men, women and children, and about 200,000 people went missing. The number of women abducted by Hindu extremists varies from 256 to 27,000 because of unreported cases. Evidence shows that the Hindu maharaja oversaw the pogrom (Snedden, 2001; Chowdhary, 2015). Many survivors fled to Azad Kashmir and Pakistan. The subsequent census showed many uninhabited villages. The large-scale killings and displacement of Muslims caused significant demographic changes, which were most likely engineered to sway Kashmir towards India if the plebiscite was ever held.

In the current demographic context, the most important is the policy of separate townships and residential colonies for Hindu Pandits who are ethnic Kashmiris. In the early 1990s almost 90% of the Hindu Pandits, who form 4% of the total population and are dominantly pro-India, migrated to Jammu and India. Since the insurrection was Muslim-supported the Pandits became increasingly fearful as they suffered killings in their community, as did a section of pro-India Muslims. The number of Muslims killed by militants has been approximately three times that of Pandits (Bose, 1997).

Over the years the pain and suffering of the Pandit Kashmiris has been weaponised more by the BJP, casting an unwavering communal shadow over the Kashmiri movement. However, analysts conclude that most of the selective killings in the early militancy were 'inspired by some sort of political motive, rather than simply pan-Islamic fundamentalism' (Bose, 1997: 74). In the atmosphere of unpredictability, the Hindu Pandits and a section of Muslims favouring India swiftly left Kashmir. While the Hindu Pandits, some of whom have returned, are not settlers, the policies for their rehabilitation present a fresh set of problems. The Kashmiri resistance leaders and masses have always welcomed the return of Pandits, but insist segregated townships as planned by the Indian government would ghettoise them and set the stage for a communal conflagration.

As the pandemic refuses to recede, Kashmiris are still under partial siege; rather, a double lockdown. And while the Indian government is projecting normalcy, education, the economy, trade and tourism remained affected.[8] In recent years, Kashmiri Muslims have become more wary, with the Indian government, through local proxies, pushing for policies including the allocation of land to retired army officers and non-Kashmiris. After removing Article 370, even as the pandemic continues, the Indian government unilaterally amended the domicile law. It has opened pathways for designated categories of Indian citizens to become domiciles of the erstwhile state. Thus far, 125,000 domicile certificates have been issued under a speedy procedure. Thus, for Kashmiris, demographic alteration and settler colonialism has become a reality. However, political resistance is in the DNA of Kashmiris. Despite most resistance leaders being in detention, the resistance to Indian occupation, which is largely people-driven, continues. The fear of settler colonialism and passionate resistance to it is likely to frame political rationality in Kashmir for the foreseeable future.

Notes

1 'Women's voice; Fact-finding report on Kashmir' (24 September 2019), http://en.maktoobmedia.com/2019/09/24/full-text-womens-voice-fact-finding-report-on-kashmir/ (accessed 10 June 2020).

2 See 'Kashmir caged: A fact-finding report by Jean Drèze, Kavita Krishnan, Maimoona Mollah and Vimal Bhai' (4 August 2019), www.nchro.org/ index.php/2019/08/14/kashmir-caged-a-fact-finding-report-by-jean-dreze-kavita-krishnan-maimoona-mollah-and-vimal-bhai/ (accessed 13 July 2020).

3 'Let Kashmir Speak', Amnesty International (2019), www.amnesty.org/ en/get-involved/take-action/let-kashmir-speak/ (accessed 13 June 2020).

4 See *Kashmir Civil Disobedience: A Citizen's Report* by Anirudh Kala, Brinelle D'Souza, Revati Laul and Shabnam Hashmi, October 2019. https:// kashmirscholars.files.wordpress.com/2019/10/kashmir-civil-disobediance-a-citizens-report.pdf (accessed 9 May 2022).

5 See Deshmane (2019). Also see the interview by Karan Thapar with Faizan Mustafa, an Indian jurist, refuting arguments made by the Indian government against Kashmir's special status Article 370, www.youtube.com/ watch?v=YiKuTsnR4VM (accessed 10 June 2020); Ather Zia, 'Straw man arguments and the removal of Article 370', *Asia Dialogue* (2019), https:// theasiadialogue.com/2019/09/27/the-long-read-straw-man-arguments-and-the-removal-of-article-370/ (accessed 10 June 2020).

6 *Kashmir's Internet Siege: An ongoing assault on Digital Rights*, Jammu and Kashmir Coalition of Civil Society (JKCCS) (2020), https://jkccs.net/ report-kashmirs-internet-siege/?fbclid=IwAR2e6wli3SNiny9fZD2KT cP02vk-unus5xSDusA15d07k5fd2S4vS41kc7Y (accessed September 2021).

7 'Asifa Bano: The child rape and murder that has Kashmir on edge', BBC (18 August 2018), www.bbc.com/news/world-asia-india-43722714 (accessed 10 June 2020).

8 *Zulm, Zakhm, Azaadi … The Voices of Kashmiri Women*, https://wssnet. org/2019/10/05/zulm-zakhm-azaadi-the-voices-of-kashmiri-women/ (accessed 10 June 2020).

References

Aslam M. J. (2020). 'Genocide of Jammu Muslims of 1947 that changed demography & history of J&K', *Countercurrents*, 6 November. Available at: https://countercurrents.org/2020/11/genocide-of-jammu-muslims-of-47-that-changed-demography-history-of-jk/ (accessed 10 June 2022).

Bhandari, P. (2019). 'The Jammu and Kashmir Reorganisation Bill 2019 portends a future hope', *Financial Express*, 8 August. Available at: www. financialexpress.com/opinion/a-win-for-democracy-the-jammu-and-kashmir-reorganisation-bill-2019-portends-a-future-hope/1669470/ (accessed 10 June 2020).

Bose, S. (1997). *The Challenge in Kashmir: Democracy, Self-Determination and a Just Peace* (London: Sage).

Chowdhary, Z. (2015). *Kashmir Conflict and the Muslims of Jammu* (Srinagar: Gulshan Publishers).

Deshmane, A. (2019). 'Kashmir: Scrapping Article 370 "unconstitutional", "deceitful" says legal expert A. G. Noorani', *Huffington Post*, 8 August. Available at: www.huffpost.com/archive/in/entry/kashmir-article-370-scrapping-constitutional-expert-reacts-noorani_in_5d47e58de4b0aca341206135 (accessed July 2021).

Duschinski, H. and Ghosh, S. (2017). 'Constituting the occupation: Preventive detention and permanent emergency in Kashmir', *Journal of Legal Pluralism and Unofficial Law*, 49(3): 314–337.

Hussain, S. (n.d.). *Kashmir: Palestine in the Making* (Srinagar: Kashmir Institute).

Lancet (2019). 'Editorial: Fear and uncertainty around Kashmir's future', *Lancet*, 394(10198): 542. https://doi.org/10.1016/S0140-6736(19)31939-7

New Indian Express (2019). 'Jammu and Kashmir sees 300 stone pelting cases', *New Indian Express*, 11 October. Available at: www.newindianexpress.com/nation/2019/oct/11/jammu-and-kashmir-sees-300-stone-pelting-cases-2045954.html (accessed 11 July 2020).

Noorani, A. G. (2010). 'A cruel hoax', *Frontline*, 12 February. Available at: https://frontline.thehindu.com/the-nation/article30179216.ece (accessed 10 June 2022).

Noorani, A. G. (2011). *Article 370: A Constitutional History of Jammu and Kashmir* (Oxford: Oxford University Press).

Office of the High Commissioner for Human Rights (OHCHR) (2018). *Report on the Situation of Human Rights in Kashmir: Developments in the Indian State of Jammu and Kashmir from June 2016 to April 2018, and General Human Rights Concerns in Azad Jammu and Kashmir and Gilgit-Baltistan* (n.p.: United Nations OHCHR).

Raghavan, V. R. (2014). *Conflicts in Jammu and Kashmir: Impact on Polity, Society and Economy* (Chennai: Vij Books).

Rajalakshmi, T. R. (2019). 'Kashmir's development statistics: Nailing a lie', *Frontline*, 30 August. Available at: https://frontline.thehindu.com/cover-story/article29054385.ece (accessed 3 August 2020).

Snedden, C. (2001). 'What happened to Muslims in Jammu?', *Journal of South Asian Studies*, 24(2): 111–134.

Thapar, K. (2019). 'We cannot be selective about the past in Jammu & Kashmir. Opinion', *Hindustan Times*, 15 September. Available at: www.hindustantimes.com/columns/we-cannot-be-selective-about-the-past-in-j-k/story-ELfaDpC6UoAfMbBNQTgIsO.html (accessed 12 June 2020).

Times of India (2019). 'We diluted Article 370 twelve times without controversy: Congress', *Times of India*, 3 November. Available at: https://timesofindia.indiatimes.com/india/we-diluted-article-370-twelve-times-without-controversy-congress/articleshow/71881833.cms (accessed June 2021).

Zia, A. (2019). 'Blinding Kashmiris. The right to maim and the Indian military occupation in Kashmir. Interventions', *International Journal of Postcolonial Studies*, 21(6): 773–786.

Zia, A. (2020). '"Their wounds are our wounds": A case for affective solidarity between Palestine and Kashmir', *Identities: Global Studies in Culture and Power*, 26(5): 357–375.

Part IV

Women, gender and love

10

Love taboos: Hindus, Muslims and moral panics

Charu Gupta

On 7 September 2014, Rashtriya Swayamsevak Sangh, the right-wing Hindu body, widely regarded as the parent organisation of Bharatiya Janata Party, the ruling party of India, published cover stories on 'love jihad' in its weekly mouthpieces *Panchjanya*, in Hindi, and *Organiser*, in English. 'Love jihad' was alleged to be a conspiracy under which Muslim men were targeting vulnerable Hindu girls and forcefully converting them to Islam by feigning love through trickery and marriage. The publications urged people to raise the slogan 'Love ever, love jihad never!' *Panchjanya*'s cover had an illustration of a man wearing a traditional Arab headdress, the *kaffiyeh*, a beard in the shape of heart, and sinister sunglasses in which red hearts were reflected. The magazine asked on the cover, 'Love blind or trade?' – *pyar andha ya dhandha*?

The 'love jihad' campaign has been compelling on several accounts. It epitomises construction of Muslim men – as evil and licentious – by politicised Hindu nationalism. It also calls for Hindu male prowess, fabricates declining Hindu numbers, reveals threats at religious conversions, formulates a homogenous Hindu identity, frames a 'vulnerable' Hindu woman, and reinstates familial patriarchies. Above all, it signifies taboos on the expression of love that defies boundaries, and anxieties around women's independent-individual expressions of desire. 'Love jihad' is inseparable from the imperative of disciplining desire, where a Hindu-coded nation is deciding the rules of love and intimacy. The anxieties underpinning the campaign of 'love jihad' played no minor role in mobilising and consolidating support for the BJP in the 2019 general election.

Feminists have emphasised that 'love jihad' has actually been a 'jihad' against love – a mythical and violent campaign, a 'delicious' political fantasy, and an attempt at mobilisation in the name of women by the Hindu right (Gupta, 2014; Nair, 2014; Sarkar, 2014). This chapter discusses how Hindu women are often constructed as victims in such campaigns, and why interreligious marriages underscore recalcitrant desires. It reflects on how the arc of Hindu female love for men outside the community, even while reifying heteronormativity, has meant that such desire is visceral and tactile, though it can only be acknowledged when it is being regulated as transgression, producing disciplining and everyday violence, along what Foucault calls the alliance model of sexuality, where – through arrangement of marriages – boundaries of religion and caste are policed (Foucault, 1978: 106–111). At the same time, 'rule breaking' by women has often aided a transformative politics of intimate religious rights. Interreligious desire in India has been a site which produces cracks and fissures in dominant embodiments.

Hindu women as victims

The motif of 'love jihad', while asserting Hindu male prowess, and marking the spectre of illegibility as Muslim, acquires its emotional bonding through imaging 'victimised' Hindu woman. Interestingly, the Syro-Malabar Church in Kerala was among the early proponents of the idea that a 'love jihad' was being waged: the idea has subsequently been appropriated and amplified by Hindutva supporters. Scholars have explored 'changing configurations of power' in histories of victimhood, where images of hapless victims stand in contrast to the brutal perpetrator (Ronsbo and Jensen, 2014: 6). For politicised Hinduism, one's religious identity is a protean category, and managing the domestic is crucial to it. The troubled intimacies of domestic spaces have coalesced around gender and family in Hindutva vocabularies. Who is bedding and wedding Hindu women is embedded in distinct Hindu nationalism. 'Muscular nationalism' rests on a gendered binary of 'martial man versus chaste woman' (Banerjee, 2012: 2). The converted Hindu woman is metamorphosed into a symbol of sacredness *and* humiliation. Campaigns like 'love jihad' privilege moral panic and familial controls over constitutional ethics.

The Hindu woman has often been regarded as an exclusive preserve of Hindu man, and safeguarding her virtue is identified as his exclusive prerogative. In the name of protecting 'our' women, which they have never asked for, all violence against Muslim men and 'disobedient' Hindu women is justified. Even before the term 'love jihad' was coined, Hindu organisations like Bajrang Dal and Ram Sena ran a 'Save the Honour of Daughter-in-Laws and Daughters' *(Bahu Betiyon ki Izzat Bachao)* campaign and a 'Movement to Save Daughters' *(Beti Bachao Andolan)*, whose central focus was to enforce love taboos by keeping Hindu girls away from Muslim men.

The formation of 'anti-Romeo squads' in Uttar Pradesh is also significant here. It is to be noted that 'love jihad' has sometimes also been called 'Romeo Jihad'. In this context, the launch of anti-Romeo squads by the BJP government in Uttar Pradesh, while supposedly meant to counter sexual harassment – euphemistically called 'eve teasing' – have often become a source of harassment and fear for women and men and a means to perpetuate love taboos. Prashant Bhushan, a lawyer, perhaps not in good taste, but tongue-in-cheek, said in a tweet: 'Romeo loved just one lady, while Krishna was a legendary eve teaser. Would Uttar Pradesh Chief Minister Yogi Adityanath have the guts to call his vigilantes anti-Krishna squads?' Another wrote, 'Alas for Shakespeare! … Yogi Adityanath's Anti-Romeo squad in Uttar Pradesh has conjured Romeo up to be a feckless hoodlum, a creature who has exponentially gained an identity of carnal calling and is now a viral disease infecting a pure and sacred state!' Feminists have reiterated that there is a sharp distinction between consensual friendship, flirtation and love between adults, irrespective of class, caste or religion in which nobody has the right to interfere, and between sexual harassment and stalking of women.

The term 'love jihad' is also interesting as both 'love' and 'jihad' are perceived as 'foreign' terms, alien to the Indian soil. 'Love' thus sits more comfortably here than say *ishq* or *prem*. And in 2014, relying on stereotypes that Muslim women are slaves of husbands, various posters appealed to Hindu men to protect their daughters and sisters from becoming 'victims' of love jihad. Repeated use of words like *sachet*, *savdhaan* and *jagruk*, which are synonyms for being beware and careful, invoke the need to watch over oneself and over women. Separate cases have been constructed as a coherent morality drama, whereby every interfaith romance and marriage has been rewritten as deception. The 'Love jihad' campaign represents the woman as 'foolish', 'lured' and 'brainwashed' into the 'trap', with no mind or heart of her own. Armed with peacock feathers and blessed water, a godman, Baba Rajakdas, advocates love taboos by selling a love 'cure' in parts of north India to save Hindu girls who, according to him, get easily carried away by Muslim boys as they do not understand that they are being exploited. The courts too often take on the mantle of paternal patriarchs. In the case of Hadiya/Akhila, the homeopathy student who embraced Islam, and thereafter married a Muslim man, the court initially grossly infantilised Hadiya. Eroding her agency and silencing her voice, the court ordered an annulment of the marriage. Her vociferous denial of charges of force was dismissed with assertions about her mediocre intelligence, young age and incapacity to think independently. A woman's turn to Islam, it appears, can only be interpreted in the legal matrix of terrorism. In convoluted ways women are told that interreligious romance is undesirable for the good of women themselves. There appears a consensus among Hindu groups against any exercise of choice by women to love or convert as individuals, sans familial and community approval. Equally, the Muslim male is denied the language of love.

In 2015, *Himalaya Dhvani*, a magazine of Durga Vahini, the women's wing of Vishwa Hindu Parishad, had on its cover the image of a leading Bollywood actress, Kareena Kapoor, who has married a Muslim actor, half covered in the *burqa*, arguing that this was the 'dreadful fate' of Hindu women who married Muslim men. Through such constructions, as Wendy Brown argues: 'Certain facts are selected and highlighted while other crucial information is omitted; … moralism is subtly and almost imperceptibly secreted into the narrative; fear is induced and mobilised; metonymic chains of victimization are established; demonization of the enemy is artfully staged' (Brown, 2006: 126).

Hindu women's everyday lives have been bombarded with instructions, imposing not only love taboos but multiple restrictions. All-out attempts have been made to keep Hindu women away from Muslim men and from symbols, customs and culture perceived as 'Muslim'. Not only intimate liaison, but day-to-day contact with Muslims is perceived as a threat to Hindu community identity. It has been emphasised that since races, religions and castes share the most extended and close contact – routine, cumulative, mundane – in the workplace, love and desire arise most frequently, if almost counter-intuitively, in the context of work relations. The metaphor of 'love jihad' attempts to penetrate the everyday lives of women. Hindutva's cry for segregation expresses a geography that maps power and hierarchy through women's bodies. In various meetings held in Uttar Pradesh, instructions have been given to Hindu women, including 'not to wear green clothes' and 'not to go to Muslim tailors and hairdressers'. Everyday public spaces like schools, colleges, theatres, ice-cream and juice parlours, mobile charge shops and private spaces like television and the internet are identified as sites where Hindu girls are 'wooed'. Pramod Muthalik has written a book, *Love Jihad: Red Alert for Hindu Girls*, which gives instructions on how to impose love taboos on Hindu women and how to forestall them from 'becoming victims'. It has instructions like: 'Be cautious about her wearing a headscarf since it becomes difficult to recognise a girl who wears a headscarf and sits behind a two-wheeler. … Since some cases of love jihad have taken place with the help of mobile phones, check incoming calls. Remember that saved numbers may be under a false name. … To get help from Hindus in a difficult situation, apply *kumkum* on the forehead' (Quoted in Johnson and Verma, 2014: 13). In the wake of the massive electoral mandate won by the BJP, its government in Uttar Pradesh went on to promulgate the Uttar Pradesh Prohibition of Unlawful Conversion Religious Ordinance (2020), which criminalised interfaith marriages as 'love jihad'. With this, the Uttar Pradesh government declared and stamped itself as a Hindu patriarch.

The minute instructions reveal the need felt not so much to protect the Hindu woman but to facilitate penetration of disciplinary regimes and love taboos. The passionate attempt to 'protect' Hindu women is embedded within ill-concealed masculinist rationalities. The language of protection actually means that women have to be kept on watch on a daily basis, as Sneha Krishnan shows in her contribution to this volume. All private–public spaces then need to be patrolled, and if so-called 'love jihadists' take on Hindu names to 'fool' women, then all love affairs are presumptively suspect, since an apparently Hindu boy may actually be a love-toting jihadist, which in turn means that the only way that 'love jihad' can be thwarted is by launching a jihad against love, thus imagining that all interfaith marriages are also 'love jihad' (Desai, 2014).

There functions a grim coercive power behind avowals of protection. These are attempts at codification through instructions, as they mandate a set of behaviours on the part of Hindu women, insulate their social spaces, and signify assiduous control over their movements. Such desires remain 'radically unthinkable' and lead to various constraints, including, as Butler says, the 'radical unthinkability of desiring otherwise, the radical unendurability of desiring otherwise, the absence of certain desires, the repetitive compulsion of others' and 'the abiding repudiation of some sexual possibilities' (Butler, 1993: 59). Instructions to women attempt to erase female subjectivity and desire. Such a woman is an enemy within, a menace for Hindutva. The intermeshing of romance, marriage and conversion produces choreography of everyday violence, framed around women's bodies. These women are actually not 'vulnerable victims', but 'risk-taking subjects'.

Recalcitrant desires, intimacies and love

The meaning of desire is context based; yet desire can be a source of creativity, producing new optimism and new narratives of possibility. Historian Michele Birnbaum remarks that desire can be 'an interracial and interpersonal dynamic, a kind of synapse on the color line rather than an individual site of intention, hopes, dreams, wishes' (Birnbaum, 2003: 17). Lauren Berlant argues that desire can measure 'fields of difference and distance. It both constructs and collapses distinctions between public and private: it reorganizes worlds' (Berlant, 2012: 13–14). Love and desire destabilise the very things they are disciplined to organise, and reopen the utopian to more promises, providing a language of intimacy and rights. Located in politics, and the everyday, intimacy is constantly in flux, contestable, and rewritable, disrupting presumably seamless boundaries. Anthony Giddens observes that 'the possibility of intimacy means the promise of democracy' (Giddens, 1992: 188). Intimacy provides us with new ways to talk of ideas made material through the physical body.

Interreligious romances and intimacies destabilise the seemingly unambiguous agenda of a triumphant Hindu majoritarianism. The metaphor of 'love jihad' also epitomises fears of Hindutva politics regarding female free will, the subversive potential of love, non-normative embodiments, pliable religious identities and syncretic practices. Reclaiming messier practices of sexual desire that constantly transgress prescriptions from within are important sites of resistance. The desires of Hindu women often do not conform to dominant ideas in the public life of a Hindu nation. Many women have negotiated intimacies beyond its moral and social parameters, reflecting shifting registers of unspoken ambivalences. Thus comes a phenomenal statement from a woman:

> I am Saldon, I am Shifah. I choose to be both. It saddens me that my marriage and spiritual choice are misused to stoke fear and hatred. … Nobody asked me my view as if I don't matter in this game of misogyny played in my name. … It is a brazen attempt to suppress and threaten a woman who has shown the courage to follow her heart. (Saldon, 2017)

There has been a substantial increase in inter-caste/interreligious marriages, particularly in the past few decades, in spite of several adversities and threats. Interviews with interfaith couples persuasively challenge 'love jihad'. Such localised and embodied practices require social courage and show how some people, particularly women, have taken control of their lives. Such women and men implicitly place themselves between two worlds, deftly dealing with both. It is their ephemeral existence and their 'instability' as fixed religious and national beings, which is a source of hope. As Nivedita Menon says, 'Young men and women *are* falling in love, across caste and religious divides, and this is rocking the foundations of caste and religious identity. … Even in these terrible times, every single day, another young woman decides to risk her very life on the strength of a glance, another young man defies death for a smile. Subversive youthful desire – it's enough to cheer up the most jaded of middle-aged anti-romantics' (Menon, 2014). Janaki Nair says, 'Indian women have taken control of their lives at a much faster pace than expected' and are 'no longer passive bearers of caste, religious, ethnic or other meaning – but the makers of meaning'.

The India Love Project, which gathers stories of love and marriage that transcend caste, religion, ethnicity and gender, has curated on Instagram and Facebook several first-person accounts and garnered a considerable following. Dhanak, an NGO mostly comprising interfaith and inter-caste couples, has evolved organically, and over the years has emerged as a champion organisation working for the promotion of the 'right to choice' in matters of marriage and relationships. More recently, a group of young people in Bhopal have come together in a campaign they call Ishq Par Zor Nahi ('No compulsion in love'), which is working to fight against the propaganda of 'love jihad' and give a face and voice to interfaith couples. The left-wing All India Student Association has started a nationwide campaign called 'Love Azad', to counter the lies of 'love jihad' and the unconstitutional laws against interfaith marriages.

Ambedkar, the great anti-caste ideologue, upheld inter-caste marriages as one way to annihilate caste, since it produced fissures in maintenance of caste purity and control of women's sexuality – even if implicitly, they produce cracks in orthodox Hindu mandates and on love taboos. Such an exercise of choice, even when partial, can perhaps aid a transformative politics of intimate religious rights. The recalcitrance of desire and interreligious marriage can throw up emancipatory possibilities of rights, where highly ritualised acts of conversion and marriage could at times become a metaphor for a new vocabulary of body, of interiority, of subjectivity.

References

Banerjee, S. (2012). *Muscular Nationalism: Gender, Violence, and Empire in India and Ireland, 1914–2004* (New York: New York University Press).

Berlant, L. (2012). *Desire/Love* (New York: Punctum Books).

Birnbaum, M. (2003). *Race, Work and Desire in American Literature, 1860–1930* (Cambridge: Cambridge University Press).

Brown, W. (2006). *Regulating Aversion: Tolerance in the Age of Identity and Empire* (Princeton, NJ: Princeton University Press).

Butler, J. (1993). *Bodies That Matter: On the Discursive Limits of 'Sex'* (London: Routledge).

Desai, S. (2014). 'A jihad against love?', *Times of India*, 1 September.

Foucault, M. (1978). *The History of Sexuality*, Vol. 1, trans. Robert Hurley (New York: Vintage).

Giddens, A. (1992). *The Transformation of Intimacy: Sexuality, Love and Eroticism in Modern Societies* (Stanford, CA: Stanford University Press).

Gupta, C. (2014). 'The myth of love jihad', *Indian Express*, 24 August.

Johnson, T. A. and Verma, L. (2014). 'Who loves love jihad', *Indian Express*, 7 September.

Menon, N. (2014). '"The Meerut Girl", desperate Hindutvavaadis and their jihad against love', *Kafila*, 14 October. Available at: https://kafila.online/2014/10/14/the-meerut-girl-desperate-hindutvavaadis-and-their-jihad-against-love/ (accessed 26 October 2014).

Nair, J. (2014). 'Why love is a four-letter word', *The Hindu*, 6 October.

Ronsbo, H. and Jensen, S. (2014). 'Introduction: Histories of victimhood: Assemblages, transactions, and figures' in S. Jensen and H. Ronsbo (eds) *Histories of Victimhood* (Philadelphia, PA: University of Pennsylvania Press), 1–22.

Saldon, S. (2017). 'I am Saldon I am Shifah', *Indian Express*, 19 September.

Sarkar, T. (2014). 'Love, control and punishment', *Indian Express*, 16 October.

11

Why is romance political?

Sneha Krishnan

In August 2019, the re-elected Bharatiya Janata Party (BJP) government in India abrogated Article 370 of the Indian constitution, which gave Kashmir special rights as a territory that had acceded to the Indian state in 1947 under considerable pressure. This abrogation in many ways consolidates India's military occupation of Kashmir. It would also allow Indian citizens from beyond Kashmir to buy land and make business investments in the region. Interestingly, however, within hours of the abrogation, social media was full of Hindu men from elsewhere in the country declaring their excitement at now being able to marry or have sex with Kashmiri women. As many pointed out, there has never been any restriction against marriage with Kashmiris.

What this slippage reveals however is the centrality of ideas about romance and love, as well as the reproductive female body, to debates on territory and the (Hindu) nation in India. As feminist geographer Sara Smith (2012: 1513) writes in the context of contested Muslim–Buddhist marriages in Ladakh, gendered bodies and their reproductive potentials 'can not only be territory but can also make territory'. In conflating the occupation of territory with claims over women's bodies, the outpouring of Hindu nationalist machismo on Twitter confirmed the centrality of questions about sex, love and romance to mainstream political debate in India. Indeed, emotions are central to the country's broader political landscape, as the other authors in this volume have so ably demonstrated. This chapter will highlight some key flashpoints in the last decade that have been symptomatic of the ways in which love and romance – or the politics of desire that maps territory onto bodies – feature centrally in questions about the ways in which caste and community engage the nation.

Risk and reputation

Since 2015, the Pinjra Tod (break the cage) movement, led by young female college students predominantly in New Delhi, has drawn attention to the surveillance that young women endure in educational settings, as well as in Indian cities more broadly. Often justified as essential for 'safety', these restrictions keep young women from accessing libraries and other educational services in the evening, as well as disallowing them from using the public and commercial spaces of cities. In 2017, Maneka Gandhi, then Union Minister for Women and Child Development, refused to consider repealing curfews at women's hostels because she believed that young women might have 'hormonal outbursts' that render them incapable of making sound decisions (Scroll staff, 2017). This discourse about 'risk' in the city is, as many scholars have shown (Phadke, 2007; Krishnan, 2016), really suggestive of anxieties about young women's exercise of sexual agency outside marriage, as well as potentially beyond the lines of caste and community. While sexual violence is indeed a major concern in Indian cities, restrictions on young women's mobility typically speaks instead to fears about reputation and respectability.

In my research in Chennai, where curfews are as early as four in the afternoon and never later than seven in the evening, I found that questions about reputation informed ideas about risk in young women's own lives. Indeed, while feminist scholarship on consent has been overwhelmingly focused on young women's capacity to say 'no' in sexual encounters, the young women I met found it equally difficult to say 'yes' without loss of reputation, or risk to their position as respectable middle-class women. As such, for instance, many young women I met believed it best to say 'no' initially, if only to mark themselves as being 'not easy'. One young woman, Malar,[1] told me about a young man she met at a sports event in which they had both participated, and whom she became interested in. Though they spent hours staring at each other across the stadium over many weeks, Malar refused him when he asked her out and continued to do so for six months. When he persisted during this period rather than give up and move on to someone else, she told me she was sure he really loved her and then felt able to accept him. This same persistence – which for Malar was a sign of his respect for her as a 'good' woman – might have been experienced as sexual harassment if she had not wanted his overtures. Concerns about reputation and the performance of respectable middle-class femininity thus blur the lines between sexual harassment – often cast as 'eve teasing' – and consensual romance.

Caste and class

These concerns were especially heightened for women who came from so-called lower caste and lower middle-class families. A lot has been made both of the social mobility that members of the Other Backward Classes (OBC) – the cluster of communities historically oppressed as 'lower caste' but not 'untouchable' – and even some Dalit communities have gained in the last two decades. In Tamil Nadu, where my research is focused, this social mobility – particularly through education – has a longer duration, owing to the decades-long history of caste-based mobilisation in the region (Subramanian, 2015). This has meant that a growing number of women from OBC and Dalit communities attend prestigious women's colleges in cities like Chennai, and live in the city's hostels. For many of these young women, protecting their reputations while at college was key to actually consolidating the social mobility gained through education. As scholars like Manuela Ciotti (2010) have shown, becoming middle class in India has historically been achieved through the embodied marking of respectability on women's bodies. Given also that the wardens and other authorities in these hostels still tend to be relatively high-caste women, OBC and Dalit women also face discrimination and are often labelled as 'loose' or 'uncontrolled' – or in the words of one Brahmin Dean at a college, whom I interviewed in 2013, 'like untethered donkeys'.

Another means through which caste and class enter this debate is in the simultaneous stigmatising of lower-caste and working-class men's bodies as threats to middle-class women. The much-celebrated unshackling of Indian women's sexualities since the dawn of 'liberalisation' in the 1990s has located these freedoms in the globalised upper middle-class spaces of malls, cafes and bars. This discourse simultaneously marks the lower-caste and working-class men – particularly migrants to cities – who people the city's public spaces as threats to these newfound freedoms. This was particularly evident in the wake of the widely reported rape and murder of Delhi student Jyoti Singh in 2012 (Shandilya, 2015). The much-debated documentary *India's Daughter* by British filmmaker Leslee Udwin, for instance, tells the story as a tension between two Indias: that of Jyoti Singh, who is presented as a good global subject who speaks English and has high ambitions, and that of her rapists whose violence is firmly located in their rural origins and 'backwardness'. This is, of course, unreflective of the reality in which feminist scholars all over the world show that sexual violence predominantly occurs within intimate settings and is perpetrated widely across different classes and communities. Indeed, this would suggest that sexual violence is not so much correlated with 'backwardness' as with a widespread culture of impunity as well as ideas about reputation and honour which consolidate men's claims over women's bodies. In my ethnography, I found that college and hostel authorities perpetrated the myth of the sexual harasser as necessarily lower class or caste and 'backward'. The young women I met also typically internalised this narrative, even if their own experiences of sexual violence were overwhelmingly within their own homes – and from relatives and members of their own social milieus – rather than in public spaces in the city.

That this stigma also conflates sexual violence with consensual sexual activity outside the boundaries of caste and community is evident from the recent debate on 'love jihad' – as Charu Gupta shows in Chapter 10 – as well as the violence that Dalit men increasingly face when they enter relationships with women of higher castes. In 2017 in Tamil Nadu, a young Dalit man named Ilavarasan was found dead after his wife Divya's family – members of the Vanniyar OBC caste – alleged that he had kidnapped her against her will. Between 2016 and 2018, in a high-profile case, a young Malayalee woman called Hadiya found her marriage annulled and herself remanded first to her parents' home and then to her college's hostel after she converted to Islam and married a Muslim man of her own choosing. Hadiya's father filed a habeas corpus petition in the Kerala High Court – this legal instrument is widely used in India to 'return' young women to their families when they have married outside the bounds of caste and community (Baxi, 2006) – alleging that his daughter was a victim of 'love jihad'. In both cases, the parties involved were all well over the legal age of majority, and as such should not have faced legal barriers to marriage regardless of caste or religion. However, in both cases, the matter at the heart of the debate in court was the young women's capacity to make decisions that were at odds with their families' wishes, as well as the state's own investment in consolidating caste hierarchies as well as (Hindu) national territory. Although the passions fomented by these debates did not translate into electoral benefits for the BJP in these two southern states during the 2019 general election, their resonances with broader national anxieties are unmistakable.

We might note here that the hostel enters this story as well, indicating the carceral significance of these institutions. Indeed, Indian courts have long been known to use private and university-affiliated hostels as remand homes for non-criminal women. This is particularly so in cases where the matter being litigated is the young woman's right to marry outside her caste or religious community. In 2013, when I was doing fieldwork in Chennai, the daughter of a South Indian filmmaker – a young woman well over the legal age of majority – eloped with a partner of a different caste, of whom her parents did not approve. The young woman was eventually remanded to her former school's hostel while the court debated her capacity to make this decision. The school hostel authorities made statements that positioned them squarely as advocates for her parents' position in the matter, and the young woman eventually returned home to her family. At the hostels where I did fieldwork, young women who eloped or entered relationships with men who were considered 'inappropriate' found themselves severely sanctioned. At one hostel, the typical punishment for such behaviour was 'gating': i.e. confinement in a room except to attend classes. Young women I met were gated for as long as three or four months – the duration of an entire semester – and often expressed feelings of suffocation and exhaustion that came from such punishment. In other cases, families were informed immediately and in some cases – especially where evidence of an ongoing sexual relationship was found – students found themselves expelled on grounds of having violated a morality clause written into the contract they signed with the college on accepting admission. Questions about hostel curfews and surveillance in these institutions are thus significant to a broader debate on the ways in which women's bodies are mapped onto ideas about (Hindu) national and communal honour.

Conclusion

In concluding, I will use one final example to illustrate the ways in which love and marriage enter debates on nation and territory in India. In 2018, various Hindu nationalist groups protested against the impending release of the film *Padmavat* by Sanjay Leela Bhansali, a retelling of the epic story by Sufi poet Malik Mohammad Jayasi. The poem and the film tell the story of the *jauhar* or sacrificial suicide of Rani Padmavati of Chittor in the thirteenth century, when faced with potential rape or murder by the armies of Alauddin Khilji, a Muslim ruler of Delhi. The protesters alleged that the film showed Padmavati as being in love with Khilji and that this was unacceptable to Hindus. These same groups eventually acquiesced to the film's screening after it was found that the film in fact depicts Khilji as deranged and violent – among other things, eating meat raw – in direct opposition to Padmavati's evident grace and beauty. As many scholars pointed out in the wake of the fracas, the film's telling of the story is problematic. Rape as an instrument of war was widely used by both Hindu and Muslim armies in that period, and continues to be used by armies all over the world. In its depiction of a feminised Hindu territory – embodied in Padmavati – who would rather burn herself than be ravaged by a rapacious Muslim ruler, the film bolsters the logic undergirding the discourse of 'love jihad': that India is essentially a Hindu territory, and that its (Hindu) women must be protected from their own desires and the designs of cunning Muslim men, even through acts of violence. Love and romance in contemporary India are thus deeply political problems that cut to the heart of the contemporary moment of Hindu nationalist ascendance.

This volume is premised on the argument that passions lie at the heart of electoral politics. This chapter has shown that the disciplinary institutions of the state – the courts and police – as well as educational institutions are all imbued with passionate attachments. They seek to materialise particular visions of nation and community by regulating gender and sexuality.

Note

1 All personal names from my research are pseudonyms, used to protect my informants' privacy.

References

Baxi, P. (2006). 'Habeas corpus in the realm of love: Litigating marriages of choice in India', *Australian Feminist Law Journal*, 25(1): 59–78.

Ciotti, M. (2010). '"The bourgeois woman and the half-naked one": Or the Indian nation's contradictions personified', *Modern Asian Studies*, 44(4): 785–815.

Krishnan, S. (2016). 'Agency, intimacy, and rape jokes: An ethnographic study of young women and sexual risk in Chennai', *Journal of the Royal Anthropological Institute*, 22(1): 67–83.

Phadke, S. (2007). 'Dangerous liaisons: Women and men: Risk and reputation in Mumbai', *Economic and Political Weekly*, 42(17): 1510–1518.

Scroll staff (2017). 'An early hostel curfew is necessary to protect girls from "hormonal outbursts": Maneka Gandhi', Scroll.in, last modified 7 March. Available at: https://scroll.in/latest/831079/an-early-hostel-curfew-is-necessary-to-protect-girls-from-hormonal-outbursts-maneka-gandhi (accessed 3 December 2020).

Shandilya, K. (2015). 'Nirbhaya's body: The politics of protest in the aftermath of the 2012 Delhi gang rape', *Gender & History*, 27(2): 465–486.

Smith, S. (2012). 'Intimate geopolitics: Religion, marriage, and reproductive bodies in Leh, Ladakh', *Annals of the Association of American Geographers*, 102(6): 1511–1528.

Subramanian, A. (2015). 'Making merit: The Indian Institutes of Technology and the social life of caste', *Comparative Studies in Society and History*, 57(2): 291–322.

Part V

What young Indians want

12

In pursuit of *Parivartan*: Youth agency and the 2019 general election in Sikkim

Mabel Denzin Gergan and Charisma K. Lepcha

The Indian general election, with all its fervour, fury and fanfare, when observed from the vantage point of the country's eight Northeastern states,[1] can be a disorienting experience given the region's dismal parliamentary representation and geographic disconnect from the rest of the country. India's eight Northeastern states send only twenty-four members of parliament to the Lok Sabha, the bulk (fourteen) of whom come from a single state, Assam. Historically, regional parties have dominated the political landscape (with a few exceptions) in Northeastern states, and national political parties, particularly the Bhartiya Janta Party (BJP), have commanded little allegiance. However, since 2014 the Narendra Modi-led National Democratic Alliance (NDA) has mounted an aggressive campaign to expand its presence in the region, forming a regional political alliance, the Northeast Democratic Alliance (NEDA) with the aim of uniting non-Congress parties, while poaching charismatic leaders from other parties behind the scenes. The 2019 general election bore rich dividends for the NDA, with the party and its allies increasing their share of seats from ten out of twenty-four in 2014, to seventeen in 2019, leading political analysts to observe that the 'saffronisation' of the Northeast was complete. In a region that is home to many religious, ethnic and linguistic minorities, the BJP's strategic expansionism has sharpened local anxieties and discontent. As we illustrate here, this emotional response is entangled with regional political and development rationalities.

This chapter offers a grounded perspective on the growing influence of the BJP in Northeast India through a focus on the 2019 general and assembly elections in Sikkim and the response of educated youth. In 2019, Sikkim, along with four other states, held its Lok Sabha (general) and assembly (state-level) elections, simultaneously. Up until this point, Sikkim's legislative assembly was the only one in the Northeast with no political representation from either the Indian National Congress or the Bhartiya Janta Party. These elections were also significant since the Sikkim Democratic Front (SDF) led by Pawan Kumar Chamling had been in power for five consecutive terms with virtually no opposition. In 2014, the entry of the Sikkim Krantikari Morcha (SKM), whose younger leader Prem Singh Tamang (Golay) had defected from the SDF, shifted the scales of power when the SKM won ten of the thirty-two assembly seats. For the first time in twenty years, Sikkim had an opposition party. The 2019 general and assembly elections in Sikkim saw the slow unfurling of mounting frustrations with the SDF's political hegemony, and culminated with two key events – the defeat of Chamling, and the maiden entry of the BJP into Sikkim's legislative assembly.

Celebrations over the end of Chamling's twenty-five-year 'rule' were marred by local anxieties and anger at the political sleight of hand that resulted in the BJP securing twelve of the thirty-two assembly seats. We detail later in the chapter how this came to be, but suffice it to say, not many voters were pleased by this turn of events. While many young people took to social media to express their disappointment at the entry of the BJP, Chamling's defeat was celebrated as a victory of the democratic electoral process. Moreover, Sikkim's sole Lok Sabha seat was won by the SKM's Indra Hang Subba, a 30 year-old PhD scholar from the Department of Physics at Sikkim University. While the SKM selected Indra Hang Subba, the SDF replaced its veteran two-term member of parliament, Prem Das Rai, with the younger D. B. Katwal. And as is standard in Sikkim, neither the Congress nor the BJP were anywhere in the reckoning for the Lok Sabha elections. Subba's age and educational status propelled him into dinner table conversations as the much-needed change required in Sikkim politics. Subba's victory was especially significant for students at Sikkim University, who were overjoyed that one of their peers would be representing the state as a member of parliament in the Lok Sabha.

For Sikkim's youth critical of the ruling party, participating in the 2019 general and assembly elections restored their faith in the electoral process and perhaps even the state's democratic future.

This is politically significant since Sikkim's youth, much like other young people in the Northeast, have grown cynical and restless in the face of state apathy, as they contend with uncertain ecological futures, a shrinking public sector and the lack of private sector opportunities (Gergan, 2014; Koskimaki, 2017; Chakraborty, 2018; Deka, 2019; Deuchar, 2019).

This chapter is structured as follows: we first provide some brief context to Sikkim's success story as a 'model' state. We then trace political developments in Sikkim between the 2014 and 2019 state elections, with special attention to the role of young people as both candidates and voters, and demonstrate how their growing political participation is indicative of the shifting landscape of regional politics in Sikkim. Both authors' primary research is based in Sikkim – while Gergan has conducted fieldwork on the Indigenous Lepcha anti-dam movement in Dzongu, North Sikkim, Lepcha's research has centred on religious transition among the Lepchas in India and Nepal.

A 'model', disciplined frontier state

Sikkim, a Buddhist monarchy bordering Nepal, China and Bhutan, was annexed to India in 1975 after a controversial referendum, in a story familiar to many sovereign, independent entities in India's Himalayan borderlands. Remnants of Sikkim's former kingdom and its symbols of sovereignty can still be found on display in the state, the Sikkimese national flag on taxis being the most visible of these. This kingdom nostalgia notwithstanding, since its merger with India Sikkim has proven to be a 'model' disciplined frontier state. Notably, Prime Minister Modi lauded Sikkim for being a 'model' state for the world, while defence analysts have observed that the state is a 'model of stability' that bolsters India's geopolitical security. During Chamling's five-term rule, Sikkim won numerous national and international accolades for its environmentally conscious policies, tourism, public works and organic agriculture. In 2002, Sikkim was included in the North East Council (NEC), becoming the eighth state of India's Northeast region. It is important to note that Sikkim's 'model' status is often juxtaposed with political conditions in other Northeastern states that are often a product of state-sponsored violence through draconian laws like the AFSPA (Armed Forces

(Special Powers) Act). By most accounts, Sikkim is the poster child for a peaceful Indian state, while in a gross generalisation other Northeastern states are seen as a hotbed for insurgency and ethnic conflict.

Sikkim's history as an independent Buddhist kingdom with a traditional feudal system and its relatively recent transition from monarchy to democracy provides important historical context to its 'model' status. Since its annexation in 1975 and up until 2014, Sikkim has had only two full-term chief ministers, both of whom enjoyed absolute majority in the state legislative assembly during their successive terms. In addition, Sikkim, like many other Himalayan and Northeastern states, is a special category state. The 36th Amendment to the Indian constitution guarantees Sikkim special constitutional provisions under Article 371F. Article 371F is an illustration of asymmetric federalism, a unique constitutional arrangement in India that guarantees protections for local customary laws, land ownership and preferential financial assistance from the Centre. Indian asymmetric federalism can be understood as an attempt to accommodate subnationalist demands from sovereign states and Tribal nations incorporated into the Indian Union post-Independence (Suan, 2014). However, these provisions, instituted to ensure the cultural integrity of Sikkim post-annexation, have in many ways made Sikkim beholden to the Centre.

Sikkim's image of tranquillity also belies the growing precarity faced by its youth. For the younger generation of voters, the resentment felt by their parents' and grandparents' generations towards the Indian state for annexing Sikkim is slowly giving way to resentment closer to home. For many years now Sikkim has had one of the highest national unemployment and youth unemployment rates (ages 15–29) (*Times of India*, 2013). Educated unemployed youth in particular argue that the fruits of Sikkim's economic prosperity have not been distributed evenly, accusing Chamling and his political cronies of corruption and nepotism. Chamling's gradual consolidation of power, which some have referred to as a 'benign dictatorship' (Clement, 2014), ensured political stability, making it lucrative for outside investors. Hydropower development is one such industry that is backed by both public and private investors. While some sections of civil society vehemently opposed these projects, hydropower was promoted by Chamling as a panacea for Sikkim's unemployment problem. However, as the projects progressed it became evident that a majority of both skilled and unskilled labour was being drawn from outside the state, further alienating the young electorate. The anxieties of a youthful, educated electorate were therefore the product of a precarious political economy.

In his twenty-five-year rule, Chamling established a political empire built on a pro-poor platform, with almost no opposition. But as Huber and Joshi (2015:15) have argued, contentious hydropower development 'has served to catalyze a politicization of environmental and political decision-making, a counter-hegemonic mo(ve)ment, which exposed a long-standing democracy deficit'. Critics of hydropower development see it as an imposition of the Central government that does not benefit Sikkim's local population, due to the ecological precarity caused by drilling tunnels in earthquake- and landslide-prone landscapes. During Gergan's doctoral fieldwork, Indigenous Lepcha anti-dam activists explained how most people in their communities were opposed to hydropower development but feared political reprisals from the SDF which had a stranglehold on grassroots politics. During the 2014 state election, those who came out in support of the new opposition party Sikkim Krantikari Morcha, were accused of being troublemakers threatening Sikkim's peace and tranquillity. As Sikkim's stability was at the time closely entangled with the Chamling rule, any challenge to SDF was in turn a threat to the state and by proxy a threat to both public and private investors.

Time for *Parivartan*?

During the 2014 state-level election a major electoral issue was the steady increase in educated unemployed youth across Sikkim. The following quote from a disgruntled youth on the SKM website summarises these concerns:

> Unemployment has reached new level [sic] with over 5000 candidates filling up the exam forms for a vacancy of 20 or 30. Well-educated youth whose only mistake was coming back to their hometown to work are being employed on adhoc and contract basis putting their career and future in jeopardy. I personally have a lot of respect for our Chief Minister but if he has become too powerful to ignore what's going on beneath his nose then I am sorry sir, next year I am voting for change.

SKM promised *Parivartan*, or change, personified in Prem Singh Tamang (Golay), whose political rallies saw an incredible turnout of young people across the state. In the 2014 elections, SKM even had the support of anti-dam activists in the state, one of whom, Dawa Lepcha, ended up contesting the election from his home constituency. Though Dawa lost, for those opposed to hydropower development, SKM's open critique of dams was especially significant. As mentioned in the introduction to this chapter, the 2014 elections saw SKM winning ten of the thirty-two assembly seats. However, as soon as the dust settled, seven of the ten SKM members of the legislative assembly defected to SDF, collapsing any possibility of building a legitimate opposition in the legislative assembly. The feeling of betrayal was palpable in social media posts, but despite this setback the 2014 elections provided a sliver of hope and the possibility that the cracks in the SDF's edifice could be pried open wider in 2019.

In Sikkim, the 2019 general election was largely overshadowed by the state assembly elections. For SDF loyalists, SKM and Golay represented the 'goonda' party – i.e. a party of rowdy, corrupt goons, a narrative that Chamling repeated often in his political rallies. While Golay, much like Chamling, had several corruption charges against him, the hyper-focus on the rowdiness of SKM's supporters was a reminder to lay folks that any opposition to Chamling threatened Sikkim's stability. But by 2019, the SKM had gained considerable ground at the grassroots level. And as the rest of India either celebrated or grieved the BJP and Modi's second term, Sikkim's assembly elections took a nail-biting turn. Of the thirty-two assembly seats, SKM had won seventeen and the SDF fifteen. However, since three seats belonged to candidates who had contested and won in two constituencies, by-elections, to be held in November 2019, were required to settle the fate of those three seats. These three seats would determine the winner of the elections.

In the meantime, the debate regarding the chief minister position raged. Prem Singh Tamang (Golay) was expected to be the next chief minister, but since he had been sentenced to a year in prison on corruption charges this officially disbarred him from holding the position. In the months leading up to the crucial November by-elections, both SDF and SKM party members made several trips to New Delhi to negotiate their party's attempts to come to power. It is important to reiterate here that until 2019 Sikkim was the only Northeastern state where the BJP had been unable to win a single assembly seat despite contesting in both the 2014 and 2019 elections. Concerns were raised by SKM party members belonging to Buddhist and minority Tribal communities regarding an alliance with the BJP. The general understanding was that such an alliance would go against the interests of Sikkim's population. In August 2019, two months before the by-elections, ten of the SDF's fifteen MLAs switched over to the BJP in the capital city of Gangtok, making it the main opposition party in a state where it had not won a single seat.

This political sleight of hand marked the BJP's maiden entry into Sikkim's political landscape. The SKM would later bargain with the BJP for two of the three seats being contested in the by-elections in exchange for a clean chit for P. S. Tamang, allowing him to become eligible to hold the chief minister's position. The alliance with the BJP by both the SDF and SKM was shocking to many in the electorate, who expressed a sense of betrayal. On social media people lamented that their votes had been wasted and that whether one voted for the SDF or SKM, it was the BJP who eventually came to power. While Sikkim, like many other Northeastern states, has little investment in Indian general elections as compared to states with more parliamentary representation, the Modi-led NDA's majoritarian politics has had a profound impact on the regional political landscape.

Young people as agents of *Parivartan*

Chamling and the SDF party's vice-like grip on Sikkim's political landscape had stifled democratic participation and civil society critique. However, as some argued, this same grip had deterred even national political parties from cultivating an alternative political base. While the entry of the BJP into Sikkim has many worried, the expanding space for debate and critique within the state has been heartening, especially for the younger generation of voters. The defeat of Chamling in the assembly elections in April 2019 was significant for this generation, many of whom had known no other ruling head of state for their entire lives. Chamling was the god of Sikkim politics, above reproach, seemingly eternal and omniscient (especially with regard to those who opposed him). To topple a god with the power of the ballot opened a new horizon of political possibilities.

In Sikkim University, where one of the co-authors (Lepcha) teaches, university elections were held on 27 September 2019, a few months after the general and state assembly election results were declared. This was the third student election taking place at the university, although it is barely a decade old. However, with each passing year, a growing number of students are showing interest, enthusiasm and active participation in the university-level electoral process. In 2019's university elections, students organised themselves into three parties – United, Ideas and Progressive parties that represented the right, centre and left respectively. While the left lost, student leaders from the right and centre parties formed the student government. Sikkim University is no Delhi University or Jawaharlal Nehru University when it comes to student politics, however university spaces have the potential to be crucial sites for the formation of political identities. In the Indian context, where university politics closely mirrors national politics, with student parties effectively representing national and regional political parties, university politics enables student engagement with the ideals and values of representative democracy.

Student elections at Sikkim University were witness to a whole new generation of young people interested in politics, not only at the university but even the regional and national levels. Indra Hang Subba winning the only Lok Sabha seat propelled Sikkim University into local news. Compared to his SDF predecessor P. D. Rai, an alumnus of India's prestigious IIT and IIM schools, Subba was seen as approachable by the common people. Hailing from a small village in West Sikkim and belonging to the Limboo community of Sikkim, Subba had a fresh appeal that many believed was missing from the SDF's candidate D. B. Katwal. Subba's appeal also went beyond party lines. After voting, people could be overheard saying that while they voted for the 'party' – a euphemism for the SDF – for the legislative assembly seats, their vote for the Lok Sabha seat was reserved for the SKM's young candidate. In addition to Subba, three other students from Sikkim University contested the assembly elections from different political parties, in a somewhat unprecedented representation of university-educated students in Sikkimese politics. Analysed together, Subba's victory and Chamling's defeat represent both a generational shift and a break from politics-as-usual in Sikkim. While the discontentment with the BJP's entry and the SKM's betrayal have overshadowed local political discourse, a focus on the role of young people offers a glimpse into how hope and optimism are anchored in a political rationality eager for change.

Conclusion

In the Himalayan and Northeastern states, young people have become a focal point as they prepare for a future in which their homelands' relationship to the nation is uncertain, and where unemployment looms large. Most recently, the passage of the Citizenship Amendment Act has opened up a can of worms in borderland states. The defeat of Chamling and the end of the SDF's twenty-five-year 'rule' warrants celebration, however this shift in the regional balance of power also produced favourable conditions for the BJP's entry into Sikkim. Given recent national events, particularly the revocation of Article 370 in Jammu and Kashmir, anxieties have been mounting in Sikkim over the future of constitutional protections like Article 371F in the face of resurgent Hindu nationalism. Notably, Indra Hang Subba was the sole member of parliament from the Northeast that voted against the Citizenship Amendment Bill in the Lok Sabha.

This chapter offers a window into how elections in Sikkim are passionate affairs, much like elsewhere in India. Despite the lack of 'mainstream' media attention and the setbacks and betrayals, the 2019 general and state assembly elections were a watershed moment in Sikkim politics. Subba's victory was an inspiration for many young people and more so for Sikkim University students, one of whom even predicted that in 2024 there might be more than ten candidates from Sikkim University. In recent days, students from the university have been organising and raising their voices on diverse issues. From protests demanding a permanent campus for the university to opposing a dress code during convocation, we see the makings of a conscientious citizen, and the expansion of civil society in Sikkim. While the entry of the BJP into Sikkim is worrying, for the younger generation of voters the April 2019 state and national elections were a crucial lesson in democracy that demonstrated that even a veteran like Chamling can be defeated and a young rookie like Indra Hang can become a member of parliament.

Note

1 These eight states are Arunachal Pradesh, Assam, Manipur, Meghalaya, Mizoram, Nagaland, Tripura, and Sikkim. A 14-mile-wide land corridor in Siliguri, West Bengal connects these eight states to the rest of the country. As many prominent scholars have noted, 'Northeast' India is a flawed category; our use of the term reflects its political life and is not intended to flatten difference or naturalise this designation.

References

Chakraborty, R. (2018). 'The invisible (mountain) man: Migrant youth and relational vulnerability in the Indian Himalayas', PhD dissertation, University of Wisconsin-Madison.

Clement, T. (2014). 'India: "Benign dictatorship" constructs dams, erodes democracy', blog post in the Pulitzer Center for Crisis Reporting. Available at: http://pulitzercenter.org/reporting/asia-india-sikkim-dam-construction-Chamling-hydropower (accessed 10 November 2015).

Deka, K. (2019). 'Youth and infrastructure development in Northeast India', Heinrich Böll Stiftung, Regional Office New Delhi. Available at: https://in.boell.org/en/2019/03/19/youth-and-infrastructure-development-northeast-india (accessed 10 October 2019).

Deuchar, A. (2019). 'Strategically "out of place": Unemployed migrants mobilizing rural and urban identities in North India', *Annals of the American Association of Geographers*, 109(5): 1379–1393.

Gergan, M. D. (2014). 'Precarity and possibility: On being young and Indigenous in Sikkim, India', *HIMALAYA, the Journal of the Association for Nepal and Himalayan Studies*, 34(2): 67–80.

Huber, A. and Joshi, D. (2015). 'Hydropower, anti-politics, and the opening of new political spaces in the Eastern Himalayas', *World Development*, 76: 13–25.

Koskimaki, L. (2017). 'Youth futures and a masculine development ethos in the regional story of Uttarakhand', *Journal of South Asian Development*, 12(2): 136–154.

Suan, H. K. K. (2014). 'Assymetric federalism and the question of democratic justice in Northeast India', *India Review*, 13(2): 87–111.

Times of India (2013). 'Sikkim has maximum unemployed; Chhattisgarh lowest: Report', *Times of India*, 19 September. Available at: http://timesofindia.indiatimes.com/india/Sikkim-has-maximum-unemployed-Chhattisgarh-lowest-Report/articleshow/22767495.cms (accessed 25 November 2015).

13

What do young people want from elections?

Sneha Krishnan

Early in 2013, I sat in a college canteen in Chennai, speaking with Shankari,[1] an 18 year-old computer science student at the women's college on whose campus we were now drinking hot coffee. I had known Shankari for a few months, having met her soon after she started college the previous year. Now she was telling me about the plans she and her boyfriend of four years had been making for the future. They wanted to live in a three-bedroom house, she told me – no less would do. One room for themselves, one for the children, and another for his mother, from whom she would prefer to live apart but she had resigned herself to the idea of having to share a home with her. If they could afford four bedrooms it would be even better. That way, if her parents came to visit they would have a guest room in which to sleep. She herself had grown up in a small one-bedroom flat with her parents and two siblings. The children slept on mattresses in the living room, or bunked in with their parents. Any visiting relatives slept on the floor too, or on mats in the kitchen and hall. To live that way when she married, Shankari believed, would be a step down and she did not want that. What she wanted, she told me, was 'sophistication', by which she meant a life in which she would have choices and privacy. She laughed that she and Manohar, her boyfriend, had spent so much time sneaking around their families and finding spaces for physical intimacy on the beach, in the cinema and even in secluded corners of a nearby temple. At least when they were married, she felt, they ought to have enough space in the house to shut the door on the rest of the family and enjoy their time together as a couple.

In 2013, an election was fast approaching: a key poll for India which would be won by the BJP, propelling Narendra Modi to Prime Minister status. To those I had grown up with in the 1990s, Modi was memorable as the Chief Minister of Gujarat who had presided over a violent anti-Muslim pogrom in the state in 2002, as well as the region's rampant anti-Dalit politics. Most of the young women I interviewed – born between 1994 and 1997 – did not have any political memory of this event. One of my roommates even asked, in late 2012, as I started a conversation about the next year's election, 'Who is Modi?'

In answering the question 'what do young people want from elections', this chapter will suggest that, while broadly speaking the women I met all wanted security, better choices and the capacity to imagine prosperous futures, they did not all see the path to this in the same way. While some – like Shankari – did not speak at all of national or electoral politics as having anything to do with their own dreams, many others saw Modi and his promises of development as a way to the 'sophistication' they sought. Yet others – typically Dalit or other 'lower caste' students – expressed a strong wariness of Modi's development rhetoric, telling me instead that they wished to return to a time when public sector employment offered the best promise of a secure future.

Affect theorists like Lauren Berlant and Sara Ahmed use the concept of 'attachments' (Ahmed, 2004; Berlant, 2007) – an embodied sense of fixation upon a future object – to understand processes of social reproduction. Resonating with the centrality of passions in politics that motivates this volume, what I hope to show in this chapter is that these attachments to imaginaries of security shape young women's electoral choices. Such attachments are not individual, but shaped through structural experiences. At the same time, this scholarship shows that the things we are encouraged to aspire for within a neoliberal discourse leave us blaming ourselves for structural failings that leave us unable to achieve a sense of security.

Sophistication

'Sophistication' – in English, even when used in a Tamil sentence – was a word I heard a lot that year from the young women I interviewed.

For many, their immediate goals for the future had to do with social mobility: being in a different milieu than the ones in which they had grown up, having choices with regard to marriage and the capacity to imagine a less precarious future for the children they hoped someday to have. Sometimes they talked about 'sophistication' in terms of the capacity to access and inhabit global capitalist imaginaries – through the consumption of products like Apple iPhones, as well as through travel to Europe and North America. Indeed, sometimes the young women I lived with in Teresa Hostel while conducting fieldwork spoke about each other as an 'iPhone person' or a 'Scooty girl', referring not so much to possession of the product in question, but to the range of lifestyle characteristics associated with these products. For instance, an iPhone girl was a stylish person, who was seen to inhabit a global imaginary of youth. A Scooty girl – referring to the popular brand of motorbikes marketed to women all over South Asia (Brunson, 2013; Krishnan, 2022) – was street-smart and independent. In this, sophistication for my informants was the range of material possessions that both rendered tangible and emotionally anchored the aspirations that other scholars have written about as central to the emergence of a new middle class in India in the last two decades (Radhakrishnan, 2011; Gilbertson, 2014).

This is reminiscent of Geeta Patel's (2000: 47) formulation of postcolonial gender as 'a domesticated insinuation into gender in which a woman desires and represents both timeless tradition and modern commodities'. Sophistication entailed a 'balancing act' (Gilbertson, 2014) in which young women populated fantasies of futurity that were in keeping with traditional ideals of 'good woman-hood' – caste endogamous marriage and motherhood, with many even hoping to quit employment when they had children – with desires for globally circulated commodities. In the pursuit of this 'sophistication', ideas about development were often close to the surface of conversations on personal aspiration, and even romantic love and marriage.

Shankari, with whom I began this chapter, had pushed her boyfriend to do a degree in engineering rather than fine art – he had, by her own admission, a talent for painting and had wanted to become an artist – because she believed this would lead to a job in a multinational corporation, and ultimately the lifestyle she sought. If he became an artist, she worried that she would have to be the main breadwinner – a situation that clashed with her conviction that true social mobility would be marked by her ability to quit her job when she became a mother. For Shankari, it seemed, electoral politics mattered little except that she hoped whatever government came to power would expand employment opportunities so that her boyfriend might easily find a job. She was aware that a growing number of engineers in India do not find highly paid employment, and she herself knew of graduates of engineering colleges who worked as salesmen in small firms, making as little as they might have done if they had taken less demanding degrees.

Others, however, had firmer ideas on their electoral preferences. Ranjana, who lived in Teresa Hostel, was staunchly pro-Modi despite being a member of a minority Christian community. This was because she believed that the BJP would most reliably champion what she referred to as 'choices' and 'change' in the lives of middle-class women like herself. The Congress and its regime, Ranjana held, had been corrupt and in the hands of political dynasties for too long. She had spent part of her childhood in Dubai, a city she remembered fondly as offering the lifestyle she wanted to inhabit: with opportunities for branded consumption, and food from all over the world, as well as a rootedness in local culture. Indeed, for Ranjana, Dubai was a way of 'being abroad without really being somewhere foreign', and this she believed could be done in India. Ranjana, too, used the word 'sophistication', and to her this was only possible through a Modi government. When I brought up the BJPs track record of instigating communal disharmony, Ranjana told me that this was 'old news', which her generation, unlike mine did not care about. (I am only eight years older than her, but crucially I am old enough to remember both the demolition of the Babri Masjid in the 1990s and the 2002 anti-Muslim pogrom in Gujarat, the latter occurring during Modi's Chief Ministership.) Indeed, Ranjana was strongly of the belief that with 'development', communal differences would fall away.

A third perspective on sophistication and its link to electoral politics came from Kalaiselvi, a young woman who came from a fishing community in a village near Madurai and had won a sports scholarship to a college in Chennai. Kalai, as I came to know her, had grown up in a home with fluctuating means: her parents had had years in which the catch was good, and the business had allowed them to expand the small home in which they lived. Other years, Kalai remembered hunger and the threat that she would have to stop going to school and go to work as a domestic labourer instead. Kalai's excellence as a long jumper and the mentorship she had received from a coach in Madurai had allowed her to come to college, and now that she had a foothold in the city, and in a middle-class life, she intended to keep it. Also using the word 'sophistication' sometimes, Kalai described the future she envisioned in which she would have a government job, preferably in the railways. This is a common route for sportsmen and women in the region, and Kalai saw it as a means to stability. She saw herself marrying a man who came from a similar background – someone who had also worked hard for social mobility – and eventually owning a home somewhere in the outskirts of Chennai. What she hoped for most, she told me, was the ability to buy a pair of gold earrings for the daughter she hoped to have some day. It was something her mother had attempted to save up for many times and failed. And now Kalai saw the earrings as a sure sign that she had gained social mobility. Kalai was staunchly against the BJP in her electoral leanings, seeing the party as aligned with big business. And coming as she did from a so-called lower caste background, Kalai saw the party's Hindu nationalism as threatening to the caste quotas that had enabled her to gain the social mobility she had. Indeed, Kalai told me that she did not care for any of the national-level parties, but remained a supporter of the Dravida Munnetra Kazhagam (DMK) in Tamil Nadu which has long set itself up as a champion of caste rights.

As these three vignettes on sophistication show, 'young people' – even young women – are not a uniform voting bloc by any means, but are rooted in their own socio-economic contexts and visions of futurity and aspiration. The structural aspect of these political subjectivities is also evident: for Kalai, for instance, there is no escaping caste, whereas Ranjana, as an upper-middle-class woman, as well as a Syrian Christian – the community is largely composed of upper-caste converts to Christianity – does not see caste and communal disharmony as a matter that is pertinent to her life.

Conclusion

Young people's involvement in Indian politics has been brought into relief of late by progressive student movements that have been at the vanguard of resistance against the rise of the Hindu right. Simultaneously, as the above vignettes suggest, 'students', or 'youth' do not necessarily vote as a unified bloc. Rather, aspirations for better lives and liveable futures take diverse forms, some of which align themselves with the rise of the Hindu right, and especially its development agenda. I did not meet any young people who actively agreed with the polarising communal politics of the BJP, but many held, like Ranjana, that things were not as bad as they seemed.

In conclusion, I will reflect on another flashpoint at which the complexity of young women's political leanings was made evident: the aftermath of the widely reported rape and murder of a young female student on a New Delhi bus in December 2012. This incident sparked protests from among young women all over the country – a movement in which both the left and the right actively participated. Calling for the death penalty for the perpetrators, and advancing a protectionist discourse about 'mothers and daughters of the nation', a conservative discourse aligned with the communal politics of the BJP was widely visible in the mobilisation at this point. Simultane-ously, groups of young women – such as the feminist organising at Delhi University that would eventually become Pinjra Tod (break the cage) – critiqued this discourse of protection, asserting instead women's right to the city (Roy, 2016). At the hostel in Chennai where I was living at the time as I conducted fieldwork, these faultlines were visible, as the women I lived with argued over the meaning of asserting 'women's rights' and an anti-sexual violence politics.

In voting, therefore, it would seem that young women seek to secure for themselves futures that allow them to inhabit the many different – and often parallel-seeming – worlds that make up their present as subjects of a rapidly changing polity. The political emotions that motivate them are quite disparate, anchored as they are in often divergent rationalities that reflect the complex ideational and material worlds they inhabit.

Note

1 All personal names of my informants, as well as the names of specific institutions with which they were affiliated, are pseudonyms.

References

Ahmed, S. (2004). 'Affective economies', *Social Text*, 22(2): 117–139.

Berlant, L. (2007). 'Slow death (sovereignty, obesity, lateral agency)', *Critical Inquiry*, 33(4): 754–780.

Brunson, J. (2013). '"Scooty Girls": Mobility and intimacy at the margins of Kathmandu', *Ethnos*, 79(5): 610–629. doi: 10.1080/00141844. 2013.813056.

Gilbertson, A. (2014). 'A fine balance: Negotiating fashion and respectable femininity in middle-class Hyderabad, India', *Modern Asian Studies*, 48(1): 120–158.

Krishnan, S. (2022). 'Scooty girls are safe girls: Risk, respectability and brand assemblages in urban India', *Social & Cultural Geography*, 23(3): 424–442. doi:10.1080/14649365.2020.1744705.

Patel, G. (2000). 'Ghostly appearances: Time tales tallied up', *Social Text*, 18(3): 47–66.

Radhakrishnan, S. (2011). *Appropriately Indian: Gender and Culture in a New Transnational Class* (Durham, NC: Duke University Press).

Roy, S. (2016). 'Breaking the cage', *Dissent Magazine*, Fall. Available at: www.dissentmagazine.org/article/breaking-cage-india-feminism-sexual-violence-public-space (accessed 3 December 2020).

Part VI

The economics of India's passionate politics

14

Social oppression and exploitation of Adivasis and Dalits in contemporary India

Jens Lerche and Alpa Shah

In the 2019 general election in India, the Bharatiya Janata Party (BJP) succeeded in gaining more of the Dalit, Adivasi and Other Backward Classes (OBC) vote (Jaffrelot, 2019). While the politics of wooing voters for elections is often different to the everyday politics faced by communities, electoral politics cannot be abstracted from people's lived realities. This chapter highlights the everyday politics of social oppression and exploitation faced by Dalits and Adivasis in India.

India is a society of graded inequalities (Thorat and Madheswaran, 2018), with Adivasis and Dalits – who make up 25% of the population – at the bottom of the economic hierarchy. They continue to fare worse than all other groups on all main social and economic standard indicators.[1] Our focus is on how the historical relations of oppression of Dalits and Adivasis have been given new life and new meanings in modern India, shaping the passionate politics depicted by the various authors of this volume. Contrary to the expectations of the founders of independent India, caste as a social category and caste-based discrimination have not withered away (Shah et al., 2006). Modi's regime has exacerbated this, but the modern oppression of Dalits and Adivasis was in place well before the BJP came to power: the previous Congress Party-led governments have been part and parcel of this development.

The chapter is based on a research programme we led that investigated the reasons for the continued oppression and exploitation of Adivasis and Dalits, drawing on fieldwork living with Dalits and Adivasis in sites in Telangana, Maharashtra, Tamil Nadu, Kerala and Himachal Pradesh as well as our long-term field research in

Jharkhand and Uttar Pradesh.[2] Here, we draw on the main publication of the research programme, the book *Ground Down by Growth: Tribe, Caste, Class and Inequality in Twenty-First-Century India* (Shah et al., 2018), and reproduce some of the arguments we have presented in other forms (Lerche and Shah, 2018, 2021; Shah and Lerche, 2020, 2021).

The changing oppression and exploitation of Adivasis and Dalits

It is well known that, historically, caste as a system of ritual purity and impurity kept the Dalits firmly at the bottom of society as 'untouchables', an 'impure' and 'filthy' class of agrestic (i.e. agricultural) slaves – i.e. hereditary unfree agricultural labourers (Habib, 1963; Kumar, 1992). The Adivasis, in comparison, lived in relatively independent communities, with much more direct access to land and forest resources, and without the domination from higher caste groups faced by Dalits; but they were stereotyped as 'wild' and 'savage'.

The oppression of Dalits and Adivasis has changed over time but it continues to be pervasive. Most notably, in spite of the rapid economic growth from the mid-1990s, Adivasis and Dalits continue to be economically worse off than all other groups across India, with significantly higher levels of poverty. While the economic growth did lead to some decrease in poverty, it also entailed rapidly growing inequality which to a large extent followed broad lines of caste, tribe and ethnicity. Using the World Bank poverty line of $2 a day in 2009–10, 82% of Adivasis and Dalits were poor, compared to 45% of the high castes (Kannan, 2018: 35). One important reason for this is that regular employment in the formal sector, government service and high-end business and capital is dominated by the higher castes. But the overwhelming majority of the Indian working population – 92% – are treated as second-class labourers as they work in the small-scale informal sector or on short-term contracts for Indian and foreign-owned formal sector enterprises as informal and precarious casual labour, without job security, social security or sick pay. Dalits and Adivasis are overrepresented in this kind of work.[3] They are historically disadvantaged and they suffer from discrimination in the labour market and in access to skills (see e.g. Thorat and Newman, 2010; Deshpande, 2011; Kannan, 2018). Adivasis' exploitation is exacerbated by land grabs by government and private sector interests, often at odds with the constitutional protection of their lands (Shah, 2018). All this means that a huge pay gap is maintained. Adivasis earn less than half the income of general castes, and Dalits not much more.[4] No wonder they are poorer than all other groups.

We have argued elsewhere that the exploitation, oppression and discrimination against Dalits and Adivasis take place through three interrelated processes. The first is that inherited inequalities of power continue to enable dominant groups to control the incorporation of Adivasis and Dalits in the modern economy, keeping them at the bottom of social and economic hierarchies. In all the study areas of our research programme, access to land and assets, to education, and to networks of power differ, leaving the Dalits and Adivasis significantly worse off than all other social groups. All-India data shows this too (on access to land, assets, education source) with the exception that Adivasis in their heartland still tend to have access to plots of mainly poor lands. Even where Dalits and Adivasis have the same levels of education as castes above them in the traditional hierarchy, in the study areas as well as in all-India data (Kannan, 2018: 41) it is the latter who get the better jobs. Our research shows that top managerial jobs in the modern non-agricultural economy are the preserve of higher castes, who are close to – or come from – the groups that dominated village life. In line with all-India data, semi-skilled and skilled jobs mainly go to non-Dalit/Adivasi castes, while Dalits and Adivasis must make do with the lowest skilled segments, with the lowest social status and poorest remuneration. In many of our sites the old locally dominant groups were also actively regulating access for Dalits and Adivasis even to the low-end jobs in the modern economy.

The second, interlinked process is the exploitation of Dalits and Adivasis as circular seasonal migrant casual labour in the Indian economy. Across India, from the 1980s onwards, there has been a rise in circular seasonal labour migration, with labourers travelling to faraway states for a part of the year for work. Estimates suggest that each year up to 100 million people work as circular migrant labour (Deshingkar and Akter, 2009). Adivasis and Dalits are overwhelmingly represented among the circular migrant labour force, with both men and women migrating for work in sectors such as brick kilns, construction, agricultural labour and low-end informalised factory work.[5] They are often hired through labour contractors, with those in the most precarious conditions becoming bonded through advance loans and delayed payments (Lerche, 2007; Shah and Lerche, 2020). Across our field sites, Adivasi seasonal migrant labour from central and eastern India was employed on worse terms and conditions even than local Dalit labour.[6] Seasonal migrant labour also has no access to Fair Price Shops which provide cheap food to local people, nor to schools.[7] They have no local voting rights, and they often do not speak the local language which makes it even more difficult for them to be heard. Our research (Shah and Lerche, 2020), as well as other studies, shows that everywhere their living conditions are appalling, they are worked harder than the local workers and often paid less (Abbas, 2016; Jain and Sharma, 2019; Mander et al., 2019). They are treated as second-class citizens, if citizens at all.

The income of low-end seasonal migrant workers is not sufficient to cover the basic needs of themselves and their households throughout the year – and even less able to provide for the full life cycle of the household from childhood to old age. They are super-exploited, i.e. paid less than the cost of their own reproduction. This is only possible because their household back in the home areas provides for the reproduction of the seasonal worker, from childhood to retirement age, in what we have called an 'invisible economy of care' (Shah and Lerche, 2020). At the same time, seasonal labour migration is also driven by the conditions in the home areas. Land alienation by government and corporate development and mining projects is undermining Adivasi local forest-based and agricultural livelihoods (Shah, 2018). In other parts of India, such as East Uttar Pradesh and Bihar, economic inequality, oppressive social relations and the absence of non-agricultural work opportunities likewise leave Dalits and others with little choice but to seek seasonal work elsewhere. Most Dalit and Adivasi rural households from these parts of India are involved in seasonal migration, as are significant numbers of Muslims and OBCs (Lerche, 1999; de Haan, 2002; Roy, 2016).

Thirdly, these exploitative class relations are inextricably linked with social oppression on lines of caste, tribe, gender and region.

This produces an overall experience of what Philippe Bourgois labelled conjugated oppression: when class-based exploitation and ethnic discrimination 'interact explosively' and produce 'an overwhelming experience of oppression that is more than the sum of its parts' (Bourgois, 1988, 1989, 1995: 72).

Our research documents that while direct untouchability has declined, stereotyping and stigmatising of Adivasis and Dalits still provide the backdrop for labour discrimination. This includes everyday use of abusive language and taunts, and the stigma that Adivasis and Dalits are ignorant, lazy, dishonest, dirty and ill-educated (Shah and Lerche, 2018). The consequences can be extreme. For example, in Tamil Nadu textiles and garment factories Dalits have to hide their surnames and caste background for years, including from their non-Dalit co-workers, to get work and accommodation (Raj, 2018). Importantly, this is set in the context of both implicit and increasingly also explicit government support of such oppression. Vigilante beatings, rapes and even killings of Adivasis and Dalits, reinforcing conjugated oppression, more often than not go unpunished. Swathes of the Adivasi lands in central and eastern India are militarised, villages burnt, rape is weaponised and locals killed in so-called 'encounters', justified as part of the fight against the Naxalite–Maoist insurgency by government forces and vigilante groups (Shah, 2018). Recent Congress governments have played a major role in amplifying these policies. However, since the Modi-led BJP government came to power in 2014, things have gone from bad to worse.

On the one hand, there is the BJP's project of rewriting history to consolidate a Hindu identity (see Chapter 1), promising certainty in uncertain times (Chapter 3) and the prospects for equality and solidarity within the Hindu fold (Chapter 6). On the other hand, the oppressive social and economic conditions of the overwhelming majority of Adivasis and Dalits are cemented. Apart from the attacks on Adivasis in their home regions, there has been a marked increase in organised vigilante attacks with impunity on seasonal migrants, Muslims and Dalits across India (Jogdand et al., 2020), and 'encounter' killings of Muslims and Dalits (Dixit, 2018). Moreover, a number of intellectuals and human rights activists protesting against this oppression have been jailed for being 'antinational' and silenced, the most high-profile case today being that of the 'Bhima Koregaon

16'. The government has even sought to ban the term 'Dalit' from public media discourse (Sahu, 2018). The message to Dalits, Adivasis and activists is that no protest will be tolerated, while their oppression, on the other hand, is acceptable.

Politics for and against conjugated oppression in India and beyond

India has some of the world's most comprehensive affirmative action policies for Dalits and Adivasis. There are reserved quotas for government jobs and in higher education, and certain parliamentary seats and other elected posts are reserved for Dalits and Adivasis. There are anti-discrimination laws in place such as the Prevention of Atrocities Against Scheduled Castes and Scheduled Tribes Act 1989, as well as constitutional guarantees for Adivasi land rights in some states.[8] These policies have been fought for over generations and should not be belittled. They have benefited many individual Dalits and Adivasis, have secured spaces for their voices and serve as platforms to claim their rights. Many grassroots groups and activists undertake important work in fighting against oppression and for better conditions for Dalits and Adivasis. However, in spite of all this, Dalits and Adivasis remain economically at the bottom of society. In fact, it is hard to see how their situation can be significantly improved if the existing inherited inequalities of power are left untouched, if super-exploitation of seasonal migrant labour is encouraged, and if all of this is underpinned by government-sanctioned conjugated oppression.

India is not unique in its oppression and exploitation of minority groups. Conjugated oppression is common across the world. Inequality and discrimination along the lines of race, ethnicity and gender are well documented in many countries, including in the UK and the US (Lerche and Shah, 2021). The treatment of migrant labour as second-class citizens is all too familiar globally (see e.g. Ferguson and McNally, 2014). In fact, a number of scholars concerned with race, gender, ethnicity and migration across the world have long been arguing that there are systemic reasons for this. They argue that 'othering' parts of the labour force – oppression and exploitation along the lines of existing difference, whether based on race, ethnicity, caste, tribe or gender, etc. – is inherent to capitalism.[9] This indicates that sweeping changes to this are not easy to achieve, as they would go to the core of existing economic and social systems.

In India, no government has tried to go down this route. Still, some governments have done more than others. The affirmative action that was put in place just after Independence, under immense pressure from the Dalit leader Dr Ambedkar and his movement, is one important positive example. The Congress–Left UPA alliance of 2004–09 is another, albeit smaller, example. Its Mahatma Gandhi National Rural Employment Guarantee (MGNREGA) led to a fall in poverty amongst Dalits and Adivasis, somewhat mitigating the abysmal poverty reduction record for these groups in the earlier phases of neoliberal growth under shifting Congress and BJP governments (Kannan, 2018).

The 2014–19 BJP government has gone in the other direction and starved the MGNREGA of funds. After that followed the demonetisation and the introduction of the Goods and Services Tax in 2017, which together had a serious impact especially on low-end employment such as the cash-in-hand-based construction sector. Finally, the government has begun work on watering down existing labour laws.[10] For the first time, employment in India actually fell. Dalits and Adivasis were hit by the fall in construction work, sometimes with severe consequences (Dewan and Sehgal, 2018), but the wider impact on Dalits and Adivasis is not known.[11]

Commentators and scholars must take these developments extremely seriously. But there is also a need to put in perspective the economic hardship that no doubt was felt by at least some Dalits and Adivasis as a result of demonetisation. For most Dalits and Adivasis such hardship is nothing new. Illness, disability, bad harvests or being cheated out of wages by an employer are part of life for them.

There is little doubt that the BJP government also increased the conjugated oppression of Dalits and Adivasis. The rights of Dalits and Adivasis and activists working with them have been even more under attack under the Modi government. But it also remains that no government has seriously sought to bring an end to the oppression and exploitation of Dalits and Adivasis. In this sense, the BJP's policies are not entirely out of line with the already existing oppressive regimes that came before it, however serious their increased oppression.

Notes

1 Measured by the multidimensional poverty index (MPI) which covers deprivation in health, education and living standards, 81% of Adivasis and 66% of Dalits were poor, compared to only 33% of Others (primarily 'higher' (non-OBC) Hindu castes). Also, 55% of Adivasi and 48% of Dalit children under five suffered of malnutrition compared to 34% of Others. The literacy rates were 59% for Adivasis and 66% for Dalits, compared to an all-India average of 73% (no figures for Others available) (Daniel et al., 2017).

2 The Programme of Research on Poverty and Inequality of Dalits and Adivasis was based in the Anthropology Department at the LSE and was led by Alpa Shah (PI) and Jens Lerche. The five postdoc scholars were: Richard Axelby (whose research sites were in Himachal), Dalel Benbabaali (Telangana), Brendan Donegan (Tamil Nadu), Jayaseelan Raj (Kerala) and Vikramaditya Thakur (Maharashtra). We are grateful to the ESRC (ES/K002341/1) and the ERC (ERC-2012- RtG_20111124) for funding the research.

3 In 2017–18, working as a casual labourer was several times more common among Dalits (41%) and Adivasis (31%) than among high castes (14%) (the statistical group 'Other'). 26% of Muslims and 23% of OBCs were casual labourers (GoI, 2019: A-401–402, A-440).

4 In 2017–18, the average wage incomes of Adivasis, Dalits, Muslims and OBCs were only, respectively, 48%, 57%, 66% and 67% of the average wage income of general caste people (Kannan, 2019).

5 Government statistics suggest that Dalits and Adivasis constitute 45% of seasonal labour migrants even though they constitute only 25% of the population (Srivastava, 2020: 174). However, the statistics significantly underreport seasonal labour migration and this figure is therefore approximate.

6 See Jain and Sharma (2019) for a comparable study of Adivasi and other seasonal migrants from Rajasthan to Gujarat.

7 Recent changes that formally allow seasonal migrants to access Fair Price Shops unfortunately mean that households must choose between either the seasonal migrant or the family back in the village accessing these shops (Srinivasan, 2020).

8 Some of these affirmative actions have also been extended to other groups, including quotas for the OBCs and reserved constituencies for local government institutions for women.

9 See Shah and Lerche (2018) and Lerche and Shah (2018) for reviews.

10 During the 2020 Covid-19 pandemic, the BJP government went even further and allowed the suspension of the now reformed labour laws. This means that states like Gujarat, Rajasthan, Haryana, Punjab and Madhya Pradesh have now legalised twelve-hour working days (Madhavan, 2020)!

11 The only available statistical data, the Periodic Labour Force Survey, shows that while employment for other groups (OBCs, Muslims) fell between 2012 and 2017–18, Dalits and Adivasis did not see an overall fall in employment (Kannan and Raveendran, 2019). It is too early to know how to interpret this, and it is not *necessarily* a positive sign: the fact that employment held up amongst Dalits and Adivasis could be because people on the breadline simply have to make do with whatever work is available, irrespective of how poor conditions and pay may be, if they are to survive. Since then, things have gone from bad to worse as the government's compassionless Covid policies are estimated to have led to an additional 75 million people falling into poverty (measured as falling below a $2 a day poverty line in 2020) (Kochhar, 2021). This is unprecedented in independent India and among the worst pandemic records in the world.

References

Abbas, R. (2016). 'Internal migration and citizenship in India', *Journal of Ethnic and Migration Studies*, 42(1): 150–168. doi: 10.1080/1369183X. 2015.1100067.

Bourgois, P. (1988). 'Conjugated oppression: Class and ethnicity among Guaymi and Kuna banana workers', *American Ethnologist*, 15(2): 328–348.

Bourgois, P. (1989). *Ethnicity at Work* (Baltimore, MD: Johns Hopkins University Press).

Bourgois, P. (1995). *In Search of Respect: Selling Crack in El Barrio* (Cambridge: Cambridge University Press).

Daniel, E., Johns, H. and Nikarthil, D. (2017). *Progress Towards Inclusive Sustainable Development in India. A Study of Dalits and Adivasis in 2030 Agenda* (New Delhi: Asia Dalit Rights Forum/Swadikar). Available at: www.slideshare.net/hrfchennai/asia-dalit-forum-report (accessed 29 June 2020).

de Haan, A. (2002). 'Migration and livelihoods in historical perspective: A case study of Bihar, India', *Journal of Development Studies*, 38(5): 115–142. doi.org/10.1080/00220380412331322531.

Deshingkar, P. and Akter, S. (2009). *Migration and Human Development in India*, Human Development Research Paper 2009/13 (UNDP). Available at: https://hdr.undp.org/en/content/migration-and-human-development-india (accessed 29 June 2020).

Deshpande, A. (2011). *The Grammar of Caste: Economic Discrimination in Contemporary India* (New Delhi: Oxford University Press).

Dewan, R. and Sehgal, R. (2018). *Demonetisation: From Deprivation to Destitution* (Mumbai: Himalaya Publishing House).

Dixit, N. (2018). 'A chronicle of the crime fiction that is Adityanath's encounter raj', The Wire, 24 February. Available at: https://thewire.in/rights/chronicle-crime-fiction-adityanaths-encounter-raj (accessed 29 June 2020).

Ferguson, S. and McNally, D. (2014). 'Precarious migrants: Gender, race and the social reproduction of a global working class', *Socialist Register*, 2015: 1–23.

Government of India (GoI) (2019). *Periodic Labour Force Survey (PLFS) (June 2017–June 2018)* (NSO, Government of India). Available at: https://cse.azimpremjiuniversity.edu.in/resources/#government-reports (accessed 17 May 2022).

Habib, I. (1963). *The Agrarian System of Mughal India, 1556–1707* (London: Asia Publishing House).

Jaffrelot, C. (2019). 'Class and caste in the 2019 Indian election: Why have so many poor started voting for Modi?', *Studies in Indian Politics*, 7(2): 149–160. doi:10.1177/2321023019874890.

Jain, P. and Sharma, A. (2019). 'Super-exploitation of Adivasi migrant workers: The political economy of migration from Southern Rajasthan to Gujarat', *Journal of Interdisciplinary Economics*, 31(1): 63–99. doi.org/10.1177/0260107918776569.

Jogdand, Y., Khan, S. and Reicher, S. (2020). 'The context, content, and claims of humiliation in response to collective victimhood' in J. Vollhardt (ed.) *The Social Psychology of Collective Victimhood* (New York: Oxford University Press), 77–99.

Kannan, K. P. (2018). 'The macro picture' in Shah et al., *Ground Down by Growth: Tribe, Caste, Class and Inequality in Twenty-First-Century India* (London: Pluto Press), 32–48.

Kannan, K. P. (2019). 'Focus on wage inequality', presentation at ISLE 61st conference, Mimeo.

Kannan, K. P. and Raveendran, R. (2019). 'From jobless growth to job-loss growth: India's employment performance during 2012–18', *Economic and Political Weekly*, 54(44): 38–44.

Kochhar, R. (2021). 'In the pandemic, India's middle class shrinks and poverty spreads while China sees smaller changes', Pew Research Center. Available at: www.pewresearch.org/fact-tank/2021/03/18/in-the-pandemic-indias-middle-class-shrinks-and-poverty-spreads-while-china-sees-smaller-changes/ (accessed 29 June 2020).

Kumar, D. (1992). *Land and Caste in South India* (Delhi: Manohar).

Lerche, J. (1999). 'Politics of the poor: Agricultural labourers and political transformations in Uttar Pradesh', *Journal of Peasant Studies*, 26(2/3): 182–241.

Lerche, J. (2007). 'A global alliance against forced labour? Unfree labour, neo-liberal globalization and the International Labour Organization', *Journal of Agrarian Change*, 7(3): 425–452. doi:10.1111/j.1471–0366. 2007.00152.x.

Lerche, J. and Shah, A. (2018). 'Conjugated oppression within contemporary capitalism: Class, caste, tribe and agrarian change in India', *Journal of Peasant Studies*, 45(5–6): 927–949. doi:10.1080/03066150.2018.1463217.

Lerche, J. and Shah, A. (2021). 'Capitalism and conjugated oppression: Race, caste, tribe, gender and class in India', *Broadsheet*, 15: 13–16. Available at: www.anveshi.org.in/broadsheet-on-contemporary-politics/broadsheet-pdfs-english-and-telugu/ (accessed 29 June 2020).

Madhavan, M. R. (2020). 'Legal but not appropriate', *The Hindu*, 12 May. Available at: www.thehindu.com/opinion/op-ed/legal-but-not-appropriate/article31560223.ece (accessed 29 June 2020).

Mander, H., Roy, I., Jain, P., Raman, V., Guha Ray, R., Bhattacharya, A. and Siddiqi, U. J. (2019). 'Stolen citizenship, stolen freedoms', *Esclavages & Post-esclavages*, 1(1): 1–17. doi.org/10.4000/slaveries.602.

Raj, J. (2018). 'Tea belts of Western Ghats' in Shah et al., *Ground Down by Growth: Tribe, Caste, Class and Inequality in Twenty-First-Century India* (London: Pluto Press), 49–81.

Roy, I. (2016). 'Labour migration from (and in) Bihar. Continuities and change', IGC working paper. Available at: www.theigc.org/publication/labour-migration-from-and-in-bihar-continuities-and-change/ (accessed 17 May 2022).

Sahu, S. N. (2018). 'Telling people not to use "Dalit" contravenes both the law and the Dalit cause', The Wire, 11 September. Available at: https://thewire.in/caste/telling-people-not-to-use-dalit-contravenes-both-the-law-and-the-dalit-cause (accessed 29 June 2020).

Shah, A. (2018). *Nightmarch: Among India's Revolutionary Guerrillas* (London: Hurst).

Shah, A. and Lerche, J. (2018). 'Tribe, caste and class – new mechanisms of exploitation and oppression' in Shah et al., *Ground Down by Growth: Tribe, Caste, Class and Inequality in Twenty-First-Century India* (London: Pluto Press), 1–31.

Shah, A. and Lerche, J. (2020). 'Migration and the invisible economies of care: Production, social reproduction and seasonal migrant labour in India', *Transactions of the Institute of British Geographers*, 45(4): 719–734. doi.org/10.1111/tran.12401.

Shah, A. and Lerche, J. (2021). 'Black Lives Matter, capital and ideology: Spiralling out from India', *British Journal of Sociology*, 72(1): 93–105. doi.org/10.1111/1468-4446.12815.

Shah, A., Lerche, J., Axelby, R., Benbabaali, D., Donegan, B., Raj, J. and Thakur, V. (2018). *Ground Down by Growth: Tribe, Caste, Class and Inequality in Twenty-First-Century India* (London: Pluto Press).

Shah, G., Mander, H., Thorat, S., Deshpande, S. and Baviskar, A. (2006). *Untouchability in Rural India* (New Delhi: Sage Publications).

Srinivasan, A. (2020). 'For India's "one nation-one ration card" plan to succeed, it must overcome three key obstacles', Scroll.in, 26 January. Available at: https://scroll.in/article/950953/for-indias-one-nation-one-ration-card-plan-to-succeed-it-must-overcome-three-key-obstacles (accessed 29 June 2020).

Srivastava, R., Keshri, K., Gaur, K., Padhi, B. and Jha, A. (2020). *Internal Migration in India and the Impact of Uneven Regional Development and Demographic Transition across States: A Study for Evidence-Based Policy Recommendations. A study prepared for the United Nations Population Fund (UNFPA)* (New Delhi: Institute for Human Development). Available at: www.researchgate.net/publication/342169988_Internal_Migration_in_India_and_the_Impact_of_Uneven_Regional_Development_and_Demographic_Transition_across_States_A_Study_for_Evidence-based_Policy_Recommendations_E-Book (accessed 29 June 2020).

Thorat, S. and Madheswaran, S. (2018). 'Graded caste inequality and poverty: Evidence on role of economic discrimination', *Journal of Social Inclusion Studies*, 4(1): 3–29.

Thorat, S. and Newman, K. S. (2010). *Blocked by Caste: Economic Discrimination in Modern India* (New Delhi: Oxford University Press).

15

Two large shocks and a long-term problem: The economic performance of the Modi government, 2009–14

Kunal Sen

Prior to the Indian general election in May 2019, there was considerable interest among commentators and observers of Indian elections about whether the economic events that had occurred in the first term of the Modi government would have any discernible effect on the voting behaviour of Indian citizens. It was felt that the slowdown in the Indian economy prior to the election would make voters less likely to vote for the National Democratic Alliance (NDA) government (Al Jazeera, 2019). However, the NDA stormed to power with an electoral majority not seen in over three decades. Furthermore, its support among poorer voters actually increased (Jaffrelot, 2019; Chapter 5). It is tempting to infer that their increased support for the Bharatiya Janata Party (BJP) suggests that passion, rather than reason, guided their electoral choice. However, as clarified by Roy in the introduction to this volume and reiterated by Mahajan in Chapter 19, emotions are entwined with rationality. Emotions support rationality, providing it with salience and goals.

In this chapter, we describe two large economic shocks that occurred in the first term of the Modi government and discuss their implications for the 2019 general election. The first of these economic events was demonetization, and the second was the introduction of the Goods and Services Tax across the country. We discuss both the material effects of these shocks as well as the emotional value that they may have had for Indian voters, providing their political rationality (of supporting the BJP) with motivation. We also discuss one other salient aspect of the economic performance of the Modi government – the lack of job creation in the Indian economy – and reflect on why this did not hurt the BJP's electoral prospects.

Demonetisation[1]

In the campaign leading up to the Lok Sabha election in spring 2014, one of the more important promises that Narendra Modi made was to 'clean up' the economy by bringing back to India all the illicit money that was purportedly stashed away overseas. After coming into power, the government led by Modi's BJP made a series of attempts to recover the black money held abroad, but without great success.

Then on 8 November 2016 the Modi government made an unexpected announcement, that it was demonetising all 500 and 1,000 rupee notes. It also announced the issue of new 500 and 2,000 rupee notes in exchange for the demonetised banknotes.[2] The aim of the demonetisation policy was to deal a death blow to the black economy by reducing the use of illicit cash to fund terrorism and illegal activities. The secondary objective was to create an impetus for the formalisation of economic activity by incentivising the use of credit and debit cards in ordinary transactions instead of cash. The available evidence suggests that the primary objective of the policy has not been achieved. Most strikingly, by 2018 around 99% of the demonetised banknotes had been deposited with the banking system, suggesting that the government's premise that a large proportion of the 500 and 1,000 rupee notes in circulation were counterfeit or black money was not correct. It seems there has been more success with the secondary objective of enhancing digital payments and hence formalising economic activity, with an increase in digital payments following demonetisation – although this increase has not been sustained over time.

What were the ramifications of the demonetisation episode for the 2019 general election? Was Modi's bold policy move likely to lead to electoral dividends? To address this question, we need to distinguish between the actual economic impact of demonetisation and its emotional value.

In terms of economic impact, there is very little doubt that the Indian economy contracted significantly following demonetisation. The economy was negatively affected by two large shocks: (a) an aggregate demand shock due to the reduction in the money supply because of the withdrawal of high-value currency notes; and (b) an aggregate supply shock due to the shortage of cash in sectors such as agriculture which depend on the availability of liquid funds for the purchase of critical inputs such as fertiliser and seeds. As a consequence, economic growth slowed to a four-year low in 2018.

The negative impact of demonetisation on the livelihoods of agricultural workers as well as those working in the informal sector, which is also cash-intensive, may well have a dampening effect on intentions to vote for the Modi government. This is particularly the case when the median voter is likely to be rural and poor, given that a great many voters live in India's rural areas and belong to the working poor.

Some suggestive evidence that economic losses caused by demonetisation resulted in voters being less likely to vote for the BJP is provided by the experience of the state assembly elections held in Uttar Pradesh soon after the demonetisation episode. Here, a 100% decrease in sales at the mandi (market) closest to the constituency resulted in a 1% fall in the BJP mean vote share in that constituency. However, it is also possible that the negative economic impact of demonetisation, which was relatively short term, was of less salience to voters in the run-up to the 2019 elections, and therefore it may not have had an appreciable effect on voting behaviour in the general election.

While the economic impact of the demonetisation policy on voting behaviour was likely to be negative (and at best zero), the emotional value of demonetisation was more likely to have a positive effect on voting behaviour in favour of the BJP. This is because even though many voters were adversely impacted by the demonetisation episode, they might nonetheless consider Modi's policy initiative to be a high-risk but laudable attempt to take concrete steps towards reducing the role of the black economy in India, in a context where news of corruption among India's elites had become commonplace.

Whether demonetisation worked in rooting out corruption or not (and the evidence suggests that it did not), this may have been less relevant to voters than Modi's symbolic gesture in trying to do something about the problem. Hence the adage about the determinants of voting behaviour – 'it's the economy, stupid' – seems to be less true when it comes to demonetisation, where political symbolism and the emotional appeal of a leader committed to uprooting corruption may well have trumped economic reality at the ballot box.

The Goods and Services Tax

The Modi government's second bold policy step was to launch the Goods and Services Tax (GST) in July 2017. The new GST system replaced many different central and state taxes on the same base with a country-wide common framework and minimised its complexity by applying a common base and rates across the entire country. The system largely used four rates of taxation (5%, 12%, 18%, 28% and additionally 0.25% for precious stones and 3% for gold) along with several exemptions. The new GST system removed any taxation applied when goods cross state borders, allowing for minimum tax-based restrictions on trade. The new system also sought to improve tax compliance by applying strong data reporting requirements electronically and cross-matching of the reported data (World Bank, 2018). The aim of the GST policy was to create a unified tax system in India, as opposed to the many different sales taxes that existed in different Indian states. The initial effect on the economy of the introduction of the GST was negative. This was especially the case for India's large informal sector – which employs the vast majority of people outside of agriculture.

The initial implementation of the GST was not handled well – small businesses in particular were confused about the onerous reporting requirements, which placed a large compliance burden on them. At the same time, the GST policy could be seen as one of the most important policy initiatives since the country's landmark 1991 economic reforms, and as the noted political scientist Pratap Bhanu Mehta noted, 'The GST, if fully enacted, will not just be one of the most significant economic reforms since 1991. It will also be one of the most significant constitutional innovations since 1950. It radically rewrites the nature of Indian federalism. The enactment of a bill of this magnitude showed glimpses of what Indian democracy can be at its best' (Mehta, 2016). While the initial effect of the GST policy on the Indian economy was a negative shock, the long-term impact is likely to be strongly positive. Firstly, GST will add up to 1–1.5% of GDP to the government's revenue.[3] In addition, the introduction of a uniform tax system across India will lead to the creation of a common market, and the removal of internal taxes which act like tariffs on cross-state trade in goods and services. This is likely to lead to a strong positive effect on India's economic growth in the medium to long term.

The GST Bill, as with the demonetisation policy, was crafted by the BJP to have a positive emotional value, with the slogan 'one nation, one tax'.[4] Yet the fact that a variety of exemptions was accorded to several states suggests that this slogan was not consistent with reality. Again, it is unlikely that voters calculated the economic benefits or losses of the GST while casting their ballot. Rather, the emotional appeal of nationalist consolidation on which the policy drew may have been more salient.

The lack of job creation

Perhaps the most disappointing feature of the Modi government has been its lack of success in creating jobs for the large proportion of India's labour force who are unskilled and poor. Unemployment rose to a forty-five-year high, according to a leaked report from India's National Sample Survey Office.

The Modi government's weak record in job creation is particularly surprising, given its original intention to rejuvenate the manufacturing sector as a source of job creation, with the much-heralded Make in India programme. The roots of India's manufacturing malaise run deep, and cannot be attributed to the performance of the Modi government per se. They are more linked to India's inability to foster the kind of labour-intensive industrialisation that has taken place in China and other East Asian countries.

Why has India not been able to foster job-creating growth of the type witnessed in East Asia? There are several reasons for this. Firstly, the nature of the trade regime in India is still biased towards capital-intensive manufacturing, in spite of reforms which have reduced the protection given to the capital goods and intermediate goods sectors. Tariffs in India still remain high compared to the regional average (Athukorala, 2009). In addition, as recently as 1996–2000, the shares of intermediate inputs and consumer goods subject to non-tariff barriers were as high as 28% and 33% respectively (Das, 2003).

Secondly, stringent employment protection legislation – among the most protective of formal workers in the world – has reduced the incentive for firms, especially those in the purview of employment protection legislation, to hire workers on permanent contracts, and pushed them towards more capital-intensive modes of production than would be warranted by existing costs of labour relative to capital. Dougherty (2008) found that for large firms (those with 100 or more workers), almost all the increase in employment has been in the form of contract workers – workers employed through intermediaries, who do not benefit from employment protection legislation – while the employment of permanent workers has decreased. The employment protection legislation is only applicable to firms with 100 or more workers, so this shows that labour laws have led to firms shedding regular labour in favour of temporary labour. On the other hand, the employment of permanent workers increased for firms with fewer than 100 workers. Gupta et al. (2008) have shown that Indian states with relatively inflexible labour legislation have experienced slower growth in labour-intensive industries and slower employment growth overall. Saha et al. (2013) found that states with labour legislation that favours permanent workers have shown a higher growth of contract workers relative to regular workers.

A third reason behind the growth in joblessness, especially in formal manufacturing, has been infrastructural bottlenecks (particularly in access to electricity) and other impediments to entrepreneurial growth in small firms (such as high costs of formalisation), along with a long history of small-scale reservation policy which prohibited the entry of large-scale units into labour-intensive industries. Finally, the opening up of the economy, leading to the availability of cheap capital goods from abroad, and the increased pro-competitive forces brought about by the economic reforms have led to increased skill and capital intensity of firms, even those located in the informal sector, to ward off foreign competition (Sen, 2008; Kathuria et al., 2010; Raj and Sen, 2012).

Conclusion

The economic performance of the Modi government in 2009–14 was not stellar, yet this did not seem to have a negative impact on the electoral fortunes of the BJP in the 2019 general election. The two large negative shocks to the Indian economy – demonetisation and the introduction of GST – did not seem to have any political fallout, as widely anticipated by commentators in the run-up to the election. Emotional value seems to have trumped economic reality in these two cases, and certainly contributed to Modi's landslide win in the 2019 election. This may also explain why the government's weak performance in job creation did not seem to hurt them in the election: India's aspirational youth were willing to give the Modi government another chance to deliver on the promises of an economic renaissance that were made when the government first came to power. It remains to be seen, however, how the crisis brought about by Covid-19 will have an impact on how voters perceive the performance of the government in 2019–24.

Notes

1 This section draws from the author's earlier piece: Kunal Sen, 'India's general elections 2019: The potential electoral consequences of demonetisation', Asia Dialogue, 30 April 2019, https://theasiadialogue.com/2019/04/30/indias-general-elections-2019-the-potential-electoral-consequences-of-demonetisation/ (accessed 9 May 2022).
2 See https://en.wikipedia.org/wiki/Indian_2000-rupee_note (accessed 10 June 2022).
3 See www.imf.org/external/pubs/ft/fandd/2018/06/impact-of-indias-new-GST-tax-on-the-economy/trenches.htm (accessed 9 May 2022).
4 See https://transformingindia.mygov.in/infographics/gst-one-nation-one-tax/ (accessed 10 June 2022).

References

Al Jazeera (2019). 'India's economy slows before national election', Al Jazeera, 28 February. Available at: www.aljazeera.com/economy/2019/2/28/indias-economy-slows-before-national-election (accessed 9 May 2022).
Athukorala, P. (2009). 'Export performance in the post reform era: Has India regained the lost ground?' in R. Jha (ed.) *The Indian Economy Sixty Years After Independence* (London: Palgrave Macmillan).

Das, D. K. (2003). *Quantifying Trade Barriers: Has Protection Declined Substantially in Indian Manufacturing*, Working paper no. 105 (New Delhi: Indian Council for Research on International Economic Relations).

Dougherty, S. (2008). *Labour Regulation and Employment Dynamics at the State level in India*, OECD Economics Department Working Papers, No. 624 (Paris: OECD).

Gupta, P., Hasan, R. and Kumar, U. (2008). 'Big reforms but small payoffs: Explaining the weak record of growth and employment in Indian manufacturing', paper presented in the India Policy Forum 2008.

Jaffrelot, C. (2019). 'Class and caste in the 2019 Indian elections: Why have so many poor started voting for Modi?', *Studies in Indian Politics*, 7(2): 149–160. doi: 10.1177/2321023019874890.

Kathuria, V., Raj S. N., R. and Sen, K. (2010). 'Organised versus unorganised manufacturing performance growth in the post-reform period', *Economic and Political Weekly*, 45(24): 55–64.

Mehta, P. B. (2016). 'GST: A constitutional adventure', *Indian Express*, 6 August. Available at: https://indianexpress.com/article/opinion/columns/indian-eonomic-reforms-institutionalisation-of-the-gst-regime-a-constitutional-adventure-2956335/ (accessed 9 May 2022).

Raj S. N., R. and Sen, K. (2012). 'Did international trade destroy or create jobs in Indian manufacturing?', *European Journal of Development Research*, 24(3): 359–381.

Saha, B., Sen, K. and Maiti, D. (2013). 'Trade open-ness, labour institutions and flexibilisation: Theory and evidence from India', *Labour Economics*, 24: 180–195.

Sen, K. (2008). *Trade Policy, Inequality, and Performance in Indian Manufacturing*, Routledge Advances in South Asian Studies (London: Routledge).

Sen, K. (2019). 'India's general elections 2019: The potential electoral consequences of demonetisation', *Asia Dialogue*, 30 April. Available at: https://theasiadialogue.com/2019/04/30/indias-general-elections-2019-the-potential-electoral-consequences-of-demonetisation/ (accessed 9 May 2022).

World Bank (2018). *The Challenges of Goods and Services Tax (GST) Implementation in India* (Washington, DC: World Bank).

16

Agrarian crisis, farmers' protests and women's assertion

Nitya Rao

India has witnessed a large number of farmers' protests, escalating since June 2017, when six farmers in Madhya Pradesh's Mandsaur district were killed in police firing. This became a flashpoint for protests not just across Madhya Pradesh, but in several other states of India, with over 500,000 farmers participating (Saberin, 2018). Expressed in different forms, as rallies and marches, throwing of produce outside warehouses and onto main roads, refusal to harvest, wearing garlands made of skulls, and in the most extreme instances suicides, these protests reflect the massive agrarian distress being experienced by the farming community across the country. They symbolise in many different ways the sense of non-viability, even the death of farming as a livelihood. Despite these escalating protests, and an anticipation of rural consolidation against the National Democratic Alliance (NDA) government led by Prime Minister Narendra Modi in the 2019 parliamentary election, this did not happen. In this short chapter, I seek to explain this puzzle of why farmer dissatisfaction did not convert into an electoral loss – rather the NDA returned to power with an unprecedented mandate. If anything, the NDA *increased* its vote share in the countryside (Maiorano, 2019).

It may be tempting to infer that the increased support for the BJP was driven by passion rather than reason. However, as Roy clarifies in the introduction to this volume, emotions are entwined with rationality, providing it the necessary push: a point reiterated by Mahajan in Chapter 19. In this chapter, I suggest that the BJP's re-election in 2019 was spurred on by hope ignited by the Prime Minister's statements on easing rural distress as well as social provisioning in the countryside that specifically addressed rural women's work burdens.

The agrarian crisis and farmers' demands

Returning to the spate of farmers' protests, one needs to recognise that 82% of Indian farms are small and marginal (FAO, n.d.). In fact, the average land-holding size has been steadily declining from 2.2 hectares in 1950 to 1.33 in 2000 (GoI, 2008), and 0.592 in 2013 (NSSO, 2013). Yet over 50% of rural households still depend primarily on agriculture for their livelihood, with the UN Food and Agriculture Organization (FAO) reporting a figure of 70% (FAO, n.d.).

For a majority of these farmers, the major crop is still dependent on the monsoon rains, and hence subject to its vagaries. In the context of climate variability and change in precipitation, temperatures and the occurrence of extreme events, yields and outputs remain uncertain, as while seeds may not germinate due to the lack of rains, the standing crop can equally be destroyed by storms prior to harvest. Alongside this uncertainty of losing their crop in the event of a drought or flood, farmers are also confronted by unpredictable markets. Even when they have a bumper harvest, the absence of assured procurement at minimum support prices, which can at the very least cover their costs of cultivation, implies the possibility of losses due to price crashes. In fact, protests mounted in 2017 following a good potato harvest in Uttar Pradesh and pulses harvest in Madhya Pradesh. Markets were flooded with the harvested crops and prices nosedived. The state did not step in to procure the produce at the announced support prices. With prevalent prices not even covering the costs already incurred on inputs, many farmers decided not to spend any additional money on harvesting the crop or transporting it to market.

As protests simmered across the country, in July 2018, at the start of the planting season, the government approved an increase in the minimum support prices for twenty-three crops, fourteen of them being kharif (monsoon) crops (Damodaran, 2018). Yet, once again, in the absence of procurement at these prices, the crisis deepened and protests mounted, culminating in two massive rallies in the month of November, first in the city of Mumbai, the capital of Maharashtra and the financial capital of India, and then in Delhi, India's national capital (BBC News, 2018). The protesting farmers had three major demands – procurement of their crops at the minimum support price, compensation for losses due to enduring drought and a waiver of loans taken for the purchase of inputs. These protests received considerable media attention, and were supported by farmers' organisations, activists and opposition political parties. As the farmers occupied the streets of Mumbai, residents of the mega-metropolis came out in their support, bringing them food and water. Middle-class solidarity with farmers was a new development on the Indian political stage and contributed to legitimising the issue of farmer distress on the national agenda. It drew the nation's attention to the livelihood crisis confronting almost half the Indian population, if not more.

The farmers' demands have an economic basis, but equally raise issues of equity and justice. While agriculture has always had good years and bad years, through till the 1970s and even 1980s, the growth rate was close to 10%. This was in line with the investments in agricultural research and extension, alongside the expansion in irrigation infrastructure. Post-1991, there has been a stagnation in agricultural investment in the public sector, and with this, a decline in agricultural growth rates, though they still hover at 4–6%. Since 2014, there has been a sharp decline in agricultural growth, with the sector performing very poorly since 2014–15, with either negative or less than 2% growth (Pincode India, 2018). The contribution of agriculture to national GDP was between 17% and 18% in 2018, pointing to the relatively low incomes of farmers, which as per official statistics were less than INR 20,000 per annum (US$298) in 2016 (Chand, 2017). While the figures may not be precise, the response of the farmers clearly reflects a slowing down of agricultural growth in the last five years leading to a crisis of survival, given that agriculture is still a major contributor to rural livelihoods.

Agrarian distress is not new, and has been building up over the past two decades. The push to voice their distress, however, has been a direct response to the promise by Prime Minister Narendra Modi in his 2014 election campaign and party manifesto to implement the recommendations of the National Commission on Farmers (2004–06). While some nominal measures were taken, key recommendations relating to procurement, pricing and distribution, alongside climate-proofing (including micro-irrigation and drought compensation), critical to sustaining farming livelihoods, have not been implemented.

The National Commission on Farmers

Given its centrality to the farmer protests, it is worth briefly recounting what the National Commission on Farmers was, its mandate and recommendations. The commission, chaired by renowned agricultural scientist M. S. Swaminathan, hence often popularly called the Swaminathan Commission, was appointed in 2004 by the NDA government led by Prime Minister Vajpayee. The first such commission to be appointed post-Independence, its mandate was to examine the strengths of and problems confronting Indian agriculture and make recommendations for its future – importantly, the wellbeing of farm families and the security of their livelihoods. Over a period of three years, based on visits to and discussions with farmers across the country, the commission submitted five reports to the Government of India, then led by the United Progressive Alliance (UPA). Giving voice to farmers' issues and representations, these reports contained a series of practical recommendations to support farming and farmers.

Three pillars were central to these recommendations. First was the need for a degree of market security to stimulate surplus production, through the announcement of a minimum support price, to be calculated using a formula of total cost (includes input costs, imputed costs for family labour and cost of land rentals) plus 50%, for all major cultivated crops. Second, emphasis was placed on guaranteed procurement by the state at this minimum support price. Third, alongside price and procurement, was public distribution to ensure food security, given that most farmers in India are poor, small and marginal farmers, who are not just producers, but also net consumers of food.

Additionally, the commission sought to improve productivity and incomes in farming through creating an enabling environment for research, innovation and extension, with a focus on water security, soil health and access to credit, insurance, technology and other essential services (Swaminathan, 2016). This vision, combining the economic viability of farming with opportunities for creating non-farm employment and meeting youth aspirations, is reflected in the draft of the National Policy for Farmers (adopted in 2007), presented as part of the commission's final report.

Unfortunately, none of these guarantees, in terms of prices or procurement, have been implemented fully by either the UPA or NDA governments. While the adoption of the total cost + 50% formula has been debated extensively, there has been little procurement at these announced prices (Gulati et al., 2018; Kaur, 2018). Farmers have been left to the vagaries of the market, whether they have a good or bad crop. Neither has there been investment in agricultural research and extension, credit or other support services, to reverse the stagnation in agriculture. Drought and climatic variability have only made the situation worse. The saving grace has been the near-universal public distribution of basic food, resulting from the legal enactment of the right to food through the National Food Security Act (NFSA) in 2013 (GoI, 2013).

Elections, hope and protest

The decade 2006–16 was one of hope for farmers: a hope that their voices would be heard, and their livelihoods supported and secured. The passage of the NFSA in 2013 strengthened this hope, as did the promise by Prime Minister Modi to implement the recommendations of the National Commission on Farmers, if he was voted into power in 2014. He promised to change the condition of farmers which the earlier UPA government had failed to do. This included a doubling of farmers' incomes in the subsequent five-year period (Chand, 2017). Yet little changed, leading to growing frustration and protest.

The Prime Minister's explicit espousal of the farmers' cause and promise to implement the National Commission on Farmers' recommendations, giving them wide publicity, then frames the current round of protests by farmers across the country. Activists, civil society groups and farmers' organisations found the commission report to be a concrete tool for the mobilisation of farmers to both demand accountability from the state and advocate for improved regulation and governance in the farm sector. This is especially true as the report suggests a range of practical measures for improving both farm productivity and farmer wellbeing. Given the growing disparity in incomes and lifestyles of the urban and rural, rich and poor, across the country, farmers now view the implementation of the 'Swaminathan report' as the only way to survive and move ahead.

Feminisation and women's assertion

With low growth rates and returns from agriculture, rural households have, since the 1980s, been diversifying their sources of income (Rao, 2017). Given the gender wage differentials in labour markets, alongside patriarchal social norms that constrain women's mobility, rural men have increasingly been migrating out in efforts to supplement household incomes. Opportunities for gainful employment at destination towns or villages, whether brick kilns, construction sites or other forms of non-formal and informal employment, are however unpredictable, effort-intensive and often risky. Even if they are able to earn incomes, they often return home in poor health, and a good part of their savings is then directed to health expenditure. Livelihoods therefore can only be secured by production on household farms, small plots, now largely managed by women (Rao and Mitra, 2013).

While women's contribution to agriculture is well accepted in the public domain, and at least from the Sixth Plan (1980) onwards in official discourse, they still have few entitlements as farmers. The National Policy for Farmers (GoI, 2007) broadened the definition of farmers to include anyone engaged primarily in farming or allied activities, thus bringing most rural women into the ambit of 'farmers'. Given the social meaning of land inheritance in India, which largely denies women rights to land, the policy suggested that local governments (panchayats) could certify women as farmers, to enable them to access bank credit, other inputs, technologies and services, including access to farmer cooperatives, needed for the farming enterprise. This was, however, not implemented. In 2011, M. S. Swaminathan, then a member of the Rajya Sabha (upper house of Parliament), introduced a 'Women farmer's entitlement bill' in Parliament, as a private member's bill, to enshrine in law women's claims for recognition as farmers with equal entitlements. Unfortunately, the draft bill was not accepted for discussion and lapsed at the end of the parliamentary term in 2014.

The recent protests have seen the participation of large numbers of women, providing visibility to women as farmers on the ground. Given that land titles remain in men's names, the Indian farmer continues to be imagined as male by most public institutions. Alongside demands for the implementation of the report of the National Commission on Farmers, a secondary agenda has now emerged, voiced mainly by women farmers participating in these protests. This relates to the recognition of women as farmers, making significant contributions to both the production economy and household survival. The women protesters are demanding policies to address their needs, provide them with support and guarantee their entitlements, as farmers, not just as home-makers or 'unpaid household helpers'. This is an interesting development, as women's claims and gendered interests often tend to get sidelined in class-based or identity-based social movements.

To compensate farmers and demonstrate willingness to address their concerns, in the lead-up to the forthcoming elections, loan waivers were announced across several Indian states. Additionally, following the large rallies in November 2018, the central government announced its intention to work towards doubling farmers' incomes. To this end, a cash transfer scheme named PM-Kisan was launched. INR 6,000 was to be transferred to all small and marginal farming households for purchasing inputs or services in the current year. The first instalment of INR 2,000 was transferred prior to the parliamentary elections held in April–May 2019. While not targeting women farmers, this act nevertheless appears to have given farm households renewed hope that promises might still be fulfilled. Rather than translating into rural consolidation against the government, as some observers predicted, these steps contributed to ensuring the resounding victory of Prime Minister Modi in the elections.

Some concluding thoughts: the absence of rural consolidation

Of course, elections are not just about material needs and interests, and the 2019 elections were foregrounded with issues of national security arising from border conflicts between India and Pakistan.

There was a call to vote for nationalism and to protect national interests, and given the splintered character of the opposition, the only source of stability and the strength required to implement policies that would ameliorate rural distress appeared to be the NDA led by Prime Minister Modi. Voting behaviour thus represents more than immediate needs; while farmers are fully aware of their situation, and farmers' movements remain vibrant across different parts of the country, clearly in the election farmers voted not as farmers, but as citizens of a nation potentially under threat. The emotive appeals of nationalism were thus entwined with a political reasoning that gauged the BJP to be best placed to implement reforms that would improve farmers' economic conditions.

A further reason for the absence of consolidation of their voice as farmers is the diversity within the farming profession itself – from upper-caste absentee landowners to middle caste smallholders and sharecroppers, and lower caste agricultural labour households, differentiated also by religion and location. While the climate and markets affect them all, their ability to respond is shaped by the particular relations of production in which they are embedded. Distinctions between different social classes in the countryside are far more concrete and real than imagined dichotomies between rural and urban, making rural consolidation extremely difficult to achieve in practice.

A closing word on women's assertion. While women still remain marginalised as farmers, and statistics point to a decline in women's participation in the productive domain, they perceive several programmes initiated by Prime Minister Modi, addressing the domestic domain, as having contributed to an improvement in their everyday lives – whether it be the construction of toilets under the Swachh Bharat Abhiyan, provision of LPG cylinders under the Ujjwala Scheme or indeed the education of girls under Beti Bachao, Beti Padhao. While there may be problems with implementation, the discourse around improving women's lives is definitely widespread. And with rural women's time increasingly under pressure, from both production and reproduction, these provisions do appear to ease at least some of the burden (Rao and Raju, 2019).

Prime Minister Modi's victory was then a resounding vote for hope. The cash transfers to farmers played a part, as did the discourse on improving women's everyday lives. It remains to be seen how issues of price, production and investment, especially by the public sector, will now be addressed.

References

BBC News (2018). 'India farmers: Tens of thousands march against agrarian crisis', BBC News, 30 November. Available at: www.bbc.co.uk/news/world-asia-india-46396118 (accessed 15 October 2019).

Chand, R. (2017). *Doubling Farmers' Income: Rationale, Strategy, Prospects, and Action Plan*, NITI policy paper no. 1/2017 (New Delhi: NITI Aayog, Government of India).

Damodaran, H. (2018). 'How the 1.5-times formula works out MSP', *Indian Express*, 6 July. Available at: https://indianexpress.com/article/explained/how-the-1-5-times-formula-works-out-msp-5247688/ (accessed 19 May 2022).

Food and Agriculture Organization of the United Nations (FAO) (n.d.). *FAO in India: India at a Glance*. Available at: www.fao.org/india/fao-in-india/india-at-a-glance/en/ (accessed 15 October 2019).

Government of India (GoI) (2007). *National Policy for Farmers* (New Delhi: Ministry of Agriculture). Available at: http://agricoop.nic.in/sites/default/files/npff2007%20%281%29.pdf (accessed 15 October 2019).

Government of India (GoI) (2008). *Agricultural Statistics at a Glance* (New Delhi: Ministry of Agriculture).

Government of India (GoI) (2013). *National Food Security Act (NFSA)* (New Delhi: Department of Food and Public Distribution). Available at: https://dfpd.gov.in/nfsa-act.htm (accessed 28 September 2019).

Gulati, A., Chatterjee, T. and Hussain, S. (2018). *Supporting Indian Farmers: Price Support or Direct Income/Investment Support?*, working paper no. 357 (New Delhi: Indian Council for Research on International Economic Relations).

Kaur, B. (2018). 'New MSP: Govt fails to meet Swaminathan standards, yet again', Down to Earth, 4 July. Available at: www.downtoearth.org.in/news/agriculture/new-msp-govt-fails-to-meet-swaminathan-standards-yet-again-61031 (accessed 28 September 2019).

Maiorano, D. (2019). 'The 2019 Indian elections and the haprassy on of the BJP', *Studies in Indian Politics*, 7(2): 176–190.

National Sample Survey Office (NSSO) 2013. *Household Ownership and Operational Holdings in India: NSS 70th Round* (New Delhi: Ministry of Statistics and Program Implementation, Government of India).

Pincode India (2018). *Agriculture Growth Rate in India*. Available at: www.pincodeindia.net/agriculture-growth-rate.php (accessed 25 September 2019).

Rao, N. (2017). 'Assets, agency and legitimacy: Towards a relational understanding of gender equality policy and practice', *World Development*, 95: 43–54.

Rao, N. and Mitra, A. (2013). 'Migration, representations and social relations: Experiences of Jharkhand labour to western Uttar Pradesh', *Journal of Development Studies*, 49(6): 846–860.

Rao, N. and Raju, S. (2019). 'Gendered time, seasonality and nutrition: Insights from two Indian districts', *Feminist Economics*, 26(2): 95–125.

Saberin, Z. (2018). 'Why are Indian farmers protesting?', Al Jazeera News, 5 June. Available at: www.aljazeera.com/news/2018/06/indian-farmers-protesting-180604194005599.html (accessed 28 September 2019).

Swaminathan, M. S. (2016). 'National Policy for Farmers: Ten years later', *Review of Agrarian Studies*, 6(1): 133–144.

Part VII

India tomorrow

17

The Modi government's authoritarian project in India

James Manor

Since taking power in 2014, India's prime minister, Narendra Modi, has made significant headway in turning a robust, socially rooted democracy into an authoritarian system. He has acquired substantial autonomy, radically centralised power, and used it to mount an aggressive, systematic assault on open politics. In pursuit of top-down control by the Prime Minister's Office, he has greatly weakened other state institutions and mounted an offensive on alternative power centres beyond the state – rival parties, civil society organisations, the media and independent voices. He has developed a personality cult, and promoted Hindu chauvinism, the demonisation and marginalisation of India's large Muslim minority, jingoistic nationalism and majoritarian intolerance. The contributors to this volume have usefully directed our attention to the confluence of these passions. In this chapter I want to emphasise the consequent authoritarian logics.

The result is not merely a more illiberal government, but an authoritarian effort to suffocate this great democracy. The Modi government is constricting the space for open politics so severely that it may become impossible for opposition parties to make significant gains in future national elections. He and other leaders of his Bharatiya Janata Party (BJP) of course reaffirm their commitment to democracy, a key part of their master narrative. But a forceful, carefully crafted campaign against openness is a patent reality. It has been pursued on multiple fronts. Here are several examples. (There are others.)

Rival political parties are treated with utter contempt. Modi's immensely powerful right-hand man, Amit Shah, refers to them in subhuman terms as cats, dogs, snakes and rats (ET Now, 2018). The stated aim is to bring into being an 'opposition-*mukht* (free)' India.[1]

The government's numerous investigative agencies are being blatantly misused to intimidate and undermine rival parties, civil society organisations and independent voices. One editor wrote, 'There is no doubt that the Narendra Modi government has been misusing various probe agencies ... especially through the fears of raids and arrests, for advancement of its political agenda' (Chhibber, 2019). Another report stated that 'All' of those agencies 'have been going around conducting investigations against opposition leaders, their associates and donors. ... With the naked use of anti-corruption agencies as political vendetta' (Vij, 2018).

The Modi government has also mounted an assault on the media. Proprietors of newspapers, television channels and other media outlets have been intimidated by the use of both sticks (raids and arrests by investigative agencies, plus other punitive actions that damage their businesses) and carrots (sympathetic treatment for their other corporate undertakings). As a consequence, India's once vibrant media has largely become 'an undisguised, unthinking, unquestioning mouthpiece of the reigning ideology ... conditioning minds, building myths, deflecting attention, normalising the abnormal'.[2] Two large teams – one within the BJP and a second within a ministry – monitor the views expressed in the media, especially coverage of the Prime Minister. Editors are told to reissue selected positive reports on Modi, to promote his personality cult. They are also warned when critical reports appear (Inamdar, 2019). Several proprietors have yielded to pressure by sacking editors and reporters, and pulling stories that were critical of the government. A few remain stubbornly independent, but they have lost lucrative government advertising, and/or faced defamation suits seeking crippling damages, and/or been raided by investigators on flimsy charges. One television channel even had its telecasts jammed.

These methods have enabled the BJP to achieve a vast edge over rival parties in fund raising, mainly from corporate donors. Between 2016 and 2018, it received 93% of publicly reported donations to parties. And 95% of another US$846.3 million, anonymously invested in electoral bonds, went to the BJP.[3] At the 2019 national election, the victorious BJP had eighteen times more money to spend than all other parties put together.

'Sedition' charges have been widely used against political opponents, independent commentators and non-partisan civic associations. The brazen nature of this tactic is apparent from the fact that the organisations facing sedition charges include two Nobel Peace Prize winners: Médecins Sans Frontieres, which the Intelligence Bureau has placed on what one report called its 'hitlist' (Baruah and Ahuja, 2015), and Amnesty International, whose bank accounts have been frozen. Between 2014 and 2016, 179 people and organisations were indicted for sedition on mostly flimsy grounds. Since only two convictions were achieved (Mathur, 2019), this was evidently mainly a device for harassment and intimidation. But in 2019, the then home minister indicated that the sedition law would be given more teeth to induce greater fear, 'so that even the soul of the anti-nationals would shiver'.[4]

After Modi first took power in 2014, one senior BJP member of parliament who had not been offered a cabinet post was asked if he was disappointed.[5] He laughed and said no, he had no wish to be a *chaprassi* (menial servant). He knew that as Chief Minister of Gujarat state, Modi had run a one-man government in which other ministers were ciphers, and he expected him to do the same in New Delhi. He was right. Cabinet government is a fiction. The Prime Minster is utterly dominant. Ministers learn what their policies are from their civil servants, who receive instructions from the Prime Minister's Office. No senior leader in the party can check Modi.

Nor can Parliament, which has also been undermined. During his first term (2014–19), only 26% of bills were scrutinised by parliamentary committees – far less than the 60% and 71% in the previous two parliaments. After his re-election in May 2019, this trend intensified. Only one of the first eighteen new acts passed by late July, and none of the seven further bills enacted by 7 August, were scrutinised. An opposition leader asked, 'Are we delivering pizzas or passing legislation?', and called it 'a mockery of Parliament … smothering the Opposition'.[6]

New laws constrict the space for open, democratic processes. One has crippled India's admirable Right to Information Act. A second seizes top-down control of the National Human Rights

Commission. A third draconian Act empowers the government to designate any individual a terrorist without evidence or due process (Varadarajan, 2019b). It has been aggressively applied.

The autonomy of India's Election Commission, which until recently was scrupulously neutral, has also been weakened. But during the 2019 parliamentary election campaign, it refused to intervene as Modi associated the heroism of the armed forces with himself, as hyper-nationalism was stoked, as opposition criticisms of his actions were said to show disloyalty to the nation, etc. – all of which flouted the commission's code of conduct. When one commission member dissented, it refused to reveal his written arguments. In response, he stopped attending commission meetings. Since then, investigative agencies have made frantic, flagrant efforts to uncover misdeeds committed by the dissenter, his wife (who faced several rounds of questioning and baseless threats of prosecution), his son and his sister (a paediatrician). No compromising evidence has been found.[7]

After considering the enormities noted above and other outrages – the epidemic of beatings and murders of Muslims by 'cow protection' vigilantes, criminal charges under draconian new laws against Muslims for supposedly perpetrating the February 2020 Delhi riots in which they were the main victims, the incarceration under draconian laws of peaceful protesters who demonstrated with copies of India's constitution in their hands against an illiberal new citizenship act – one immensely eminent social scientist sees India becoming a 'pretend democracy, sadly but steadily creeping from democracy to some form of thugocracy' (Bardhan, 2020).

India's politics can no longer be adequately analysed by using concepts derived from studies of democracy. To understand the new India that is emerging, we must instead draw insights from the literature on 'competitive authoritarianism'.[8] It assesses systems in which power holders do not abolish all formal democratic rules, but manipulate them in abusive ways. Elections may not be entirely free and fair. Governments curtail 'political rights and civil liberties, including the freedom of the press, freedom of association, and freedom to criticize the government without reprisal'. They 'deny the opposition adequate media coverage … Journalists, opposition politicians and other government critics may be spied upon, threatened, harassed, or arrested' (Levitsky and Way, 2002: 52–53).

What impediments remain which might check or thwart Modi's authoritarian project?

Modi has carefully avoided major economic reforms that might have reduced the state's leverage over one potential obstacle: powerful corporate interests. When he took power in 2014, many observers expected him to trigger a new surge of economic liberalisation that would empower market forces and bring fundamental changes to the balance of power between the state and capitalism in India. Despite his claims – echoed by fawning pro-government media outlets – to have implemented audacious economic reforms, and despite some modest changes,[9] this has not happened. Market-friendly advisors have quietly departed in dismay over Modi's failure to adopt bold new policies, and a few stubbornly objective liberalisers have made their disappointment plain.[10]

Dramatic reforms have not occurred because Modi has consciously avoided them – for political reasons. If he had fulfilled expectations by liberalising, he would have reduced the powers that his government needs to exercise control – and top-down control is his principal aim/concern. Punitive actions against major corporations – demands for fees and taxes, denials of preferment, etc. – and the threat, and indeed the use, of raids and probes by investigative agencies have ensured that 'Indian corporate icons are terrified of the Modi government'.[11] We often hear it said that a neoliberal order now prevails in India. That is patently inaccurate. The state has retained too many formidable powers for that to be true.[12]

Modi has not yet achieved dominance over two key institutions, the Election Commission and the higher courts. We have noted that investigative agencies have made frantic but so far fruitless efforts to discredit the one objective dissenter on the three-member Election Commission. If he cannot be dislodged, seniority rules dictate that he will become the powerful *Chief* Commissioner in 2021. That could make the commission a major obstacle to the drive for autocratic dominance.

The Modi government has sought – so far without success, as a result of resistance by judges – to change the rules for the selection of Supreme Court justices. So it has resorted to enticements to persuade justices whose rulings are 'law declared' – that is, they have the same force as legislation – to avoid obstructive decisions.

The most recently retired chief justice was provided with a seat in India's upper house – as a signal to others of the rewards that might await them. Some recent Supreme Court rulings have gone the government's way, but several have not. The government has on several occasions defied decisions by the Supreme Court,[13] but that tactic is a poor substitute for full control – over which a struggle will continue, with uncertain outcomes that could undermine the drive towards authoritarian dominance.

Some eminent analysts argue that Hindu chauvinism and the majoritarian attitudes which Modi has promoted may have taken enough root in the popular mind to sustain that drive.[14] But for that to be true, Indians must have abandoned their strong proclivity – evident over many decades – to shift their preoccupations from one of the many political identities available to them to another and then another, often and with great fluidity.[15] The BJP's failure to achieve victory at an embarrassing string of state elections in this federal system since late 2018 suggests that Hindu voters may not have fixed as tenaciously on their religious identity as Modi would wish. Indeed, Indians have demonstrated a passionate attachment to alternative identities and embedded these in regional, caste and linguistic rationalities.

Indian voters have long tended strongly to punish politicians who make serious mistakes, and Modi has made plenty of them.[16] The possibility that they may have a cumulative and damaging impact on his popularity brings us to one last – and formidable – potential obstacle for Modi: India's impatient, sophisticated voters. They are not mere lemmings. Ruling parties have been thrown out at eight of the last twelve national elections, and at roughly 70% of state elections in this federal system since 1980. The Prime Minister is still basking in his successful re-election at the 2019 national election, when his high personal approval ratings were crucial. But, as noted above, his party has fallen short of victory at a long succession of state elections since late 2018, when rival parties reminded voters that Modi would not personally head the state governments that they are electing. This suggests that while his popularity is a major plus at national elections, it may be his party's *only* significant asset.

Voters' patience with him could wear thin if mistakes mount up. And the Hindu majority's identification with their religious identities could wane as the customary fluidity reasserts itself. The struggle to frustrate Modi's authoritarian project, and to avoid the suffocation of Indian democracy, is not over.

Notes

1 The BJP national executive discussed this objective on 15 April 2017 (Mohan, 2017).
2 Krishna Prasad, former editor-in-chief of *Outlook* (Prasad, 2019).
3 Mishra (2019); and Varadarajan (2019a). They used a report by the Association for Democratic Reforms (2018).
4 IANS (2019). The bill to change the UAPA (Unlawful Activities (Prevention) Act) making it possible to designate individuals as 'terrorists' is in a similar vein. See Varadarajan (2019b).
5 Private conversation, New Delhi, 2 June 2014.
6 PTI (2019a). See also Mahaprashasta (2019) and PTI (2019b).
7 For more detail, see Manor (2019).
8 Important sources for this approach include: Levitsky and Way (2002: 51–65); Schedler (2006); Levitsky and Way (2010, 2020).
9 See, for example, Krishnamurthy (2020).
10 For the most telling indication of this, see the commentaries in the financial newspaper *Business Standard* between 2014 and 2016, by which time they had given up hoping. See also the sharp critique by a distinguished advocate of economic liberalisation and former BJP minister, Arun Shourie (2015). A systematic analysis can be found in Echeverri-Gent et al. (2021).
11 See, for example, Anandan (2019). See also this Bloomberg report (Rs 92,000 is US$13 billion): Ragini Saxena, "Modi govt refuses to waive Rs 92,000 crore dues of Airtel, Vodaphone Idea", *The Print*, 5 November 2019 (Saxena, 2019).
12 For a detailed explanation of India's far from neoliberal order, see an analysis of how senior politicians at the state level in this federal system use the powers that they retain to dominate politics and public affairs (Manor, 2016).
13 For example, on several occasions, when the Supreme Court has ruled that citizens' use of *Aadhaar* (a universal ID system) to obtain crucial services and benefits from government must be voluntary, Modi's government has continued to insist that this must be mandatory. For details, see Manor (2020).
14 This case has been made by the immensely distinguished Suhas Palshikar in: 'The BJP and Hindu nationalism: Centrist politics and majoritarian

impulses' (Palshikar, 2015); and 'The political culture of "New India": Some contradictions' (Palshikar, 2019).

15 For details, see Manor (1996).

16 See the analyses elsewhere in this collection by Nitya Rao (Chapter 16), Kunal Sen (Chapter 15) and Jens Lerche (Chapter 14).

References

Anandan, S. (2019). 'Fees of doing business: Why Indian corporate icons are terrified of the Modi government', *The Caravan*, 1 October. Available at: https://caravanmagazine.in/commentary/why-indian-corporate-icons-terrified-modi-government (accessed 9 July 2022).

Association for Democratic Reforms (2018). 'Analysis of donations from corporates & business houses to national parties for FY 2017–17 & 2017–18', Association for Democratic Reforms. Available at: https://adrindia.org/content/analysis-donations-corporates-business-houses-national-parties-fy-2016-17-2017-18-0 (accessed 9 July 2022).

Bardhan, P. (2020). 'India is steadily creeping from democracy to some form of thugocracy', *Indian Express*, 18 January. Available at: https://indianexpress.com/article/opinion/columns/pretend-democracy-minority-groups-india-muslim-caa-6222141/ (accessed 9 July 2022).

Baruah, S. Kr and Ahuja, R. (2015). 'Narendra Modi govt cracks down on NGOs, prepares hitlist', *Hindustan Times*, 24 January. Available at: www.hindustantimes.com/india/narendra-modi-govt-cracks-down-on-ngos-prepares-hitlist/story-Q9lGg6i2YimcSehgA7W4lN.html (accessed 9 July 2022).

Chhibber, M. (2019). 'Is Modi govt using CBI, ED for political battles, or is it opposition propaganda?', The Print, 5 February. Available at: https://theprint.in/talk-point/is-modi-govt-using-cbi-ed-for-political-battles-or-is-it-opposition-propaganda/188204/ (accessed 9 July 2022).

Echeverri-Gent, J., Sinha, A. and Wyatt, A. (2021) 'Economic distress amidst political success: India's economic policy under Modi, 2014–2019', *India Review*, 20(4): 402–35.

ET Now (2018). 'Modi wave uniting "cats, dogs, snakes and rats": Amit Shah targets anti-BJP front', podcast, *Economic Times*, 6 April. Available at: https://economictimes.indiatimes.com/news/politics-and-nation/modi-wave-uniting-cats-dogs-snakes-and-rats-amit-shah-targets-anti-bjp-front/videoshow/63645818.cms?from=mdr (accessed 9 July 2022).

IANS (2019). 'Sedition law will be made more stringent: Rajnath Singh', *Economic Times*, 16 May. Available at: https://economictimes.indiatimes.com/news/elections/lok-sabha/india/will-review-sedition-law-make-it-more-stringent-after-coming-to-power-rajnath-singh/articleshow/69134816. cms?from=mdr (accessed 9 July 2022).

Inamdar, N. (2019). 'How Narendra Modi has almost killed the Indian media', Quartz India, 12 March. Available at: https://qz.com/india/1570899/how-narendra-modi-has-almost-killed-indian-media/ (accessed 9 July 2022).

Krishnamurthy, M. (2020). 'Agriculture reforms: Are the recent reforms likely to double farmers' incomes?', podcast, Centre for Policy Research, 19 June. Available at: https://cprindia.org/agriculture-reforms-are-the-recent-reforms-likely-to/ (accessed 9 July 2022).

Levitsky, S. and Way, L. (2002). 'The rise of competitive authoritarianism', *Journal of Democracy*, 13(2): 51–65.

Levitsky, S. and Way, L. (2010). *Competitive Authoritarianism: Hybrid Regimes after the Cold War* (Cambridge and New York: Cambridge University Press).

Levitsky, S. and Way, L. (2020). 'The new competitive authoritarianism', *Journal of Democracy*, 31(1): 51–65.

Mahaprashasta, A. A. (2019). 'Monsoon sessions shows better laws are not Modi government's preference', The Wire, 28 July. Available at: https://thewire.in/government/monsoon-session-bills-passage-modi-governments-effects (accessed 9 July 2022).

Manor, J. (1996). '"Ethnicity" and Indian politics', *International Affairs*, 72(3): 459–477.

Manor, J. (2016). 'India's states: The struggle to govern', *Studies in Indian Politics*, 4(1): 8–21.

Manor, J. (2019). 'The prospects for a Congress Party revival', *Indian Politics and Policy*, 3(1): 129–148.

Manor, J. (2020). 'The potential – constructive and destructive – of information technology for records management' in A. Thurston (ed.) *A Matter of Trust: Building Integrity into Data, Statistics and Records to Support the Sustainable Development Goals* (London: Institute of Commonwealth Studies, University of London Press), 67–82.

Mathur, S. (2019). 'Sedition law: Pro-government or pro-nation?', Spontaneous Order, 10 May. Available at: https://spontaneousorder.in/sedition-pro-government-or-pro-nation/ (accessed 9 July 2022).

Mishra, A. (2019). 'BJP got 93% of the Rs.985 crore corporates donated to the national parties in 2016–18', The Print, 9 July. Available at: https://theprint.in/politics/bjp-got-93%-of-the-rs-985-crores-donated-to-national-parties-in-2016-18/260764 (accessed 9 July 2022).

Mohan, A. (2017). 'Vipaksh Mukht Bharat: How Modi, Shah want to herald the golden age of BJP', *Business Standard*, 2 August. Available at: https://business-standard.com/article/current-affairs/vipaksh-mukht -bharat-how-modi-shah-want-to-herald-the-golden-age-of-bjp-117051100217_1.htm (accessed 9 July 2022).

Palshikar, S. (2015). 'The BJP and Hindu nationalism: Centrist politics and majoritarian impulses', *South Asia*, 38(4): 719–735.

Palshikar, S. (2019). 'The political culture of "New India": Some contradictions' in N. G. Jayal (ed.) *Re-Forming India* (New Delhi: Penguin), 346–362.

Prasad, K. (2019). 'Democracy can die in daylight too', *The Hindu*, 14 June. Available at: https://thehindu.com/opinion/lead/democracy-can-die-in-daylight-too/article27902292.ece (accessed 9 July 2022).

Press Trust of India (PTI) (2019a). 'Are we delivering pizzas, Derek O'Brien asks over hurried passing of bills', *The Hindu*, 31 July. Available at: www.thehindu.com/news/national/are-we-delivering-pizzas-dereko-brien-asks-over-hurried-passing-of-bills/article28767394.ece (accessed 9 July 2022).

Press Trust of India (PTI) (2019b). 'Opposition accuses government of pushing through bills', *The Hindu*, 1 August. Available at: www.thehindu.com/news/national/opposition-accuses-government-of-pushing-through-bills/article28781657.ece (accessed 9 July 2022).

Saxena, R. (2019). 'Modi govt refuses to waive Rs 92,000 crore dues of Airtel, Vodaphone Idea', The Print, 5 November. Available at: https://theprint.in/economy/modi-govt-refuses-to-waive-re-92000-crore-dues-of-airtel-vodaphone-idea/316177/ (accessed 9 July 2022).

Schedler, A. (ed.) (2006). *Electoral Authoritarianism: The Dynamics of Unfree Competition* (Boulder, CO: Lynne Rienner Publishers).

Shourie, A. (2015). 'BJP govt is Congress plus a cow, never seen a weaker PMO: BJP leader Arun Shourie', *Indian Express*, 27 October. Available at: https://indianexpress.com/article/india/india-news-india/bjp-govt-is-congress-plus-a-cow-never-seen-a-weaker-a-pmo-says-arun-shourie/ (accessed 9 July 2022).

Varadarajan, S. (2019a). 'Modi and the BJP: Just follow the money' The Wire [video], 13 July. Available at: https://thewire.in/video/beyondtheheadlines-modi-and-the-bjp-just-follow-the-money (accessed 9 July 2022).

Varadarajan, S. (2019b). 'UAPA Bill: India's most dangerous law yet', The Wire [video], 26 July. Available at: https://thewire.in/video/beyond-the-headlines-11-uapa-bill-dangerous-law (accessed 9 July 2022).

Vij, S. (2018). 'Modi government is so busy throwing stones at others that it has forgotten its own glass house', The Print, 5 June. Available at: https://theprint.in/opinion/modi-govt-is-so-busy-throwing-stones-at-others-that-it-has-forgotten-its-own-glass-house/66234 (accessed 9 July 2022).

18

The 2019 elections and their implications for Muslim politics

Mujibur Rehman

The victory of the Narendra Modi-led Bharatiya Janata Party (BJP) in the 2019 parliamentary election has transformative implications for Muslim politics in India. Until the electoral rise of the BJP during the late 1980s, Muslim politics was safely ensconced within the dominant secular politics of India.

Since its inception in 1980, the BJP has sought to craft a strategy that ignored Muslim voters, perpetuating a politics of polarisation in order to forge a Hindu majority by moderating caste divisions with an unambiguous objective to launch its politics of Hindu majoritarianism as state ideology. This ideological objective called for the collapse of India's secular polity, and the annihilation of minority rights. Hence, a strategy of polarisation was needed, which had to be located in a political environment of a hate campaign against India's religious minorities, particularly Muslims, by constructing them as a visible Other. Present-day Muslim politics, at both formal and informal levels, is deeply shaped by the emotions that the BJP has unleashed in conjunction with other Hindu right organisations, such as Rastriya Swayamsevak Sangh (RSS),[1] Vishwa Hindu Parishad (VHP),[2] Bajrang Dal and many others. Of course, such emotions are entwined with majoritarian rationalities, as I demonstrate in this chapter.

Implications of ignoring Muslim voters

At the national level, the strategy of ignoring Muslim voters bore fruit for the first time in the 2014 parliamentary election, and this was repeated in 2019. However, similar experiments were tried before, for instance during the Gujarat assembly elections in 2002, 2007 and 2012 under the leadership of Narendra Modi. The strategy was later employed in Uttar Pradesh in 2017, and Karnataka in 2018. What unfolded in 2019 and 2014 was indeed the nationalisation of a strategy that was already being employed successfully in different states.

Indian Muslims (roughly 14. 2% of the population according to the 2011 census) are the largest religious minority, compared to other religious minorities such as Sikhs, Christians etc. Located at the heart of India's competitive electoral politics ever since its first election in 1951–52, they have remained central to India's political discourse owing to their numbers and also for their concentrated presence in the electoral constituencies in various regions.[3] Indeed, historically, the politics around Muslims during the early part of the twentieth century led to the partition of colonial India.[4] In an ideological sense, Indian Muslims have remained the key attraction for competitive populism as part of the politics of secularism among secular as well as non-secular parties such as the Bharatiya Janata Party (BJP) and Shiv Sena (SS). The rise of Hindutva politics and its growing pan-Indian shape has offered a new context to look at the emerging patterns of Muslim politics in India.[5]

India experienced a tectonic shift towards the right ideologically in the 2014 parliamentary election (Hasan, 2018; Rehman, 2018; Jaffrelot et. al., 2019). By winning 303 seats in the seventeenth Lok Sabha with a vote share of 37.36%, the BJP not only ensured the Modi regime's return by a greater majority with a bigger vote share compared to 2014; it marked a further perpetuation of the rightward ideological shift. This trend appears almost irreversible.

One obvious dimension of ignoring Muslim voters by the BJP is not to field Muslim candidates. The result is a shrinking in size of Muslim political elites and a weakening of Muslim voices in the long run. Muslims are depoliticised, and a growing sense that they lack rights as citizens is leading to a virtual endorsement of a Hindu majority state. Signs of such trends are already visible in the Muslim community, apparent in the widespread silence about lynchings of Muslims in various parts of India since 2014.

The dramatic decline in numbers of Muslim members of parliament (hereafter MPs) in the Indian Parliament to only twenty-three in

2014, the lowest ever in the history of Indian democracy, is robust evidence of change in the Muslim polity in India. There never was adequate representation of Muslim MPs in the Indian Parliament, but the general fervour of secular political rhetoric did not raise concerns about this inadequacy.

It is now apparent that not offering tickets to Muslims to run for office is part of the deliberate electoral strategy of the BJP. According to Christopher Jaffrelot,

> The BJP's decision not to field any Muslim candidates aims to liberate the party entirely from the 'Muslim vote' that it accuses other parties of wooing for electoral gain at the expense of the Hindu majority. The low representation of Muslims also stems from other parties, who are reluctant to field Muslim candidates in constituencies other than those with a high concentration of Muslim voters. This tactic was especially clear in the Congress' case, which the BJP accused of cultivating a Muslim vote bank by showing concern for their social and economic condition – a false concern if one goes by the impoverishment of Muslims in the UPA regime. (Jaffrelot, 2018)

The strategy of pre-empting Muslim representatives by not fielding them in the electoral fray not only weakens the community's political voice, but also bolsters indifference towards issues that affect Muslims, as was evident during the campaign in the run-up to the 2019 general election.

India's 2019 campaign and the Muslim factor

During the campaign for the 2019 elections, positive issues pertaining to the Muslim community barely figured.[6] Developmental issues that had become part of mainstream policy conversations after the publication of the Sachar report (Prime Minister's High Level Committee, 2006) (for example, education, diversity, redistributive funding to economically backward districts) have disappeared. Opposition political parties were as indifferent as the ruling BJP on Muslim issues during the campaign and after.

The spate of mob-lynchings of Muslims during the first five years of the Modi government was a non-issue during the 2019 campaign. The lynchings, as a strategy, have been devised by non-state Hindutva groups to intimidate Muslims into giving up eating beef and sacrificing cows as part of their religious rituals. Most self-styled secular parties chose to ignore the issue, given the potential polarisation any condemnation of lynchings could cause.

The BJP has almost been supportive of lynching – evidenced by the fact that the Modi government is yet to respond to the counsel of the Supreme Court to form a special law against lynching in 2018 – which the court declared as a 'horrendous act of mobocracy'.[7] This is one court decision that the Modi government seems committed to overlook, contrasted with the implementation of the Ayodhya judgement to build Ram Temple.[8] Furthermore, India's national data on crime does not keep separate information on this heinous crime as part of state policy. Indeed, even the newly installed Congress governments (for instance in Rajasthan)[9] have passed anti-lynching laws, which to some measure demonstrates some (though not substantive) difference between the Congress and the BJP.

The BJP combined its strategy of indifference towards Muslim issues with an active attempt at polarising the electorate over the National Register for Citizens (NRC).[10] Regular public statements by several leaders, including India's home minister Amit Shah, to expand the NRC to all states in India is further evidence of its politicisation.[11] Such a claim is made mainly bearing in mind that its direct victims are Muslims, and that extension of the NRC to the rest of the country will entrench the politics of polarisation. Any non-Muslims excluded from the NRC will be accommodated as citizens under the Citizenship Amendment Act (Aiyer, 2019).

Fought in the shadow of the Pulwama attack that took place only a few weeks prior to the poll, the 2019 election presented the BJP with an opportunity to create a hyper-nationalist political discourse.[12] A polarising atmosphere, largely anti-Muslim owing to the prominent presence of the Muslim-majority Pakistan factor in the political conversations, dominated the overall milieu of the political campaign. But these conversations also helped the BJP to dodge real issues, encouraging it not to respond to demands for accountability on its own performance, and its failure to live up to the political agendas it had set up for itself during the 2014 campaign.[13]

Mainstream political parties are increasingly wary of espousing issues deemed to be Muslim, a direct outcome of the politics of indifference and polarisation cultivated by the BJP. Over the years,

Muslims have also felt betrayed by the secular parties, particularly the Congress. Despite being the largest religious minority – with a population greater than those of France and Germany combined – it has remained economically backward. The Sachar Committee Report (2006) has provided credible data to demonstrate how Muslims stand out comparatively as a backward community. As early as 1983, the Gopal Singh Panel report suggested that Muslim conditions in India were identical with Dalits (Ministry of Home Affairs, 1983). All of these point to the lack of commitment of secular parties to the overall development of India, and Muslims in particular. This has led to considerable alienation among Muslims that has now deepened in the face of rising Hindu majoritarianism.

Muslim political parties and their limits

After Partition, an overwhelming number of Muslims who chose to stay in India remained loyal to the Congress Party and other secular parties such as the left parties. But as time passed and the party system transformed, Muslim voters changed their loyalties to support various other parties such as the Samajwadi Party (SP) and Bahujan Samaj Party (BS) in Uttar Pradesh; Communist Party of India (Marxist) (CPI(M)) and Trinamool Congress (TMC) in West Bengal; Dravida Munnetra Kazhagam (DMK) and All India Dravida Munnetra Kazhagam (AIDMK) in Tamil Nadu; Rastriya Janata Dal (RJD) and Janata Dal (U) in Bihar. What is important to underline here is that Muslims as voters barely sought to move out of the mainstream secular parties. Being carried away by the *Sabka Sath, Sabka Vikas* slogan of Mr Modi in 2014, some Muslims also voted for the BJP.[14]

The Muslim league which championed Partition wanted to revive itself in India, but failed miserably in all parts except the tiny corner of Kerala, from where it elected only one MP to Lok Sabha in 2019. In the 2017 assembly election in Uttar Pradesh, it renewed its efforts to gain a foothold in North India again, but all of its candidates lost their deposits. Other major Muslim political formations that have appeared include the All India United Democratic Front (AIUDF) in Assam, set up by Maulana Badruddin Ajmal in 2005 – only one MP was elected in 2019, two fewer than in 2014. Also, its vote share has declined from 14.8% in 2014 to 7.8% in 2019. On the other hand, the All India Majlis-E-Ittehadul Muslimeen (AIMIM), which was set up in 1927, has its main base in Telangana, and also has a base in Maharashtra – from where it had a member of parliament elected in 2019. Its efforts to find social bases in other states like Uttar Pradesh have not reaped any dividends however. In the Bihar assembly election in 2020, the party fielded twenty candidates in the state assembly of 243 seats and won five seats.[15] This electoral success for AIMIM has provoked several commentators to argue that the politics of polarisation has led to the precise trajectory that the BJP was expecting, which is why secular voters should be wary of the AIMIM.[16] I have however expressed deep scepticism about the potential of AIMIM's Mr Owaisi to emerge as a major figure of Indian Muslim politics that could match his media profile in a column I wrote titled 'No sole spokesperson for Muslims'.[17]

Though these political parties have accomplished marginal success, what has remained unambiguously clear is that Muslims continue to stay loyal to the mainstream secular political parties. The rise of secular regional parties in restricted regions has also contributed to the confusion among Muslim voters, as each of these secular parties fields a Muslim candidate in a constituency with significant Muslim voters, causing a split in minority votes, and helping the BJP candidate to win in a polarised campaign. Because the BJP candidate is invariably a Hindu, as the BJP does not field Muslim candidates, this makes the victory easier for the BJP candidate. This confusion among Muslim voters will help the BJP candidates in future.

Some evidence does exist of Muslim voters moving towards the BJP in 2014; but the politics of *gharwapsi*, *love jihad* and lynching has generated considerable resentment and has crystallised anger among Indian Muslims towards the BJP. Given that the BJP deliberately pursues politics of polarisation, and the mainstream parties are becoming increasingly influenced by these tactics, Muslims are likely to begin to feel more despondent and marginalised. However, their political participation in India's electoral politics will remain as it is the only vehicle by which they can negotiate their future. No particular signs of retreat of Muslims from political or electoral life is evident at this juncture, and emerging challenges would encourage them to be more proactive. Some of this is evident in the nationwide anti-Citizenship Amendment Act protests.

Meanwhile, violence and exclusion of Muslims is likely to grow as the BJP seemingly remains committed to its majoritarian agenda.[18] Nonetheless, the general commitment of Muslims to remain integral to inclusive mainstream politics remains very high, which is why Muslim parties would have no future in Indian democracy. Muslims thus continue to negotiate within the existing available secular political space for their secular and constitutional rights in the face of majoritarian aggression by the Hindu right. India's endangered secular polity will continue to encourage Muslims to assert for their rights.

Notes

1 For a comprehensive analysis of what RSS stands for and its implications for the Indian polity, see Noorani (2019).
2 For an incisive analysis of the VHP and its role, see Katju (2017).
3 Some of the important works of Muslim politics are Hasan (1997b) and Khurshid (2019).
4 There exists a rich scholarship on the subject of Partition and its implications for India's secularism. This includes Hasan (1997a) and Pandey (2001).
5 For important works on the rise of the Hindutva or BJP politics, see Chatterji et al. (2019); Jaffrelot (1998); Hansenn (1999); Rehmann (2018).
6 Similar trends were witnessed in state elections, for instance the Gujarat state elections in 2017.
7 See the report, 'Supreme Court order on mob lynching strong, but new law will be useless unless existing rules are enforced', www.firstpost.com, 27 July 2018 (accessed 19 August 2020).
8 It is in this hypocrisy that the tragedy of Indian democracy lies, a tendency that Indrajit Roy describes as 'fascist undertones' (Roy, 2020).
9 See the report, 'Rajasthan Assembly passes anti-lynching bill', www.thehindu.com, 5 August 2019.
10 See the report, 'CJI Ranjan Gogoi says NRC cures a wrong, "Critics are playing with fire"', *Indian Express*, 4 November 2019.
11 See the report, 'Government will implement NRC across the county: Amit Shah', *Economic Times*, 18 September 2019.
12 See the report, 'Pulwama attack a gift to BJP before polls: A S Dulat', *Indian Express*, 31 March 2019. Available at: https://indianexpress.com/article/india/pulwama-attack-a-gift-to-bjp-before-polls-a-s-dulat-5650995/ (accessed 18 May 2022).

13 Research has suggested that polarisation around Muslims has invariably helped the BJP in electoral politics. See the paper titled, 'Do parties matter for ethnic violence: Evidence from India by Garenth Nellis according to a report published in the *Economic Times*', 5 December 2014 (accessed 20 May 2020).

14 See Rehman (2018), particularly chapter 7, 'Explaining the inconvenient truths of Indian political behavior'.

15 See 'AIMIM wins 5 seats in Bihar, but has not made a big dent in Mahagathbandhan vote share', www.theprint.in, 10 November 2020.

16 See Yogendra Yadav, 'Asaduddin Owaisi's rise is just the opportunity Hindutva politics is waiting for', www.theprint.in, 18 November 2020.

17 See Shaikh Mujibur Rehman, 'No sole spokesperson for Muslims', www.thehindu.com, 20 December 2020.

18 For a more detailed analysis of this aspect of the puzzle, see my forthcoming book, *Shikwa-e-Hind: The Political Future of Indian Muslims*.

References

Aiyer, Y. (2019). 'The citizenship bill must be opposed', *Hindustan Times*, 31 October. Available at: www.hindustantimes.com/columns/the-citizenship-bill-must-be-opposed/story-sxrqkgvM05hizuGxz784eI.html (accessed 18 May 2022).

Chatterji, P., Hansen, T. B. and Jaffrelot, C. (2019). *Majoritarian State: How Hindu Nationalism is Changing India* (New Delhi: Harper).

Hansen, T. B. (1999). *The Saffron Wave: Democracy and Nationalism in Modern India* (Princeton, NJ: Princeton University Press).

Hasan, M. (ed.) (1997a). *India's Partition: Process, Strategy and Mobilization* (New Delhi: Oxford University Press).

Hasan, M. (1997b). *Legacy of a Divided Nation: India's Muslims Since Independence* (New Delhi: Oxford University Press, London: Hurst & Co).

Hasan, Z. (2018). 'Collapse of the Congress Party' in M. Rehman (ed.) *Rise of Saffron Power* (New Delhi: Routledge), 154–168.

Jaffrelot, C. (1998). *The Hindu Nationalist Movement in India* (New Delhi: Columbia University Press).

Jaffrelot, C. (2018). 'The dwindling minority', *Indian Express*, 30 July.

Katju, M. (2017). *Hinduised Democracy* (New Delhi: New Text).

Khurshid, S. (2019). *Visible Muslim, Invisible Citizen: Understanding Islam in Indian Democracy* (New Delhi: Rupa).

Ministry of Home Affairs (1983). *Report on Minorities*, Vol. 1 (New Delhi: Government of India). Available at: http://ncm.nic.in/home/pdf/

special_report/REPORT%20ON%20MINORITIES.pdf (accessed 10 June 2022).

Noorani, A. G. (2019). *The RSS: A Menace to India* (New Delhi: Leftword Books).

Pandey, G. (2001). *Remembering Partition: Violence, Nationalism, and History in India* (New Delhi: Oxford University Press).

Prime Minister's High Level Committee (2006) *Social, Economic and Educational Status of the Muslim Community of India: A Report* (New Delhi: Government of India). Available at: www.minorityaffairs.gov.in/en/document/sachar-committee-report/complete-sachar-committee-reportenglish-2006-6655-kb (accessed 10 June 2022).

Rehman, M. (ed.) (2018). *Rise of Saffron Power: Reflections on Indian Politics* (New Delhi: Routledge).

Rehman, M. (forthcoming). *Shikwa-e-Hind: The Political Future of Indian Muslims* (New Delhi: Simon & Schuster).

Roy, I. (2020). 'India: A year after Narendra Modi's re-election the country's democracy is developing fascistic undertones', *The Conversation*, 22 May. Available at: https://theconversation.com/india-a-year-after-narendra-modis-re-election-the-countrys-democracy-is-developing-fascistic-undertones-135604 (accessed 18 May 2022).

19

Cementing emotions: The new reasoning of majoritarian politics

Gurpreet Mahajan

Whether it is the frustration and anger expressed by the protesting farmers and other marginalised groups or the righteous indignation that was expressed when forty Central Reserve Police Force (CRPF) personnel were killed in a suicide-bomber attack in Pulwama, emotional politics seems to be the order of the day. After India executed an air strike against 'terrorist camps' across the border, passions ruled the public arena without restraint. Even though people stood solidly behind the government's decision, many sections of the media (print, electronic and social media) whipped up popular sentiment to demand complete solidarity. As emotional politics took over traditional spaces for debate and discussion, the urge to explain the current phase of Indian politics and the electoral victory of the Bharatiya Janata Party (BJP) through the lens of emotions appears to be irresistible. However, all such accounts that invoke a simple and rather indefensible binary between emotions and reason remain myopic. They fail to recognise the deeper shifts that are occurring in the political discourse – changes that often lie hidden under the effervescence of emotions. In particular, the manner in which the BJP is challenging the preceding consensus around the politics of difference remains unnoticed. While we confront the present nature of emotional politics it is equally important to reflect on the new reasoning that majoritarian politics is employing in India and many other parts of the world.

Identity politics and emotions

Since the 1990s, Indian politics has been defined by an overflow of passions, cultural iconography and symbols. Whether waving blue flags or constructing statues of elephants, owning the visible public spaces and inscribing them with one's cultural markers has been a familiar characteristic of identity politics. While identity politics of all hues brings with it a surplus of emotions, the BJP has continually added new and qualitatively different elements to it. Earlier identity politics revolved around the inclusion of specific marginalised groups in the political public domain, and each of them brought in their specific cultural symbols; this made the public domain more diverse in form and content. The BJP ushered in a new era of cultural politics. Now religious cultural identity became the connecting thread, an overarching frame that glided over caste-related differences to construct a pan-India Hindu identity, ushering in a novel form of cultural politics. In the early years when the BJP's strategy of political mobilisation revolved around temple construction, the public arena was overtaken by saffron-clad men and women, religious leaders, *Sadhus* with *tilak* on their foreheads, and men carrying a *trishul*. This was an unprecedented sight. The scale at which ostensibly religious virtuosos participated in secular affairs was a feature that Indian politics had never quite seen before. This evoked an inner tie between culture, religion and politics that connected with the Hindu population.

When Narendra Modi became prime minister, the national political discourse changed further. In 2014 the focus was on connecting directly with the people, creating the image of a strong, decisive leader, and with it a brand – 'NaMo'. This derivation from the name 'Narendra Modi' was suffused with religious cultural content, as in Sanskrit 'Namo' implies bowing before a revered deity with folded hands. The use of holograms to project a 3-D image of Narendra Modi standing in the midst of live audiences in different places simultaneously added a touch of magic to the campaign. The 2019 campaign did not have a similar kind of spectacular moment, but it consolidated the emotional and cultural dimension in fresh and innovative ways.

From 2014 to 2019, as Prime Minister, Narendra Modi was by all accounts the most popular leader. All others were trailing far behind. Throughout this period, his image as a self-sacrificing person, dedicated to serving the nation, strong in his resolve and decisive in his functioning, was carefully crafted and presented to the people. Reference to his '*chappan inch ka seena*' (56-inch chest) and stories of 'Bal Narendra' (his heroism as a child) created a larger-than-life persona – the stuff that superheroes are made of. It nurtured trust in the leader and simultaneously a sense of awe. This time around, echoes of '*Modi hai to mumkin hai*' (if Modi is there everything is possible), reaffirmed that image. Connecting with the leader directly, building trust in him, tapped positive emotions of optimism and hope, albeit in a way that suspended doubt or questioning. This was a new form of emotional politics.

At the second – equally important – level, the campaign was pegged to emotions aroused by the collective invocation of the nation. In India, cricket matches, particularly with the neighbouring country of Pakistan, invariably involve a display of heightened zeal and drama, where winning (or defeating the opponent) is critical and perhaps even more important than the game itself. This time the same, or an even more intense form of passion was stirred, centring around the idea and the image of the nation/*Bharat mata*. The Pulwama terror strike set the stage for this. Grief and anger at the attack, and the 24x7 images of the bodies of martyrs returning to their home towns, created a public sphere in which emotions ruled and the collective became more important than the individual.

The focus on nationalism changed the language of cultural politics. So far, on many occasions, the BJP campaign has brought into play religious symbols to create a sense of community among the majority Hindu community. However, religious majoritarianism is a double-edged sword; even as it consolidates and homogenises the majority community, it tends to create sharp boundaries between those who are included and those who fall outside its fold. Hence it unites at one level and divides at another. The idea of nationalism has the capacity to build a collective with strong emotional ties while using the language of unity and commonality. This was again a new form of cultural politics enacted in and through the collective.

Tapping the anxieties

Expressions of strident nationalism, along with the deepening of cultural/religious faultlines, are not unique to India. In fact we can see this pattern of political articulation and mobilisation in many other parts of the world – from Europe to America and Brazil. While there are specific circumstances and issues through which these ideas have gained popular support in different countries, nevertheless there are certain common conditions that constitute the context for these assertions.

By the end of the twentieth century the nation-state, which had been the accepted and desired unit of political life, was under steady attack. The emerging left-liberal critiques questioned the creation of rigid, artificial boundaries. They associated the nation-state with wars, unnecessary loss of life and an impediment to dealing with global issues such as climate change and environmental degradation. As concepts of cosmopolitanism and world citizenship gained momentum asking for the removal of barriers, the prevailing order at the national and international level was questioned. While these discourses focused on global justice and justice for future generations, the questions of justice and a better life for citizens within the nation-state were taken up by the right-wing forces. Groups for whom globalisation held the promise of a better future were attracted by the former, but those who were losing out, for whom the old economic and social order was crumbling, and the power to challenge capital was steadily diminishing, pushed for the latter. The nation-state, and sentiments of nationalism – an insider/outsider distinction – provided ways of regaining control. They looked for new voices in the political domain, new entrants and parties that could break with the existing trends and reassert an order in which a significant section of the majority population could hope to regain power.

New technologies of communication, social media networks, provided avenues for connecting with like-minded people and creating new solidarities. Extreme positions of all kinds which might previously have made local news now became the talking points around which opinion could be sharply polarised. The threat posed by terrorism added further to a sense of loss and anxiety that had been engendered by the new world created through globalisation (Giddens, 1999). Fear of a terror attack, something that might occur anytime anywhere, created a sense of 'generalized insecurity' (Baumann, 2006). The new right drew on these elements of fear, anxiety and insecurity to strengthen and win support for the alternative it presented.

In India, an analogous narrative of economic precariousness aggravated by corruption in high places, along with loss of faith in old forms of identity politics, strengthened the BJP. Marginalised groups that remained on the fringes of the new economic order, and had not benefited from the older system of reservation policies and identity politics, wanted a radical break in the nature of politics and leadership.[1] Industry and corporations too wanted a strong government to effect structural changes for the growth of capital. Interestingly enough, even those who wanted to hold onto the old social order longed for a break from the existing form of identity politics. The BJP under the leadership of Narendra Modi provided just that hope to a whole cross-section of people.

Reasons cementing emotions

Support for the BJP has taken many forms; when nationalism became the primary focus, an aggressive and strident display of passions was often in evidence. In the context of 'nation-under-attack', these assertions of complete solidarity tended to silence others, and this has fostered the impression that reason has fled from the public domain. But, contrary to popular belief, emotion and reason do not occupy separate and mutually exclusive spaces. The presence of emotions should not be taken as the absence of reason. Indeed the success of the BJP should be understood as the assertion of a rationality that marked a form of liberal politics in the early to mid-twentieth century. The BJP, particularly under Narendra Modi, has systematically pushed for the idea that equality entails sameness – identical treatment for all, the majority and the minorities. This is the reasoning for which emotions are in play.

The year preceding the general election of 2019 saw many protests and demonstrations, particularly from farmers in different parts of India. Given the large percentage of the population that is involved in agriculture and the numbers that came onto the streets to press their demands, it appeared that winning the election would be an uphill task for the incumbent government. Political observers felt that the deep crisis in the agrarian sector could translate, as it had in the past (for instance, in recent state elections in Chhattisgarh, Madhya Pradesh and Rajasthan), into a vote against the party in government (see Bera and Bhaskar, 2019; Das, 2019; Kazmin, 2019).

However, this did not happen. Despite the prevailing difficulties, which were aggravated by globalisation, the BJP (which was already the single largest party) consolidated its support. In fact it increased its seat share in Parliament, and after almost three decades of coalition governments, a single party, the BJP, returned with a majority at the Centre. Almost everyone would agree that electoral victory of this kind is not possible without the support of many different groups and classes in society. They must also accept that the BJP employed multiple strategies to reach out to diverse sections and communities. But was all this made possible by their brand of cultural politics? Was this the triumph of emotional politics?

No doubt strident expressions of loyalty to the nation, sacredness accorded to territory and India's sovereignty were visible everywhere and they evoked strong feelings. Several social media platforms were flooded with high-octane, combative and contentious comments; but it is important to recognise that these statements elicited mixed reactions. While some endorsed them, others were alarmed by them. One cannot therefore explain the increased support base and impressive victory of the BJP by a singular emphasis on passions and emotional politics.

In situations that are heavily charged with emotion, whether in personal or public life – for instance, when we see or hear about victims of a bomb blast – sentiment carries the day. At that time justifications are rarely spelt out, and this fosters the impression that when emotion prevails, reason vanishes. In actuality, reason may not be evident but it is present, albeit hidden under the surface. Whether we recognise it or not, reason and emotion often coexist. It is therefore necessary to go beyond the surface level and uncover the reasons that are not immediately apparent.

In the present scenario too, the visibility of emotional politics should not take our attention away from the fact that the BJP (like many other right-wing regimes in other parts of the world) is steadily owning the ground which was previously occupied by the liberal framework – a framework that emphasizes no difference and identical rights for all.

In India, since the 1990s at least, state discourse had moved towards 'politics of difference'. Represented as 'inclusive politics', the effort was to identify marginalised minorities (which included historically disadvantaged communities, socially and educationally backward communities, women, religious minorities) and give them greater representation, visibility, space and opportunity in the public domain. To put this another way, policies were carefully designed to include specific communities on the basis of their identity. This framework of accommodating marginalised identity groups (which replaced the notion of general and abstract citizenship) sought to make the public sphere more diverse; it functioned with the belief that the liberal framework (which was indifferent to social identities and claimed to represent all) implicitly favoured the majority. Hence an effort was made to give space and power to marginalised minorities. Indeed, as 'inclusive politics' became the operative norm, new alliances, configurations of groups and political parties emerged, and they claimed to speak for and represent specific communities.

As a principle, the politics of difference aimed to promote social justice and diversity. It put the spotlight on the many ways in which minority groups are disadvantaged in the framework of liberal neutrality. However, when a principle becomes ossified and fixed, it loses its vitality and becomes a victim of its own reasoning. In a way this is what happened in India. The cracks in this framework were apparent at many levels – from electoral politics and policies to emerging protests. There were demands by sections within the marginalised communities for sub-quotas, so that they could benefit from reservation policies; many states identified 'most backward classes' (MBCs) or 'extremely backward classes' (EBCs). There were also demands from communities which were facing hardships due to the crisis in the agrarian sector or the effects of modernisation, for inclusion in the list of beneficiaries of special policies. Clearly, the existing structure was not able to meet all the demands for separate recognition and accommodation. There was some disillusionment even with parties that claimed to represent the interests of the marginalised groups. The politics of difference was thus under stress and there was hardly any discussion on how the underlying principle should be operationalised to meet these emerging concerns.

The BJP effectively utilised the unease prevalent in this form of highly particularised identity politics. Taking the traditional liberal ground, it criticised the politics of difference as divisive, as it purportedly catered to specific interests rather than common interest. At another level, it took over the agenda of gender equality, valuing this over cultural diversity. In pitting the concern for women's equality against respect for diversity, it once again offered a liberal reasoning that reached out to a much larger audience. Further, by extending reservations for economically weaker groups, irrespective of their position in the social structure, it took attention away from identity and onto material needs, and reinforced the view that the needs of the majority should merit the same consideration as those of the identified minorities.

This is a new form of reasoning which draws on the liberal paradigm. It aims to be neutral by weighing the concerns of the majority on a par with those of minorities. Nevertheless it employs the language of identical rights for all, no difference, common national interest and integration, as against group or community interests and differentiation between citizens on grounds of diversity. In doing so it aligns itself with the critics of 'politics of difference' and multiculturalism the world over (Malik, 2015; Miller, 2016). The presence of this reasoning in the BJP's appeal needs to be acknowledged, for it is this that has helped it to reach out to many different groups, including those that did not appear to be its initial support base.

Notes

1 For about two decades at least, tensions have been building within the marginalised groups (see Mahajan, 2012; Assadi and Rajendran, 2000). One could see this in the emerging demands for separate sub-quotas within the OBCs and SCs, and shifts in electoral support. Election surveys conducted by Lokniti, CSDS, captured these trends. In 2014, almost a quarter of the Dalits voted for the BJP, and this support base increased to 34% in the 2019 elections (see Kumar, 2019; Rukmini, 2019).

References

Assadi, M. and Rajendran, S. (2000). 'Changing shape of caste conflict', *Economic and Political Weekly*, 6 May, 1610–1612.

Baumann, Z. (2006). *Liquid Fear* (Cambridge: Polity Press).

Bera, S. and Bhaskar, U. (2019). 'BJP poll machinery wary of farm distress amid drop in crop prices and stagnating rural wages', LiveMint, 13 March. Available at: www.livemint.com/elections/lok-sabha-elections/bjp-poll-machinery-wary-of-farm-distress-amid-drop-in-crop-prices-and-stagnating-1552418295614.html (accessed 9 May 2022).

Das, A. (2019). 'Parliament election, agrarian distress and Emerging Farmers politics', Countercurrent.org, 31 March. Available at: https://countercurrents.org/2019/03/parliament-elections-agrarian-distress-and-emerging-farmers-politics-a-view-from-the-grassroots/ (accessed 9 May 2022).

Giddens, A. (1999). *Runaway World: How Globalization is Reshaping Our Lives* (London: Profile Books).

Kazmin, A. (2019). 'India: Narendra Modi faces a backlash as election looms', *Financial Times*, 10 March. Available at: www.ft.com/conten t/1db3b51e-392d-11e9-b856-5404d3811663 (accessed 9 May 2022).

Kumar, S. (2019). 'Here's how BJP earned the massive mandate: Explained in numbers', *Economic Times*, 28 May. Available at: https://economictimes. indiatimes.com/news/elections/lok-sabha/india/heres-how-bjp-earned-massive-mandate-explained-in-numbers/articleshow/69529857.cms? from=mdr (accessed 9 May 2022).

Mahajan, G. (2012) 'Reservations' in A. Kohli and P. Singh (eds) *Routledge Handbook of Indian Politics* (London: Routledge), 144–154.

Malik, K. (2015). 'The failure of European multiculturalism', *Foreign Affairs*, March/April. Available at: www.foreignaffairs.com/articles/western-europe/2015-02-18/failure-multiculturalism (accessed 9 May 2022).

Miller, D. (2016). 'The changing face of multiculturalism in Europe', *Globe and Mail*, 18 April. Available at: www.theglobeandmail.com/opinion/the-changing-face-of-multiculturalism-in-europe/article29647990/ (accessed 9 May 2022).

Rukmini, S. (2019). 'The BJP's electoral arithmetic', Carnegie Endowment for International Peace. Available at: https://carnegieendowment.org/2019/04/04/bjp-s-electoral-arithmetic-pub-78678 (accessed 9 May 2022).

Index

Lightning Source UK Ltd.
Milton Keynes UK
UKHW022107110123
415173UK00004B/14